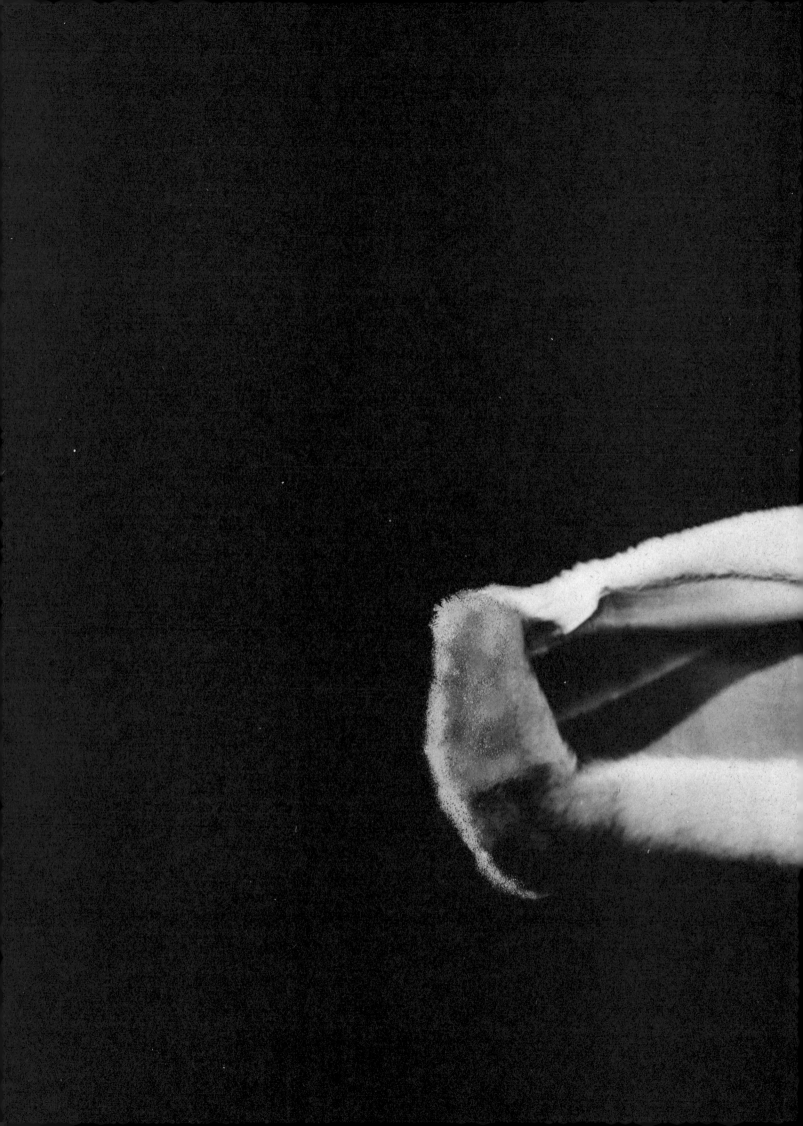

A
PICTORIAL
HISTORY
OF
SEX IN THE MOVIES

JEREMY PASCALL
CLYDE JEAVONS

HAMLYN
LONDON
NEW YORK
SYDNEY
TORONTO

For David Austin, Robert Scott and Harry Snyder

Published by
The Hamlyn Publishing Group Limited
London · New York · Sydney · Toronto
Astronaut House, Feltham,
Middlesex, England

© Copyright
The Hamlyn Publishing
Group Limited 1975
Reprinted 1976
ISBN 0 600 37058 5

Printed in England
by Jarrold and Sons Limited,
Norwich

front endpaper
Theda Bara in *Cleopatra*

title spread
Marilyn Monroe

contents spread
Christina Schollin and Jarl Kulle in
Dear John

back endpaper
Maria Schneider and Marlon Brando in
Last Tango in Paris

special research on censorship
by Guy Phelps

picture research by
Sheila Whitaker

CONTENTS

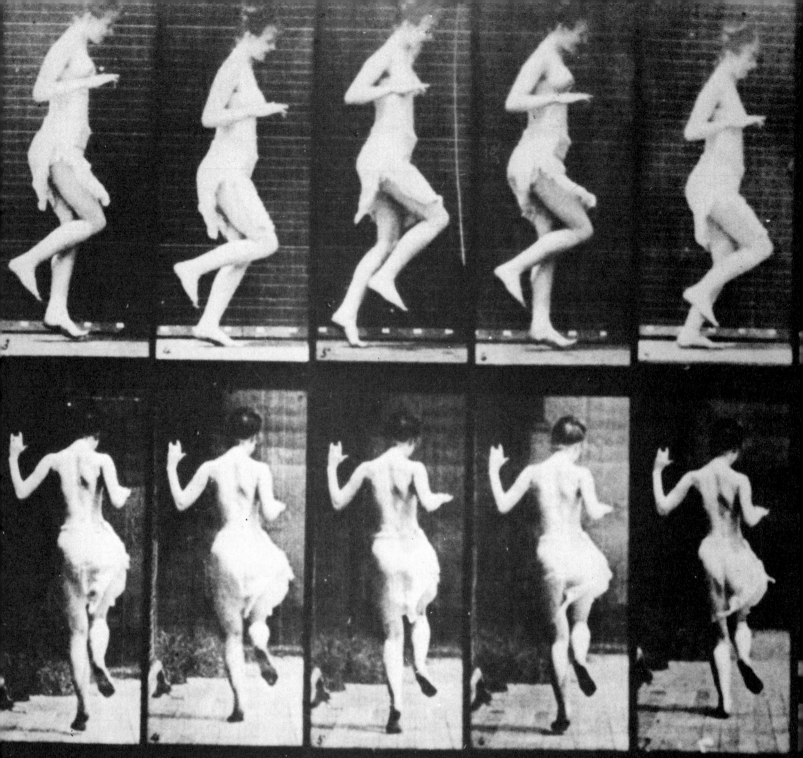

THE EARLY YEARS
Awakened with a Kiss

'The movie was born in the laboratory
and reared in the counting-house.
Filthy hands taught it to walk.'[1]

First Stirrings

'The motion picture is a genuine art,' wrote Terry Ramsaye in his book 'A Million and One Nights'. 'It is genuine in that it is strictly popular, appealing to and serving the multitudes. This art has grown out of simple, elemental wishes. The forms which it has taken are the products of now well recognized human traits. Like all the great arts its appeal is based on a few primitive, and therefore universal, instincts and mechanisms in man. Sex and combat are the chief instincts.' Even in 1926, when Ramsaye wrote that and the film was still a relatively young medium, the commerciality of sex in the cinema was widely understood. Producers had not been slow to capitalize on it and Ramsaye was able to talk about 'the startling sex frankness of the present era'.

Modern cinema audiences tend to look back to the screen's earliest days with an amused condescension, mentally lumping together the jumpy flicker-images of the Silent Era and Victorian sexual mores. The mistake is easily made. We think of the early cinema as being sexually naïve because most of the films we see from the period are either comedies or what might broadly be described as melodramas. Sadly, so few films are still in existence, and those which are have usually suffered the ravages of time and the lack of resources necessary to conserve them. The modern viewer sees only a small selection of the material which poured from the studios. Chaplin, Fairbanks, Pickford are the names which automatically spring to mind, and to most their films have a whimsical charm as curiosities from an age of innocence. To assume that producers in those pioneering days were unaware of sex and its box-office implications is as mistaken as to believe that the sons of those pioneers only really discovered sex in the late 'sixties. The main difference lies, not in content, but approach. Still, it is certainly true to say that the early film-makers were nowhere near as frank as those who followed them.

The Sex equals Good Box-Office equation was also well understood by the forerunner of the movie, the Kinetoscope or Mutoscope. Before the days of projected films these 'peepshows' were great attractions at carnivals, arcades and travelling shows. The viewer peered into a peepslit, cranked a handle and a moving picture appeared before his eyes. In the early days, *any* movement on film was a wonder to be gaped at. But after awe came the need for something more – excitement, titillation – and promoters were swift to understand that the spicier the material offered the more the nickels rolled in. Short reels with alluring titles appeared: in America 'What the Bootblack Saw' was the typical title; in Britain it was the butler who was not averse to a little voyeurism. Not all the subjects were salacious. Some were morally uplifting, some sporting. But it was the 'saucy' ones which attracted the customers.

Witness the scene at a board meeting of the Biograph Company. One director, a respectable pillar of financial society, is dubious about the choice of material offered at the company's Mutoscopes. He feels that perhaps some are a trifle more lubricious than is necessary. The time-honoured defence is mouthed: 'It's what the public wants.' The banker is sceptical, and so records from a nearby arcade are produced and show the following takings:

'U.S. Battleship At Sea'	$0.25
Joseph Jefferson in 'Rip's Sleep' . .	$0.43
'Ballet Dancer'.	$1.05
'Girl Climbing Apple Tree'	$3.65

Financial considerations overwhelm moral sensibilities and the doubting director's only comment is: 'Then I think we had better have some more of the Girl-Climbing-Apple-Tree kind.'

As Ramsaye, who records the incident, noted: 'The production policy of the motion picture was ordained forever in that decision. The dominant note had been struck.'[2]

The Biograph Catalogue of the 1890s showed that the producers – still, remember, living in Victorian times – were thoroughly acquainted with the appetites of their public and set about whetting, if not completely satisfying, them. Item No. 539 is an excellent early example of what producers down the years have learned – take a mundane story, give it a spicy title, and you can fool the punters into buying tickets. There was certainly nothing unintentional in the come-on line 'How Bridget Served The Salad Undressed'. The catalogue describes it:

'This is an old and always popular story told by motion photograph. Bridget of course mistakes the order and brings in the salad in a state of dishabille hardly allowable in polite society.'

Amusing and naïve as these vignettes now appear – and it must be remembered that the most the bootblack ever saw was his mistress in her chemise – they prove that the fundamentals of sex as a seller were understood and vigorously put into practice. Promoters and owners of peepshows had their fingers on the pulse as well. One, W.D. Stansifer of Butte, Montana, understood his patrons perfectly and wrote to a distributor requesting a certain type of entertainment. The letter he received in response speaks volumes:

Edward Muybridge, a British photographer working in America in the 1870s, anticipated cinematography by analyzing motion on film. He achieved this with a series of cameras linked to trip wires set off by the subject under study – in this case a running woman. Later he invented a form of projector which gave his pictures an appearance of continuous movement. Nudity thus unwittingly became an early feature of the cinema.

Above: Edison's Kinetoscope Arcade, San Francisco, in the late 1890s.

Right: Fatima – first victim of film censorship – before and after bowdlerization.

'We are confident that the Dolorita *Passion Dance* would be as exciting as you desire. In fact, we will not show it in *our* parlor. You speak of the class of trade which wants something of this character. We think this will certainly answer your purposes. A man in Buffalo has one of those films and informs us that he frequently has forty or fifty men waiting in line to see it.'

Dolorita's 'Passion Dance' must have been sensational by contemporary standards because the picture held the box-office record at the Kinetoscope parlour on the Atlantic City boardwalk. Indeed, it attracted so many customers that it ran into trouble. A passing do-gooder noted the queue and, moral antennae pricking, waited in line for his turn. What he saw prompted the peepshow's owner to write to the distributor two days later and say: 'The authorities request us not to show the Houchi Kouchi, so please cancel order for new Dolorita. . . .'[3]

Censorship was already rearing its head.

It is hardly to be wondered at – given the prevailing moral climate of the times, with Victoria still alive and imposing her values on millions throughout her enormous empire, and the eastern seaboard puritanical tradition flourishing in the States. Fighters against social evils like drink and turpitude were bound to poke their noses into the innocent entertainments of the huddled mass of poor and largely illiterate which thronged the streets of major American cities.

Vast numbers of these customers for peepshows and the screen-projected nickelodeons which followed not only could not read or write, they couldn't even speak English. They flocked, therefore, to see a show which was cheap, wondrous and demanded absolutely no command of language. Visual jokes were instantly understood and sight-gags on film could induce riotous laughter which cut through every ethnic barrier. The few explanatory titles which helped to clarify the action were instantly translated by anyone with the smallest grasp of the tongue, and communicated throughout the hall in a multitude of voices which must have sounded like the Tower of Babel without in any way marring anyone's enjoyment of the programme.

The middle classes who patronized the theatre – an entertainment too expensive and literary for the poor majority – looked upon peepshows and nickelodeons with the deepest suspicion and with typical hard-nosed zeal were quick to spot and stamp out anything that might inflame the passions of the lower classes. The peepshows suffered occasionally from the attentions of the local authorities but it was the technological revolution of the screen-projected film that brought the hounds of righteousness to full cry.

A peepshow was, in its way, a private entertainment. It was, after all, merely a box into which the spectator peered and, although arcades often contained rows of them like one-armed bandits in a casino, the audience for each was limited to one viewer at a time. The introduction of projector and screen changed all this. Now as many people as could be packed into a hastily converted store, cheek-by-jowl on wooden benches or standing around the walls, constituted the audience. Consequently, men, women and children crammed into these cheap entertainments to gasp as waves apparently lapped at the wall or, as the story goes, to rush in horror from the sight of a locomotive under full steam advancing out of the jury-rigged sheet and into the body of the hall! Size was what preoccupied the anti-nickelodeon lobby. Not just the size of the audience but also the dimensions of the picture. Suddenly images were transformed from little square frames to wall-sized monsters and, in the eyes of the reformers, bigger meant worse.

A sensation of the 1893 Chicago Columbian Exposition (or World Fair) had been a peepshow exhibition of the talents of Fatima. Fatima's speciality was a '*danse du ventre*', or belly dance. By current standards this display of Terpsichorean art was mild to the point of innocuousness. Excepting the navel region she was respectably clad – perhaps even overdressed – and her gyrations, while doubtless athletic, were hardly inflammatory. As peepshow entertainment they were acceptable. But when Fatima was transferred to projector and screen and enlarged beyond life-size, moral wrath descended and the censor stepped in.

However, he did not ban the exotic dancer out of hand. Instead he settled upon an extraordinary compromise. Fatima could still demonstrate the mobility of her dorsal muscles, but certain portions of her rippling anatomy were to be hidden from the public gaze by the superimposition of a screen – resembling nothing so much as a fence of white palings – which ran in two strips across the film masking those portions of her physique that were thought to be offensive. Curiously, her midriff and navel were spared and her upper torso – admittedly ample – and lower abdominal region to the knees obscured. Curiouser and curiouser was the fact that in the first place both these areas were generously clad; and, in the second, the nature of the stencil allowed the viewer tantalizing glimpses of voluptuosity between the lines! The effect must surely have served to excite the viewers' imaginations and achieve the exact opposite of the censor's wishes. Evidently, asinine decisions from the wielder of the blue pencil were not confined to later years.

Another *cause célèbre* occurred in 1896 when controversy centred around a short Vitascope production snappily entitled *The May Irwin–John C. Rice Kiss*. The start of the furore was, innocently enough, a Broadway parlour farce entitled 'The Widow Jones', starring the aforementioned Miss Irwin and Mr Rice. '"The Widow Jones" had its high moment in a prolonged kiss between the principals. It was one of those persisting, adhesive osculations, doubtless made more delightful by the sweeping model of the hero's moustache, a hirsute ornamentation of the type which reached its zenith among British cavalry officers in India and among the Texas Rangers. It was also a high-vacuum kiss, attended at its conclusions by sounds reminiscent of a steer pulling a foot out of the gumbo at the edge of a water hole. It was, in brief – and in length – the world's greatest kiss, as of that date.'[4]

Vitascope were quick to see its commercial potential. Without a thought for the rest of the play, they dragooned the stars into performing this action before their waiting cameras. The

Après le Bal – le Tub (After the Ball – the Bath) – Georges Méliès' saucy *vignette* of 1897 in which a woman, assisted by her maid, disrobes and steps naked into a shallow bathtub. The maid pours water over her and wraps her in a towel, whereupon she exits.

inter-labial activity lasted the full extent of fifty feet of celluloid, in extreme close-up, and was certainly the prototype for all such that were to become obligatory in virtually every movie produced after that date.

The Kiss, as the reel became universally known, was a box-office smash and ran the circuits to excellent business and reviews – until, that is, it played Chicago where it was seen by Herbert S. Stone, the publisher of a small circulation periodical, who, on 15 June, 1896, ran the following diatribe:

'In a recent play called "The Widow Jones" you may remember a famous kiss which Miss May Irwin bestowed on a certain John C. Rice, and vice versa. Neither participant is physically attractive, and the spectacle of their prolonged pasturing on each other's lips was hard to bear. When only life size it was pronounced beastly. But that was nothing to the present sight. Magnified to Gargantuan proportions and repeated three times over it is absolutely disgusting. All delicacy or remnant of charm seems gone from Miss Irwin, and the performance comes near to being indecent in its emphasised vulgarity.

'Such things call for police interference. Our cities from time to time have spasms of morality, when they arrest people for displaying lithographs of ballet-girls; yet they permit, night after night, a performance which is infinitely more degrading. . . . The Irwin kiss is no more than a lyric of the Stock Yards. While we tolerate such things, what avails all the talk of American Puritanism and of the filthiness of imported English and French stage shows?'[5]

The Grundys were abroad and saw, via the 'mechanically ingenious and pretty toy for that great child, the public', the collapse of all they held sacred. Stone's primary objections to the middle-aged raptures of Irwin and Rice were based, interestingly enough, on the physical unattractiveness of the participants and the size to which they were magnified. Perhaps the idea of love after forty was repulsive, and indeed one wonders whether it would be a popular theme today if, for example, an obviously middle-aged couple were seen in frankly sexual display. The movies do, after all, depend largely on the physical beauty of the leading actors and their youth. Cary Grant in

Tih Minh (1919) by French director Louis Feuillade, whose mystery serials were famous for their uninhibited realism.

his fifties, for example, could only play romantic leads opposite women half his age because he didn't look his years.

Herbert Stone's criticism might, therefore, be endorsed on aesthetic grounds – but surely not on moral ones. There's nothing lewd or depraved in the sight of two people, of whatever age, indulging in the simplest expression of love. But in the context of the times, when the ruling classes eschewed any outward show of emotion and flinched away from physical contact, perhaps it was all too shocking.

Notwithstanding Stone's bellow of outrage, *The Kiss* continued to be a highly popular film and played the smoky nickelodeons until the copies literally fell apart from use. That it should seem at all daring strikes us as extraordinary, accustomed as we are to such scenes being spliced into movies almost gratuitously. *The Kiss* is probably only remembered today for the fact that it opened the door for film censorship.

By the start of the century, the fledgling art and industry had learned a great deal, not least how to pander to public taste. In 1905 Paley and Steiner, producers of Crescent Films, were offering in their catalogue the following attraction:

'THE FLATIRON BUILDING ON A WINDY DAY This side-splitting scene was taken on January 25, 1905, when the wind was blowing a gale, and gives one à general idea of what women experience on a windy day around this noted corner. The great velocity of the wind can be plainly seen by the manner in which the pedestrians are clutching their hats and skirts and grasping at anything for support. It is at this corner where one can get a good idea of the prevailing types in hosiery and lingerie. *This is the finest picture that has ever been taken at this corner, and we can safely recommend it as something exceptionally fine.*'

As Cole Porter rightly observed, 'In olden days a glimpse of stocking was looked on as something shocking', and to glimpse not only hose and ankle but also, perhaps, lingerie and knee would have been greeted with delight by the masses and with apoplexy by the Stones of the world. It comes as no surprise to learn that the film (which was simply an action record of a popular postcard subject) was the hit of the year, but film-makers could not for much longer handle such *risqué* subjects with impunity. The watchdogs of public morals were about to close in.

In the early years of the century the film industry was most prolific not in America but in France. Indeed, one studio – Pathé – made more movies in a year than the whole American industry. The early work of Lumière and Méliès had given the French a flying start, and the genius of Méliès in particular, which grasped the fantastic freedom of the medium in the creation of spectacular effects, fairytale tableaux and magic tricks, soon made the static work of most Americans look obsolete. Méliès showed the world how to make a trip to the moon; trains flew; mermaids cavorted beneath

the waves; ladies turned into skeletons.

In addition, France was still the site of the world's Capital of Love – Gay Paree. The Naughty Nineties, with the Moulin Rouge and the Can-Can, were but recently past, and Paris was still the home of the graphic arts, of the Impressionists and, of course, of the 'French Postcard'. Lautrec's posters were displayed on every street corner and alongside them were sold their naughty offspring – 'Cartes Postales Suggestives'.

These 'éditions artistiques' were probably even more popular in America than in the land of their manufacture. They depicted women – usually described as actresses, models or dancers – in a variety of poses and varying stages of undress. Frequently they followed the currently fashionable 'high-art' style of the classical nudes which were displayed in the most respectable galleries, but quite soon bathing belles and series entitled 'Intimité de Boudoir', 'Types d'Orient' and 'A Sa Toilette' appeared, precursors of the cheesecake pin-up. Soon erotic and suggestive postcards were a major industry and in 1910 France produced 123 million of them and gave employment to over thirty thousand workers.[6]

For the French, therefore, it was a simple and obvious step from the postcard pin-up to the very much more exciting prospect of animating these beauties. France was never inhibited by the Puritanism of Britain and America; it was the home of the Folies Bergère, famous and infamous the world over for its undraped girls (who were frequently employed by Méliès to decorate his films). Before 1900 striptease and nudity had already been committed to French film. Bared breasts, if not common, were by no means rare and between 1904 and 1906 some studios even made excursions into pornography, given general release under the heading of *Naughty Subjects of a Piquant Nature*, which zeroed in on the activities of young ladies in their baths and bedrooms and lingered on nudity. These had a short run even in liberal (not to say libertine) France and were prosecuted in 1905. However, much of their output was diverted underground

The early Italian epics were notable for their lack of modest costuming. This 1912 version of *Dante's Inferno* (directed by Francesco Bentolini, Adolfo Fadovan and Emilio Proncarolo, with sets based on illustrations by Doré) even included rare glimpses of full-frontal male nudity.

One of the best and most
spectacular of the first
Italian epics was Giovanni
Pastrone's *Cabiria* (1913, *see
below*), a love story set
against the Second Punic
War, whose most memorable
character was Maciste (The
Strong Man); so memorable,
in fact, that he became the
hero of a long-running,
anachronistic and often lurid
series of spectacular
adventures, including (*right*)
Guido Brignore's *Maciste
all'Inferno* (1926), a graphic,
underclad vision of hell set
in the nineteenth century.

to become the foundation, and, for many years,
the mainstay of the blue or stag film-circuit.

Other European countries followed the
French lead in exploiting the new medium.
Germany quickly came up with *Salome* (1902),
a film of such eroticism that its showing was
restricted to its native land. It was directed by
Oskar Messter and achieved some celebrity, but
his work, according to the distinguished historian of the German screen, Lotte Eisner,
showed 'nothing which even remotely recalls
the gaiety of the comic films of Pathé or
Gaumont, the stylistic perfection of the French
films d'art or the poetic fantasies of Georges
Méliès.'[7]

The Italians were altogether more successful.
They started their industry with a bang by
virtually inventing the epic at first try. With
the glory and grandeur of a splendid past
around them they recognized how the grand
spectacular sweep of their history could be
translated into filmic terms. They were also not
slow to spot that the sexual licence and orgiastic
behaviour associated with their ancestors
would not exactly kill box-office sales. The
loosely historical or biblical theme which is a
conveniently moralistic peg on which to hang
sexual excesses and debauchery was a form
which others – notably De Mille – were to take

Bartolomeo Pagano as
Maciste in *Cabiria*.

over and perfect. By looking back on, graphically re-creating and hypocritically condemning the brutality, sadism, licentiousness and
carnality of their forebears in such films as
Lucrezia Borgia and *The Last Days of Pompeii*,
and later the seminal *Quo Vadis?*, the Italians
hit upon a cinematic formula which one historian was to describe as characterized by
'lascivity, sumptuousness, a hysterical roman-
ticism and exaggerated passions'.[8]

Many of these foreign products were imported into the States and were lapped up by
American audiences. Before sound, of course,
the market for films was much more international as no time, trouble or expense had to
be invested in costly dubbing. With the simple
expedient of cutting in a few translated title
cards the movies were speedily ready for
release and instantly acceptable to the home
audience. If Herbert S. Stone had objected to a
mere screen kiss and had railed against 'the
filthiness of imported English and French stage
shows', imagine how he and his ilk would react
to the presence of foreign breasts, naked and
larger than life-size on the wall of his down-town
nickelodeon!

Growing suspicion and ill-ease among the
moral guardians eventually came to a head in
1907. Fuelled by the outstanding success of the
nickelodeons, or 'electric theatres' as they
were now called, by their vulgar exteriors,
raucous advertising, noisy phonograph music
and perhaps most of all by the titles of the
offered reels, the middle classes – who saw their
poorer citizenry frequent these sinks of iniquity
and were convinced that such entertainment
threatened the moral fabric of society – were
waiting for the chance to pounce. It has to be
admitted that the film producers did little to
help by christening their products with such
provocative titles as *Cupid's Barometer*; *Old
Man's Darling*; *A Seaside Flirtation*; *Beware,
My Husband Comes*; *Paris Slums*; *The Biga-
mist*; *Course of True Love*; *College Boy's First
Love*; *Gaieties of Divorce*, all of which were to be
seen in the same April week in one city in 1907.

That city was Chicago, and it is Chicago
which takes the dubious honour of initiating
the first ordinance for censorship of movies in
the United States. The match which ignited the
powder keg came in March 1907, with an
editorial in the Chicago Tribune entitled 'The
Five Cent Theatre' that was a swingeing attack
on the nickelodeon. It saw these places of
entertainment as sores on the urban landscape
without a single redeeming feature, and levelled
against them such criticisms as '... ministering
to the lowest passions of childhood ... proper to
suppress them at once . . . should be a law
absolutely forbidding entrance of boy or girl
under eighteen ... influence is wholly vicious....
There is no voice raised to defend the majority
of five cent theatres, because they cannot be
defended. They are hopelessly bad.'[9]

In fact, there was a voice raised to defend
them, that of George Kleine, whose Optical
Company was perhaps the largest business
concern dealing in movies. It is no coincidence

that he was the largest importer of foreign films in America. He also claimed that the daily attendance for screenings in Chicago alone was around one hundred thousand. Impressive though such figures were they must have been read with alarm by those who believed a judge's assertion in a correspondence column that 'these theatres cause, indirectly or directly, more juvenile crime coming into my court than all other causes combined'. The fight was taken up on both sides with broadsides being fired in the daily sheets. In a very short time New York took up the banner and The Children's Society initiated a crusade against the nickelodeons.

Interestingly, though, these disputes seemed to centre more around the evils that ensued from frequenting these places than from the sexual content of the fare purveyed. Nickelodeons were seen as being comparable with gin palaces or, in later years, pool halls as hang-outs for the actual and potential criminal. Certainly the content of the films displayed was considered to be of low standard, but there appear to have been no specific charges in this period against sexually offensive displays.

However, the furore aroused in Chicago and later New York was to have serious repercussions. On 8 June, 1907, Mayor McClennan of New York was in receipt of a report from his police commissioner recommending that all nickelodeons and other such places showing movies should have their licences revoked, thus effectively eradicating them from the city. In November, the Chicago City Council passed an ordinance that gave the responsibility for the issuing of picture permits to the chief of police, which in effect endowed him with the power of censor. 'This was the first direct censorship legislation addressed to the motion picture,' asserts Terry Ramsaye.

Not to be outdone, Mayor McClennan over in New York announced a year later to the day that he would hold a hearing 'to enquire into the advisability of allowing the motion picture shows to operate on Sundays and go into the general question of the physical safety of the screen theatres'.[10] The result of the hearing was an order 'revoking the licences of all five cent motion picture theatres in Greater New York and instructing the police department to see that they were closed at midnight, December 24, Christmas Eve, 1908.'[11] The news hit the presses and 'Christmas morning the world read that New York's mayor had clamped the lid of the law down on the city's motion picture theatres as unclean and immoral places of amusement'.[12]

The people directly affected – the five hundred exhibitors whose business was so summarily closed – acted fast and, ignoring the holiday, held a stormy meeting. Much legal to-ing and fro-ing resulted in injunctions against the order, but it directly led, in the early weeks of the new year, 1909, to the setting up of the National Board of Censorship of Motion Pictures. The establishment of the board was seen as an expedient way of forestalling such a move from the outside or even the total annihilation of the industry by exultant reformers, but with it the word 'censorship' officially entered the history of the movies.

It was unfortunate, for it spurred those who wanted censorial control even further and in 1915 the body changed its name to the National Board of Review. With its institution, the motion picture industry admitted that it needed an official watchdog and undoubtedly set the scene for the many storms, fights and backlashes that have rocked the history of the cinema from that point.

Sex Comes to Stay

By 1913 the cinema's history was short but already tempestuous. The infant industry had firmly shown its understanding of the box-office potency of sex but – since Edwin S. Porter's historic *Great Train Robbery* (1903), which is generally accepted as the first film to portray a story – it had lingered more over the subject of crime. Now the first film actually to treat a controversial sexual subject was ready to make its bow.

New York in the 1890s had been much shocked, and of course intrigued, by revelations of a flourishing white-slave trade – the international trafficking in young women for immoral purposes. This 'market for human flesh' had caught the imagination of the media and the popular arts and resulted in much lurid publicity and later pulp novels and even plays set around the theme. Two of Broadway's most successful excursions into the area had been 'The House of Bondage' and 'The Lure', both of which had been so inflammatory that they had attracted police attention and had excited

the imagination of a young director named George Loane Tucker.

Tucker was a film director working for the Independent Motion Picture Company – universally known as Imp. To be a director in New York in 1913 held little of the prestige and none of the glamour associated with such a post in a later decade and in Hollywood. In fact, Tucker's duties were to hack out humdrum one-reelers

Matt Moore as the policeman hero of George Loane Tucker's sensational white-slave drama, *Traffic in Souls* (1913).

Cautionary sexploitation dramas cashing in on the success of *Traffic in Souls* included more than one adaptation of a celebrated play about syphilis, 'Damaged Goods'. The British version directed by Alexander Butler in 1919, faithfully re-created the story of a student who contracts venereal disease from a country girl turned prostitute, is 'cured' by a quack doctor, marries and sires an infected child.

on a regular basis with the main considerations being speed and cheapness. Despite his lowly situation, Tucker was inspired with an idea to do a great cinematic exposé of the white-slave trade and, indeed, make a big picture: a picture running more than two reels and, furthermore, costing an incredible $5,000. To American producers such a project was unheard of. Pictures ran for one or perhaps two reels, no exhibitor would consider anything more, and those foreign products – like *Quo Vadis?* (1912) – which had been longer, had played not in local picture theatres but in 'legitimate' venues like 'real' theatres and even opera houses. What's more, $5,000 was the approximate budget for a dozen standard Imp movies.

Tucker got a very curt brush-off from Carl Laemmle, head of Universal under whose banner the Imp product was distributed, but found a sympathetic ear in Jack Cohn, Imp's film editor. Undismayed by Laemmle's brusque dismissal of his project, Tucker, with the connivance of Cohn, determined to shoot the picture secretly. Aided by the departure of the studio manager to Europe and the smokescreen of an internal political war in the company that diverted the attention of the administrators, Tucker and Cohn went to work, literally shooting the picture in odd moments and breaks in their normal day-to-day routine. In four weeks they finished shooting and found themselves with an unprecedented ten-reel, uncut, titleless film which they called *Traffic in Souls*.

Meanwhile, however, Tucker had had an argument with the acting studio manager and left not only Imp but also America in favour of England. He also left his child – all ten reels – with Cohn with strict instructions not to edit it beneath seven reels. Cohn had the unenviable task of cutting it – to six reels including titles – and then showing it to Laemmle and admitting that it had cost an astounding $5,700. If Laemmle turned it down he and a few conspirators would have to put up the money themselves.

The first showing was not a success. The executives were more concerned with their own

power struggles and bickered throughout the run. Cohn was depressed and angry and the same night, spurred by a sense of outrage, decided to beard the lion in his den. He roused Laemmle from his bed and said, 'I've come about *Traffic in Souls*. You talked all through the picture and you didn't see it. Nobody can look at a picture and talk business all the time. Won't you come down and really see it?' Laemmle agreed.

The result was a showdown between Laemmle and his enemies in the company. Laemmle offered to buy from Universal for $10,000; his opponents, sensing he was on to a winner, bid $25,000. It stayed in Universal.

Traffic in Souls (1913) was, indeed, a winner. Helped by some typically exaggerated publicity which claimed it was a '$200,000 spectacle' including '700 scenes with 800 players, showing the traps cunningly laid for young girls by vice agents', it opened at Weber's Theatre in New York and very quickly proved to be such an attraction that it played in twenty-eight cinemas in the Greater New York area and grossed approximately $450,000. It was the first tangible proof that exploitative screen sex sold and, typically, was followed by a rash of movies on the same theme. The speed at which films could be made in those days is demonstrated by *The Inside of the White Slave Traffic*, which was prepared, made, cut and screened in under a month after *Traffic*'s opening.

Damaged Goods (1915) – a highly successful Broadway play – followed and opened with the unique feature of a lecture by one Dr Carleton Simon on 'civilization by syphilization' and grossed over half a million dollars. Despite attempts by producers to make such products respectable, the authorities – particularly New York's Department of Licences – thought the trend had gone far enough and stepped in. Five similar movies were condemned – including *Sex Lure* and *Protect Your Daughter* – and this action, coupled with a satiation of the public's appetite for such themes, killed the market and the trend swung towards things more clinical. *Where Are My Children?* followed later – 'an uplifting drama of abortion' – and, almost by way of response, came *Motherhood*. This latter was felt to be a downbeat title by one enterprising exhibitor, who changed it to *The Doctor and Your Wife!*

But although sex was on the screen to stay, it wasn't without a fight. In 1914, Arthur Hammerstein filed a suit against impresario David Belasco claiming damages on the grounds that a theatre's reputation had been seriously injured because he had allowed *Traffic in Souls* to be shown there. Hammerstein actually won his case in the first court, although Belasco – and presumably the reputation of both the theatre and the film – triumphed on appeal.

And, much more importantly, in 1915, the cinema received a crucial blow, although one whose effects were not to be immediately noticed. In the case of Mutual Film Corp. v. Ohio, the issue of prior censorship first came before the Supreme Court, who were called upon to decide whether films fell within the free-speech guarantees of the state constitution. The court ruled that films should be distinguished from the printed media in a number of ways that placed them outside the free-speech provisions. 'The exhibition of motion pictures is a business pure and simple, originated and conducted for profit . . . not to be regarded . . . as part of the press of the country or as organs of public opinion. They are mere representations of events, of ideas and sentiments published or known; vivid, useful, and entertaining, no doubt, but . . . capable of evil, having power for it, the greater because of their attractiveness and manner of exhibition.' Prior censorship was thus constitutional and the decision encouraged its spread. By 1921 thirty-six states were considering censorship legislation.

If one wanted to put a date on the beginning of the star system, then 2 April, 1910, is as good as any and better than most. It was on that day that 'The Biograph Girl' was disclosed to the world as Miss Florence Lawrence.

Prior to this, the movies had known no stars. Producers correctly suspected that to name their actors would be to open the floodgates to a deluge of demands for increased salaries commensurate with the individuals' drawing power at the box-office. Actors had therefore gone largely unnamed, although the public, in an understandable desire to relate to the people they saw on the screen, had supplied them with soubriquets, like 'The Fat Man', and made a point of going to see movies in which their anonymous favourites appeared.

Florence Lawrence was The Biograph Girl and as such was 'a star' – in that she attracted

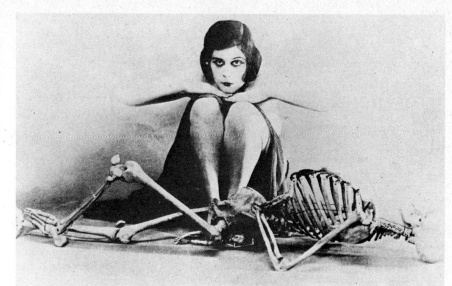

Theda Bara in her most famous publicity pose, as the man-eating vamp from *A Fool There Was* (Frank J. Powell, 1915).

people to her films – even though the industry might be unaware of the fact or wish to ignore it. Exceptionally, Carl Laemmle sensed that the actress's evident popularity with the public might be a distinct advantage and he wooed her away from Biograph and into a secret hiding-place. Soon afterwards, a newspaper story, originating from St Louis, claimed that The Biograph Girl had been killed in an accident. On 2 April, Laemmle's name also appeared in the press, strongly denying the report and claiming that Miss Lawrence was alive and well and now The Imp Girl, and he produced her in the flesh to prove it. Such was the start of the star system and also, it might be added, of the publicity stunt, for Laemmle it was who planted the death notices in the first place.

And so stars were born and the movie world was to revolve around them thereafter. Things moved apace in those early days and once the star system was established it was not long – six years to be precise – before the sex symbol was invented. She came in the unlikely guise of Theodosia Goodman, daughter of a tailor from Cincinnati – or, after some adjustments by publicists, Theda Bara, daughter of an Arabian princess from the Nile.

Few creations of the movie publicity machine were more eccentric and improbable than Bara. Because she was the first she had to be the oddest, and not even the wildest imaginings of the studio image-makers could actually compare with the utterly astonishing fact – to the modern observer – that the public actually lapped her up seemingly without noticing the brazen implausibility of her cover story. Today Bara seems farcically improbable as anyone's sex symbol. She 'had a maternal figure. She was, in fact, remarkably like a suburban housewife circa World War I, bitten by the glamour bug into imagining herself a supreme seductress of men, and by some weird turn of fate succeeding at it.'[13] But she was the woman for her time and the story of her success is as bizarre as the inventions of those who created her.

In 1897, the summer exhibition at the New Gallery in London included a painting by Philip Burne-Jones entitled 'The Vampire'. It was a

Florence Lawrence – 'The Biograph Girl' who became 'The Imp Girl' – the first real star of motion pictures.

Theda Bara as *Cleopatra* (J. Gordon Edwards, 1917).

Barbara La Marr – 'the girl who was too beautiful' – with Ramon Novarro in *Trifling Women* (Rex Ingram, 1922). Her career as a popular vamp star of the 'twenties – and her life – were cut short in 1926 by a combination of alcohol, drugs and tuberculosis.

ghoulish composition featuring a miasmic young woman of cadaverous features bending over the body of her dead lover whose skin bears the puncture marks of her teeth. A grotesque spectacle of depraved eroticism, it appealed strongly to the late-Victorians.

Rudyard Kipling – a relative of Burne-Jones – was moved to write a poem which he also entitled 'The Vampire'. Neither painting nor poem was very good and might, indeed should, have been forgotten were it not for the extraordinary trend they spawned. Kipling's verse ran, in part, as follows:

A fool there was and he made his prayer
(Even as you and I!)
To a rag and a bone and a hank of hair
(We called her the woman who did not care)
But the fool he called her his lady fair –
(Even as you and I!)

The rest of the doggerel went on to tell how the fool is ruined by his love. The painting and the poem coincided with the appearance and vast popularity of Bram Stoker's 'Dracula' and started a public fancy for things vampiric. Cashing in on a trend was as prevalent then as now, and Porter Emerson Browne – seeing the financial viability of spin-offs – transformed the poem into a stage play entitled 'A Fool There Was'. The play hit Broadway in 1909 and was an instant smash, thanks almost entirely to the heavily featured character of The Vamp.

The enormous appeal of this sexually predatory woman must be set in its time. This was still an era in which sex was more of a marital duty to the wife than a pleasurable experience. In Britain women were urged to lie back and think of England; in the States there was a whole continent still to be populated by sturdy young sons. Women were expected to be passive partners and to consider sex as a male beastliness, a price to be paid for respectability and security. Among young moderns – and spurred by the Suffragette movement – these attitudes were breaking down, but the general view of women was uncompromising. Nice girls didn't like sex; the sort that did were evil. And, as evil has always had a fascination, the sexually aggressive vamp, bent on the destruction of men, cast a spell over contemporary audiences.

During the play's run, William Fox purchased the screen rights and set about casting the major part. The play's producer and leading man warned Fox that the part tended to turn the head of the actress who played it and that he was constantly having to replace her. 'Put the girl you choose under contract, the part will make her,' he advised.[14]

Fox handed the direction of the film venture over to Frank Powell, who was, at that time, making *The Stain* (1915). A Miss De Coppett (in fact, Miss Goodman) applied for a part in *The Stain* and Powell was impressed by her and used her in a minor role in the film. Then, when the hunt for 'a rag and a bone and a hank of hair' was in full cry, presented his protégée, Theda Bara. After her success, the publicists asserted that the name was an anagram of 'Arab Death', which the public seemed to accept, along with the rest of the incredible myth. The truth was, of course, much more prosaic. Theda was a diminutive of Theodosia and Bara a contraction of a family name, Barranger. Whatever the girl's name, she was accepted, put under contract (Fox took the advice), and made the film.

A Fool There Was became an instant and immense hit in the first month of 1915. Theda Bara was a colossal attraction as, indeed, was the plot, which told of a young diplomat of upright and sober countenance, of good background and steady marriage who is sent to Europe. During the voyage he is ensnared by a vamp who, without too much difficulty, seduces him. In permissive Europe they abandon themselves to the pleasures of the flesh and wild debaucheries. The diplomat's family hear of his shame and when the reckless pair return renounce him. Coupled with this rejection is the departure of the vamp, who has taken him for all he has and leaves to find new victims. He, naturally, takes to drink and narcotics. His steadfast but broken-hearted wife attempts to win him back into the fold of marital fidelity and, just as success seems to be hers, the vamp returns and cries, 'Kiss me, my fool!' The power

of evil overcomes purity and the destroyed hero falls into her arms, broken and dying.

The vamp – the character and the word – passed into the culture and Fox, with a solid-gold sex symbol on his hands, set the publicity machinery to manufacturing a myth. Theda Bara, the studio was to claim in a barrage of information, was born in the shadow of the Sphinx, daughter of royalty, weaned on the blood of venomous snakes, and so on.

To buttress the mythology, the still cameras were enlisted to capture her at her most mystic. These shots were in themselves erotic, being heavily dependent on as little clothing and as many fetishist accoutrements as possible: breast barely concealed beneath elaborately worked jewels or diaphanous wisps of gauze; body hung about with pendants, snakes, spiders' webs, chains and other esoteric symbols; eyes heavily mascaraed to make them sunken and manic; heaped high with props to heighten dramatic effect. The vampire sucked blood, but one classic still showed her staring over a skeleton – presumably a dead lover – whom she appears to have recently eaten! The whole thing was pure hokum and, perhaps because it *was* so outrageous, press and public revelled in it.

The proof of Bara's impact as a sex symbol is that she made an astounding forty-odd films over the next three years, an incredible output of about one a month; her salary jumped in that time from $75 a week to $4,000, and she created a rage for anything vampish, including 'baby vamps'! She inspired many imitators, like Virginia Pearson and Louise Glaum, but none – apart, perhaps, from the beautiful, tragic Barbara La Marr – came anywhere near to dislodging her from her throne.

In retrospect, *A Fool There Was* is as laughable as Bara's grossly over-acted sexuality. There was no subtlety to it; she was a massive exaggeration, pursuing her male quarry with crazed eyes, luring him with animated gestures, loving him with the sensitivity of a rampaging

The scantiest dresser of the pre-'twenties period was Annette Kellerman, Australian dancer and swimmer, pioneer of the one-piece bathing suit, star of William Fox's million-dollar spectacular *A Daughter of the Gods* (J. Gordon Edwards, 1916), and (according to the Fox publicity) 'the world's most perfectly formed woman'. Her Hollywood career rapidly faded, but Esther Williams played her in a 1952 movie biography, *Million Dollar Mermaid*.

Virginia Pearson, the Fox studio's number two vamp after Theda Bara.

rhino. In the end this very travesty of desirable womanhood was what finished her career, along with the vamp's popularity (although 'vamping' – the sinuous use of body, eye-drooping and languid gesture – continued well into the next decade). Bara became a parody of herself as she prowled her destructive, emasculating way through movie after endless movie. She was trapped by her own creation – as were so many sex symbols who followed – so that when, by 1918, the public would no longer accept vamps, they also would not accept Bara as anything *but* a vamp. When she tried to break the mould and play the traditional Pickford-style heroine, the people who had made her a star rejected her.

Perhaps the paying customers were becoming more sophisticated. Perhaps they were starting to throw off the double standards of Victorian morality; certainly, by the 'twenties, they realized that illicit love – sex before or outside marriage – needn't necessarily be with a man-eater, and that because a woman recognized her own sexual needs she didn't have to be as nymphomaniacal or depraved as the Bara character.

By 1920 Bara's screen career was at an end. Her contribution to the art of film was negligible, but her contribution to the making of the sex symbol – a major figure in screen history – was considerable. Bara laid most of the ground-rules. She was the first popular star whose primary attraction was her sexuality. She proved conclusively that audiences paid vast sums of money to see women projecting a highly sexual image. She showed the industry that a star can be built from the publicity man's head and through the media. She showed that *true* sex symbols have a bisexual appeal in that they attract equally the fantasies of the opposite sex and the vanity of their own. Men adored, women emulated.

She found, too (as her rather pathetic 'At Liberty' announcements in the trade press until her death in 1955 testified) that being a sex symbol can put a millstone round your neck

that's difficult to cast aside. Bara could no more strip away her mask of erotic evil than Monroe could exorcise the demons which drove her to sex stardom. Bara's life after screen stardom, however, was a good deal happier, and although few of her films survive, and those which do, like *Fool*, are little more than cinematic curiosities, it is not strictly true to say, as Terry Ramsaye did, that 'The verb ("to vamp") may prove to be the only permanent contribution of the Fox-Theda barrage to the world.' If Bara did nothing else, she stamped the essence of the sex symbol on the public consciousness.

The infant cinema toddled, walked and finally took great strides in those first few years. In almost every aspect it developed with an astonishing speed. Sexually it reached its adolescence. It knew what sex was about and it was keen to try it, but was held back by the disapproval of repressive adults. In step with its increasing portrayal of things sexual was an equally aware Puritan lobby which saw in this mass art a spreading danger, particularly to the 'poor and criminal classes'. However, despite the growing interference of the censors, the cinema recognized that it could depict sex in a more vivid – if not more explicit – form than the post-card, novel or play. The screen's frankness, though, stopped well short of complete explicitness. Nudity, with a few exceptions, was forbidden, as were, for example, horizontal love scenes. Lingering kisses, suggestion-laden and sultry glances and much eye-rolling generally indicated deep passion. However, the film was, initially, a medium for the poor, who well understood the grim reality of life on the streets and in the ghettoes. Vice and prostitution were by no means alien to them and they instantly recognized a brothel or whore on the screen even though no overt mention was made of them.

As early as 1914 the screen had found its first genius in D.W. Griffith and the first film masterpiece in his monumental *Birth of a Nation*. The critical and popular acclaim with which the film was greeted – and, more particularly, the criticism it received to the effect that it endorsed prejudice and racialism – prompted Griffith to try for an even more spectacular production, *Intolerance* (1916).

Intolerance was to be truly enormous, but from the start it was doomed. Griffith threw huge and ever-increasing sums of money into the project, constructed vast sets, and hired armies of extras in an effort to – as the sub-title had it – depict *Love's Struggle Through the Ages*. The venture was too big, and even on its first showing the reasons became apparent to some who had worked on it. Joseph Henabery, actor and assistant director on the movie, said of that screening: 'It was a very disconnected story. I knew that Griffith had had a problem trying to utilize all this material in a sensible way. . . . He had switched from period to period and he had it all chopped up. He just had too much material.'[15]

When he had finished the film, Griffith took it from Hollywood to the East and, says Henabery, 'apparently some of the powers-that-be said, "You ought to have more sex in it." As usual, the guys that sell to the public figured that the public all think in a certain way.'[16]

As a result, Griffith cabled instructions to Henabery to 'shoot scenes of Belshazzar's Feast' and 'he described what he wanted – naked women'. Henabery was doubtful and told a colleague, 'He can't shoot naked women. You can't get away with that sort of thing.' But orders were orders and these came from the great D.W. himself, who wanted an orgy. 'So I got a bunch of people together, and as a basic shot I developed a section from an old painting known as "Belshazzar's Feast". It was a wild party. A real orgy. I had people lying around so that they weren't stark naked – almost, but not quite.' In fact, Henabery learned later that Griffith had shot some naked women for the sequence himself: 'Horrible-looking creatures . . . he'd dug up from the red-light district.' These

shots were eventually cut into the scene.

It is in many ways a sad comment that a directorial talent like Griffith's should have been forced to accede to the exploitative demands of commerciality (especially as he was a sensitive enough director to be able to appreciate the truly erotic, clear from his comment: 'There is no suspense like the suspense of a delayed coition') and sadder still that totally gratuitous sexual segments should have been indiscriminately injected into a project of honest artistic endeavour.

So, soon after the industry had taken its first hesitant step into screen sex with *Traffic in Souls* (a mere three years before), the 'filthy hands' were steering it towards a course that it wavered on thereafter – the fine line between sex as an integral part of a scenario and as a cynical, irrelevant (as far as the plot goes) come-on to set the turn-stiles clicking.

Mack Sennett's bathing beauties began a lasting Hollywood cheesecake tradition. Among the prettiest was Anglo-French star Marie Prevost, who became a popular leading lady in the 'twenties, but could not reconcile herself to supporting roles with the coming of Sound, took to the bottle and died in 1937.

21

THE TWENTIES
Hollywood's Heyday

The Movies Grow Up

Nothing was quite the same after the First World War. Movies, which had thrown themselves into the fray with intense patriotic propagandizing, seemed to grow up. With peace, the more sophisticated middle-class audience which now patronized the plush new cinemas would no longer accept the standard sexual fare of demure maidens (like Mary Pickford in *The Little American*, 1917) threatened with a fate worse than death at the hands of the brutal and licentious Boche soldiery. Even the doughboys – recruited from the farms and urban ghettoes – were more worldly wise; after all, many of them *had* seen Paree and were versed in the ways of love.

Social and sexual mores were changing, and there were those in Hollywood who registered the shift and acted upon it. Cecil B. De Mille, noting the mood of the times, jumped in with a completely new (to the screen) brand of entertainment – the film centred around the marital problems of the middle classes. Divorce, infidelity and philandering were featured. The titles of a series of such films made between 1918 and 1920 indicate the new permissiveness: *Old Wives for New* (1918), *Don't Change Your Husband* (1919), *For Better for Worse* (1919), *Male and Female* (1919) and *Why Change Your Wife?* (1920). The main theme exploited was the premise that marriage and love are not necessarily incompatible and couples should act as lovers rather than fall into the marital rut, but that if a marriage has dulled sexuality then romance is available elsewhere. Such plots, of course, questioned the whole basis on which marriage had hitherto worked.

Female sexuality was at last being recognized and the woman who admitted her sexual needs was not necessarily evil – as the vamp had been depicted – but obeying her natural drives. In *Why Change Your Wife?* Gloria Swanson – who was frequently cast in such roles – realizes that her constant hen-pecking has driven her husband into the arms of another woman and sets about winning him back by changing her image. She tells her dressmaker when ordering a new garment, 'Make it sleeveless, backless, skirtless – in short, go to the limit. I won't be dressed like anyone's aunt!' Her strategy works, she vamps (as opposed to *being* a vamp) and captures her spouse's heart. The year before – in *Don't Change Your Husband* – the roles were reversed: Swanson – bored with her lacklustre husband – runs off with an attractive but profligate cad. Husband smartens up and Swanson, her lover's true character revealed, returns.

De Mille's excursion into such subject matter paid off handsomely. The public needed an antidote to the gloom of war, and it was also starting to crave settings other than those of urban ghettoes in which poverty, honesty, fidelity, virtue and self-sacrifice were applauded and rewarded. Opulence, luxury and hedonism were great attractions; the wealthy need no longer be depicted as wicked or charitable. The black-and-white characterizations of the pre-war years were now merging into more believable shades of grey.

However, De Mille's major themes in these movies should not be seen as immoral. Indeed, although marital disharmony, infidelity and divorce were graphically portrayed, the message was always strictly 'moral'. The principal characters soon saw the errors of their ways and gratefully, lovingly returned to the shelter of wedlock.

These productions were enormously popular and, significantly, initiated one of De Mille's most characteristic and successful devices for injecting sex into his movies while keeping the scene totally inoffensive. In a masterstroke of trivial genius De Mille realized that on the screen Cleanliness *was* next to Godliness and he shifted sexual emphasis away from the bedroom to the bathroom. If bedrooms were taboo – and soon they were deemed so to be – then what better place than the bathroom to arouse the voyeur in the audience? Who could possibly object to hygiene and sanitation?

With this blindingly simple plot contrivance, the charms of Miss Swanson could be displayed with complete tact. But De Mille was, after all, De Mille. His films didn't just have bathrooms, they had Temples to Hygieia: plush, lush, exotic, where oils, salves and balms pandered and pampered the body, anointing it in near-holy ritual; where foaming bubbles and mystic ointments replaced plain soap and water; where a woman undressed about as naturalistically as Salome; where towels were never less than an acre. It was a tease from start to finish and it was all quite unobjectionable. From *Old Wives for New*, when he introduced his sexy washroom, C.B. De Mille used it regularly and added a new cliché to the movie canon.

Well-scrubbed maidens and marital mischief were two of the director's great contributions to screen sex. His third – and the one for which his name lives – came a few years later: the Biblical Epic. Even in his contemporary movies immediately following the war, De Mille had resorted to flashbacks to earlier times to help his plot along.

In 'The Admirable Crichton' – which he directed as *Male and Female* (1919) – he was faced with a problem. How could a member of

Lillian Rich played a sybaritic Southern vamp in Cecil B. De Mille's lavishly staged modern morality tale, *The Golden Bed* (1925). Her decadent, voluptuous nest epitomized De Mille's successful blend of glamour, sex and moral righteousness.

the servant classes make love to a member of the ruling classes when such things were as taboo as the portrayal of miscegenation? Easy – flashback to a former incarnation when the butler was 'a king in Babylon' and the lady 'a Christian slave'.

In 1922, he transported the story of a flapper back to prehistoric times and figure-displaying skins in order to prove that the teenage heroine of *Adam's Rib* with her bare legs and short skirts was simply a modern manifestation of an age-old type of woman. This time, however, there were those ready to shout 'Hold!' and the film took a critical beating. Seeking subject

The Swedish-made *Häxan* (*Witchcraft Through the Ages*, Benjamin Christensen, 1922), an imaginative, dramatized treatment of the history and psychology of witchcraft, described itself as an 'audacious film' which 'brings to life the sad aberrations of an age when satanism troubled the minds of many'; but its scenes of nudity, orgies, black mass and torture, despite claims to authenticity, caused it to be banned almost universally.

One of De Mille's first society sex comedies, *Don't Change Your Husband* (1919) was described by Variety as 'clean and wholesome', an indication of the director's consummate skill in wrapping up his risqué themes in good taste. Gloria Swanson (seen here with Ted Shawn) played a fickle divorcee who can't decide between her stuffy ex-husband (Elliott Dexter) and a two-timing playboy (Lew Cody).

matter for his next movie, C.B. was struck by the number of suggestions from the public he received for a biblical theme. He chose *The Ten Commandments* (1923).

He had already learned most of his important lessons, foremost of which was that the portrayal of 'historic' events allowed the director greater freedom in his depiction of subjects unacceptable in a modern context. An orgy set in 1920 Manhattan was *verboten*, but one portrayed at the times of, say, Herod or Pharaoh was quite permissible.

The formula of extravagant spectacle and detailed sexual licence was an allowable and

Above: De Mille's *Manslaughter* (1922), about an amoral society girl (Leatrice Joy) whose excesses cause the death of a policeman, contained orgiastic fantasy sequences intended to draw parallels with the decadence and downfall of ancient Rome:

Left: The legend of *Casanova* provided a popular framework for displays of period spectacle and sex in the 'twenties and 'thirties. Most opulent and revealing of them was this Franco-Italian colour production of 1927, directed by Alexander Volkoff and starring matinée idol Ivan Mosjoukine as the Latin seducer.

immense box-office draw. As De Mille pointed out, he didn't write the Bible nor did he invent Sodom and Gomorrah. However, he could peddle a pious line in hypocrisy when it suited him and some years later wrote to a Jesuit friend: 'The producers are in a state of panic and chaos and . . . they rush for the bedspring and lingerie the moment the phantom of empty seats rises to clutch them.'[17] Typically, he omitted to mention that some directors were equally fast to the bathroom and silken robe in such times!

De Mille was not alone in his divination of the public's willingness to accept new themes and a fresh treatment of sex. Erich von Stroheim was uniquely suited to the part of director of the perverse.

Von Stroheim was the sort of enigma that Hollywood at first adores and subsequently abhors. He claimed aristocratic parentage he never had. He was an Austrian but paraded more like a Prussian, bullet-headed, militarily erect and embodying in his appearance the brutal and sadistic villain he so often, as an actor, portrayed. Altogether he was an intriguing man and must, to the largely impressionable Hollywood community, have seemed

The highly exploitable *Dante's Inferno* was also frequently filmed. Fox's production of 1924 (director Henry Otto) was relatively tasteful, disguising its cast's nudity with body stockings and discreetly draped hair; this revealing shot of Diana Miller as Beatrice was cut from some versions.

Typically, Cecil B. De Mille won moral approval for his 1923 version of *The Ten Commandments* by paralleling the biblical story — complete with statutory orgy round the Golden Calf — with a modern one. Photoplay said: 'It wipes the slate clean of charges of an immoral influence against the screen.'

the quintessential Continental. With no reputation except as a 'heavy', he impressed Carl Laemmle – head of Universal – so much that he allowed the Austrian to direct his first film on the strength of a single-page scenario and gave him a totally free hand with but one proviso: the original title was *The Pinnacle*; 'What means this word pinnacle?' he demanded. 'The public won't know what it is about. There are more blind husbands about than there are pinnacles, so we'll call it *Blind Husbands*.'[18]

Von Stroheim's life in the days of the dying Austrian Empire no doubt coloured his attitudes. His was a world of decadence, in which the pleasures of the flesh were to be satisfied; where the perverse and the bizarre were very nearly the commonplace; where female Ameri-

Betty Blythe, as *The Queen of Sheba* (J. Gordon Edwards, 1921), captured the imagination of American girlhood just as for a while Rudolph Valentino, as *The Sheik*, incarnated the romantic male ideal, and trendy dating couples liked to think of themselves as 'Sheiks' and 'Shebas'.

can tourists willingly surrendered themselves in the arms of Continental, hand-kissing adventurers; where husbands were indeed blind and wives foolish.

Few of von Stroheim's films were made without controversy and studio conflict. After a decade of stormy film-making which produced, among others, *Blind Husbands* (1918), *Foolish Wives* (1921), *Greed* (1923), *The Merry Widow* (1925), *The Wedding March* (1928) and *Queen Kelly* (1928), von Stroheim became an outcast, not least because of his meticulous and expensive attention to detail (he insisted that all the soldiers in one film should be dressed in regulation silk underwear even though this was never seen), his extravagance (*Foolish Wives* was billed as 'The First Million-Dollar Picture'

Erich von Stroheim's abortive drama of female sexual jealousy, *Queen Kelly* (1928), was notable for its erotic symbolism, especially in this bath scene with Seena Owen. The production was wound up when its star, Gloria Swanson, walked off the set after learning that the character she was playing was scripted to inherit a chain of brothels (a gesture echoed more violently by mogul Louis B. Mayer, who reputedly struck von Stroheim when the latter stated his opinion that 'all women are whores'). The film was eventually released in a patched-up version.

Few of von Stroheim's films escaped mutilation, and this included his version of *The Merry Widow* (1925), which lost its line-up of semi-topless cabaret dancers (joined here by John Gilbert) in the American-released version.

Playful sadomasochism was a hallmark of von Stroheim's characterizations as the cruel Continental seducer. In this censored scene from *Foolish Wives* (1921), perhaps the liveliest of his original satires on sexual intrigue, Mae Busch was the willing playmate.

and a sign in New York's Times Square logged the daily expenditure total) and his uncomfortable obsession with the darker side of human sexuality.

'Stroheim was the true creator of a sophisticated cinema,' one critic has claimed.[19] Certainly, he treated his audience as adults in that his images and characterizations were often enigmatic and, frequently, shocking. Shocking, that is, if you were knowing enough of the byways of human carnality to spot them. After *Blind Husbands*, the studios took against Stroheim's unruly genius and sought to curb him. In many ways he suffered the same humiliations at the hands of more powerful but essentially lesser men as did Orson Welles.

Only two of his films – *Blind Husbands* and *The Devil's Passkey* (1919) – remained unmutilated. He shot his material at length, letting the camera dwell on foibles and failings, linger on symbols and totems. The studios cut them savagely. Even Irving Thalberg, the young

genius of MGM and said to be the most sensitive of all the moguls, could not countenance Stroheim's individuality. When viewing a sequence from *The Merry Widow* in which, at enormous length, the camera roves over a cupboard crammed with shoes, boots and slippers of all types, he countered von Stroheim's explanation – 'I wanted to establish that this man is a foot fetishist' – with the retort, 'You are a footage fetishist.'[20]

Fetishism, unnatural obsessions and dark lusts dripped from Stroheim films. They seldom reached the screen after the studio and then the censor had taken the scissors to them. Those that did only slipped through because the viewers had failed to comprehend their significance. 'Stroheim revealed the great festering wound which was eating away at the heart of society.' A society that was collapsing through its own depravity and inertia, that had been rudely smashed by the First World War. 'Kings, queens, princes, great barons, wealthy in-

'One of Hollywood's more genial souls, though not without a strain of Rabelais' (Will Hays on von Stroheim). In this daringly horizontal seduction scene from *Foolish Wives*, Stroheim's conquest (one of five in the film) was played by Miss Dupont (so called because her aristocratic lineage was allegedly so refined that she could not be referred to in any other fashion).

dustrialists, the glittering haute monde – locomotor ataxia, haemophilia, nymphomania, satyriasis, perversions, gluttony, rape. This was Stroheim's "high world".'[21] Perhaps Hollywood took against him so virulently because, in so many ways, it had itself become the new decadent Vienna; because it created its own aristocracy, lived by its own extraordinary moral code, indulged in its own spectacular pleasures and because, underneath the veneer, there lurked a darker side.

De Mille brought sex to the screen in a new form; von Stroheim added sophistication and an understanding of the newly vaunted work of Freud. Both made their first films in this mould in the last years of a dying decade and properly belong to the 'twenties.

The New Sodom

Soon after the announcement of Miss Florence Lawrence as the first named star, the hierarchical structure that was Hollywood until the 'fifties was conceived. Stars were the new élite, and stars were measured by their drawing power, their billing and the amount of money they were paid. As early as 1914 Mary Pickford won a contract for an unprecedented $104,000 a year; by 1916 she had been guaranteed $1,040,000 for a two-year contract. The pickings were rich indeed and the stars were living in a style and at a rate that knew no comparisons. These were Silent days: an era in which the stars worked during the daylight hours and played through the night because there were no lines to learn for the next day's shooting.

And these were film people. And film people were like theatre people but much exaggerated. They had their own code, their own morals. They were young, they were rich and they were beautiful. Sometimes they were indiscreet and, because they were the biggest international stars the world had ever seen, the eyes of the media were turned on them.

Scandal. That was what sold – and still sells – newspapers. And scandal – if any existed in the early days of the 'twenties – was a useful club with which prudes and reformers could beat the film-makers into cleaning up their products. And scandal there was. Drugs, for example, had taken hold of some of the public's favourite performers – Wallace Reid, Mabel Normand and Barbara La Marr to name only a few. Marriages were frequently breaking up in the town. The very well publicized divorces and marriage of Pickford and Fairbanks laid open the unorthodox lifestyle of Hollywood's beautiful people, and once reporters had a foot in the door they were going doggedly to pursue any other hint of illicit shenanigans.

The 'twenties had hardly started before there was a scandal which blew the lid off the town. On Monday, 5 September, 1921, Roscoe 'Fatty' Arbuckle – a $7,000 a week star of the Famous

Players-Lasky Studio and one of America's best-loved comedians – threw a party at the St Francis Hotel. In the course of the celebrations, twenty-five-year-old Virginia Rappe, a small-part player with a reputation for getting on as best she could, was taken ill and died four days later. It is still not fully known under what circumstances she received her fatal injuries; the ballyhoo surrounding the incident at the time, the allegations and counter-claims that flew across the town and the general air of mystery, have helped to blur the facts.

What is known is that everyone had been drinking heavily and Virginia Rappe retired from the main celebrations. Some claimed she had been ripping her clothes off, others that she passed out. Some said that she had been accompanied to a bedroom by another woman, others that Arbuckle had escorted her there and locked the door. Broadly, it was alleged that the comedian had sexually and obscenely assaulted her in such a way as to make her scream, 'I'm dying. He broke me inside. I'm dying.' Arbuckle's defenders denied the charge absolutely and maintained that he had done all in his power to look after her. It was, however, generally agreed that the dead Miss Rappe was no better than she ought to have been. This, of

Mary Pickford, 'America's Sweetheart', epitomized goldilocked innocence on the screen, an image only partially tarnished when she married Douglas Fairbanks amidst a flurry of divorce scandal.

In contrast to the sex
superstars of the 'twenties,
like Gloria Swanson and
Pola Negri, were the popular
romantic leading ladies and
comediennes such as
Constance Talmadge (*right*)
and her sister Norma.

Lillian Gish, perhaps the greatest of all Silent screen actresses, saved many a saccharine melodrama with her almost puritanical characterizations of distressed innocence.

course, in no way mitigated an attack – if such had occurred – that led to death. All-in-all it was a most distasteful affair which needed investigation.

Arbuckle was brought to trial on three separate occasions for involuntary manslaughter. The first two resulted in the juries being unable to agree, and the third totally exonerated him and indeed attacked the State for ever having charged him. So Arbuckle was cleared and free. But his career was ruined and the press had a field day tearing into Hollywood morals. To many it only went to support what they had always believed – that Hollywood was the new Sodom.

The censorship lobby and the moralists, shocked at the scandalous revelations, went hand-in-hand. 'The motion picture men were sinking deeper and deeper into the gloom of the industry's disgrace. They needed a friend, quickly. The flow of scandal was telling at the box-office. Censorship movements were acquiring new strength. Professional enemies of the screen were capitalizing opportunity.'[22] The friend they sought was Will H. Hays, the Postmaster General of the Harding Administration.

On 2 December, 1921, barely three months after Arbuckle's fateful party, ten of Hollywood's most important moguls wrote a letter to Hays saying that the undersigned 'realize the necessity for attaining and maintaining the highest possible standard of motion picture film production in this country and are striving to have the industry accorded the consideration and dignity to which it is justly entitled, and proper representation before the people of this country so that its position, at all times, may be presented in an unbiased and unprejudiced manner.' It went on to say that 'we feel that our industry requires further careful upbuilding and a constructive policy of progress.'

The fine words and rolling phrases actually concealed the fact that the signatories –

powerful and despotic men though they were – were unable to agree among themselves on most issues, were motivated by self-interest that made compromise in most things unthinkable, and were mortally afraid that if they didn't somehow club together and make an appearance of house cleaning, the initiative was going to be taken from them by the ever more outspoken and incensed lobbies outside Hollywood. The last thing they wanted was dictation from Washington in the shape of federal legislation.

They chose their man carefully. Hays had masterminded the Harding election campaign. He was a consummate organizer, well respected and with impeccable credentials. He knew the important people, had the ear of the politically powerful, and was recognized generally for his strongly moral and upright respectability. They may also have hoped that by appointing him themselves to an organization they had created,

Roscoe 'Fatty' Arbuckle, one of America's best-loved comedians, whose career was ruined by scandal during Hollywood's most hedonistic period prior to the Will Hays clean-up.

Rudolph Valentino dans

L'AMANT ETERNEL
(LE FILS DU CHEIK)

ASTRA PARIS FILMS

and offering him a very substantial $100,000 a year salary, he would be their man. But Hays would be sold no pups; he was no man's mouthpiece and, on accepting, he took his duties very seriously indeed. In fact, during Will H. Hays's twenty-three years as 'Czar' of Hollywood and President of the Motion Picture Producers and Distributors of America (MPPDA or, as it was universally known, Hays Office) many of those who had lobbied him so earnestly to represent them would often have cause to curse the day that they had been panicked into hiring the man.

Hays, on accepting the position in early 1922, defined his duties under a number of headings, among the most important of which were lobbying against any threatened state or federal censorship legislation and cleaning house. In fact, in the early years the Hays Office, thanks to the tireless work of its secretary Courtland Smith, did manage to defeat a film censorship bill in Massachusetts, but within months of taking office Hays lectured the film world assembled to honour him at the Hollywood Bowl: 'This industry must have towards that sacred thing, the mind of a child, towards that clean virgin thing, that unmarked slate, the same care about impressions made upon it, that the best clergyman or most inspired teacher of youth would have.' He was posting notice, in effect, that while he would work on the industry's behalf to fight legislation he would also assiduously follow a policy of self-censorship. The 'mind of a child' speech may have provoked titters among the community, may have elicited smug smiles on the faces of the moguls, but within ten years Will H. Hays was going to be the most aggravating thorn in the creative flesh of directors and producers (whom he valued little as a breed) and turn the industry and its attitude to sex upside down.

Shortly after the round robin that recruited the Czar, Hollywood was rocked by another scandal. During the night of 1 February, 1922, director William Desmond Taylor was murdered. The perpetrator of the deed was never apprehended and the headlines were filled with the case for months as police and reporters dug into the director's personal life. Will Hays took a poor view of such things and the Taylor case, together with Wallace Reid's death – he was a drug addict – and Arbuckle's trials, moved him to take action. Written into every contract

thereafter was a 'morality clause' that threatened suspension or even termination if the artist was involved in any scandal. This at least had the effect of making the wilder elements of the community more discreet in their affairs, but probably did not fundamentally affect the way in which they conducted themselves in private.

A primary object of Hays's job was 'to foster the common interest of those engaged in the motion picture industry in the United States by establishing and maintaining the highest possible moral and artistic standards in motion picture production'. In other words, self-censorship.

A first step towards this was the introduction in 1924 of the 'Hays Formula', which demanded that books, scripts and screenplays be submitted to his office for vetting. The formula soon proved unworkable and in 1926 Jason Joy was sent to Hollywood (the Hays Office was based in New York) to set up a Studio Relations Department to deal more closely with producers. In the following year a list of 'Don'ts and Be Carefuls' was introduced with the aim of pointing out areas in which censor boards were particularly sensitive. The industry paid lip service but little more. The full impact of Hays and censorship was not to hit Hollywood for another few years, spurred by the enormous upheaval of Sound.

Will Hays, 'Czar of Hollywood', with Baby Peggy, three-year-old star of a 'twenties fairytale series.

Stars in the Ascendant

Whatever the implications of Hays's arrival might be in the future, the 'twenties, The Jazz Age, had arrived, and with the new decade came a new concept of sexuality. Women's fashions showed the way; legs were in and bosoms were out; or, to be more precise, bosoms were even more in for they were practically non-existent. Short skirts revealed more of the lower limbs than had been seen for many years and fashion-

able figures were 'boyish', with breasts flattened by a bandeau. But the girls were dizzy. They laughed and danced and drank and smoked and loved speed. They were also a lot less inhibited than their mothers when it came to love.

Stars like Gloria Swanson and Joan Crawford captivated audiences in the first years of the decade, but without any doubt the biggest star to emerge was an Italian, born (so he

grossers and second in rental only to Vidor's war epic, *The Big Parade*, 1925) Valentino became a very hot property indeed. It didn't matter that in real life Valentino was a sexual dud – possibly homosexual, almost certainly impotent – and suffered two ignominious marriages, the first to dancer Jean Acker, which was unconsummated, and the second, to designer and ersatz Russian from Utah, Natacha Rambova, who dominated him and came close to wrecking his career with her

claimed) Rodolpho Alfonzo Raffaelo Pierre Filibert Guglielmi di Valentina d'Antonguolla. It was as Rudolph Valentino that he achieved stardom.

Valentino epitomized the continuing fascination of the public with exoticism. He was in direct descent from Theda Bara and, indeed, has been described as 'quite simply a male Vamp'. It's difficult today to see the magnetism that he evidently exerted; it has been said that he had the acting talents of the average wardrobe, and he certainly seemed to restrict his range to a great deal of eye rolling, eyebrow jerking and facial smouldering. This, however, was enough to ensure that during his lifetime and even fifty years after his death the name Valentino is synonymous with 'Great Lover'.

The Four Horsemen of the Apocalypse made Valentino a star in 1921. It was one of those parts in one of those movies which, by some chemistry that no one can adequately analyze, shoots the actor to the top. Valentino was right for the time. He was also, strangely, a sex symbol who did not appeal to both the sexes. Valentino was a ladies' man; men, by and large, detested him.

Valentino was different and women knew it. His patent-leather hair, his smoky eyes, his habit of kissing women on the inside rather than the back of the hand, the way his chest heaved when consumed by passion, the manner in which he turned away, tight-lipped, when nearly overcome and, most of all, his cavalier, almost brutal, treatment of women all conspired to make him the hottest, sexiest, most desirable male star of the 'twenties.

With the astonishing success of *Four Horsemen* (it made $4,500,000 in distributors' rentals, putting it up with the 'twenties top box-office

Valentino in distress in *Son
of the Sheik*.

high-flown, pseudo-artistic plans. On screen, as a matador in *Blood and Sand* (1922), a smouldering Arab in *The Sheik* (1921) and *Son of the Sheik* (1925), he was sexual dynamite. Few of the male stars whose appeal was primarily based on sexuality, including Gable, attained the peak of Valentino's near-hysterical popularity. A popularity that lingers even today among a large and fanatically faithful band of followers.

Valentino's films gave off a heady sexual aura. In *Blood and Sand*, statuesque Nita Naldi – a heavy-chested virago of a woman – clutches his hands in wonder and says (via titles), 'Someday you will beat me with these strong hands. I should like to know what it feels like.' In *Monsieur Beaucaire* (1924) he is seen near-naked and ritualistically dressed by pandering attendants. And in *The Sheik* – most famous of all his roles – he fulfils every woman's romantic and erotic fantasies by swooping out of the desert to carry off Agnes Ayres.

Valentino offered women sex without marriage, surrender without guilt. The world's women saw his films and relived them in their imaginations. They wrote to him explaining how, when making love to their husbands, they fantasized that it was with him that they were performing. He struck a deep, responsive erotic chord in the women of the 'twenties, who

reacted – over-reacted – in a rather unhealthy manner. It was as if they were suddenly freed from the dam of sexual guilt and repression and their innermost drives poured from them in a hysterical flood. They mobbed cinemas where his films played and his funeral (he died in 1926, barely into his thirties and only six years after becoming a star) was an undignified circus of mourning.

To modern eyes Valentino's acting seems clownish and his appeal inexplicable, but he brought an important change to the cinema's sexual attitudes in that he was the predator, he could take a woman so that she melted romantically or surrendered to his brutality and no stigma was attached. His love was impossible fantasy and therefore morally harmless. He was animalistic in his desires and set a trend for Latin Lovers, beautiful seducers and male

carnality that was to become staple fare.

His death provoked the studios to look for replacements. There were many candidates but none filled his shoes and robes with complete success. Perhaps the most popular was Ramon Novarro, who specialized in action films (notably the 1927 version of *Ben Hur*) and was noted for his superb physique, which he displayed always to the fullest possible advantage. Others included Antonio Moreno, Ricardo Cortez, Rod la Rocque and Gilbert Roland.

A certain coyness about sex was still manifest. To speak the word out loud was yet a little shame-making and so a word was coined by a very popular Englishwoman of good breeding called Elinor Glyn, who set Hollywood in a spin with her thoughts on the subject of 'It'. 'It' – 'the indefinable something,' said Madame Glyn, philosopher and arbiter of 'twenties sex

Evelyn Brent, glamorous star of the 'twenties, in a fully-rigged publicity pose.

In *The Four Horsemen of the Apocalypse* (1921) Rudolph Valentino played the part of Julio, an Argentinian art student in Paris at the time of the First World War — giving director Rex Ingram an excuse to include this tastefully risqué tableau.

'Someday you will beat me with these strong hands. I should like to know what it feels like.' Valentino and Nita Naldi in *Blood and Sand* (Fred Niblo, 1922).

appeal – was the rage; who had 'It' and who did not were the talking points of the late 'twenties. One who very definitely had 'It' – indeed Madame Glyn selected her personally – was Clara Bow.

Glyn was a power at MGM and used her specialized knowledge of the subject to groom the stars in the ways of love. 'I had always suspected,' she pronounced, 'that American men could not make love. Not even the leading men had any idea how to do it,'[23] (which probably explained the appeal of Valentino and other non-Americans). She crystallized her thoughts in a magazine story entitled 'It' and found herself the doyenne of matters romantic. 'It' was, she explained, 'a strange magnetism which attracts both sexes . . . there must be physical attraction, but beauty is unnecessary'.

Paramount, seeing the enormous interest in 'It' (both the concept and the novelette that bred it), determined to cash in on the fad and turn the drippy story of a thrusting young businessman who falls for an 'It'-filled shopgirl into a light romantic comedy. Mme Glyn was dragooned, willingly, into selecting the girl who personified her ideal. The choice was Clara Bow.

Bow was and remains still in the minds of the public the 'It Girl'. She was a flat-breasted, frenetic, energy-packed flapper. She epitomized the fun, freedom and pure *joie de vivre* that was the 'twenties. (Actually, Colleen Moore was the original Flapper – a term derived from the strange habit of wearing galoshes unbuckled, a direct flouting of convention! – and she made her name and created the image of the speed-crazy, cocktail-drinking Gay Young Thing in *Flaming Youth*, 1923.)

Bow 'danced even when her feet were not moving' and was billed as 'the Hottest Jazz Baby in Films'. She was no ordinary sex symbol – indeed, she described herself as 'a tomgirl' who 'doesn't care particularly about men' – but after the million-dollar-grossing *It* she was a very big star who knew precisely how to use her body, how much of it to expose and, more important, what portions of it to cover alluringly.

In a series of highly successful films after *It* in 1927, Bow summed up the spirit of the decade, but she fell foul of her own lifestyle, was attended by scandalous revelations, including – according to a personal secretary she charged with embezzlement – a propensity for drink, drugs and gigolos, and by the 'thirties – her own times past – faded. She once said: 'Being a sex symbol is a heavy load to carry, especially when one is tired, hurt and bewildered.' Possibly the most poignant epitaph ever for a breed of star she helped to create.

The great sex stars of the 'twenties seemed to split fairly neatly into two broad categories – the home-growns and the exotics. The home-growns of the Colleen Moore/Clara Bow mould included Gloria Swanson (mainstay of the De Mille marital comedies and other sophisticated roles, such as *Male and Female*, 1919, *The Affairs of Anatol*, 1921, *Prodigal Daughters*, 1923, *Untamed Lady*, 1926, and *Sadie Thompson*, 1928) and Joan Crawford, who started as a flapper and graduated to knowing career-girl parts after her début in *Pretty Ladies* (1925).

The exotics generally followed the Theda Bara tradition of sultry temptress. Foremost among them was Pola Negri, the first in a very long line of Hollywood imports from Europe. She came from Poland, had a successful career in Germany, and took America by storm with

When Valentino died of peritonitis in 1926, more than 15,000 people packed Broadway to view the body. Many women fainted, others (*above*) were knocked down by the violence of the crowds trying to get into New York's Campbell Funeral Parlour.

Most popular of Valentino's would-be successors was Mexican-born Ramon Novarro, whom the MGM publicity department described as having 'the body of Michelangelo's David and the face of an El Greco don'. His most famous role (*left*) was in *Ben Hur* (Fred Niblo, 1927).

41

Clara Bow – the 'It Girl' – was the archetypal flapper, the wild party-girl who always settled for the boy-next-door in the end. Her publicity stills, however – like the one above – were often more alluring than her on-screen image.

explicit (for the time) kiss with Dolores Costello in *The Sea Beast* (1925). His off-screen sex life was energetic and debauched, but little of this (except in later years in the ravages to his face and body) showed in his films and, anyway, he was always considered a Great Actor.

After Valentino's death, probably the most popular screen lover was John Gilbert. His peak as a romantic lead was reached opposite Garbo in *Flesh and the Devil* (1927), in which the love scenes were undoubtedly fuelled by the fact that the principals were extremely smitten with each other. Gilbert's career, however, was cut short by the introduction of Talkies. Although it is generally supposed to have been a squeaky voice that put paid to his stardom, the fact is probably that his voice – actually pleasant and well-modulated – suffered from the inadequacies and bad recording of the early equipment and, by the time engineers had ironed out most of the faults in their infant technology, the damage to his reputation had been done.

The apparent obsession with foreign stars can be seen, to some extent, as an American inferiority complex about its own sexuality. France and Italy were the traditional cradles of love, while home-grown stars tended to be handsome, attractive, steady, but not deeply sexual. Gary Cooper – whose triumphs truly belong to other decades – started making a reputation for himself in the 'twenties. He was considered a very beautiful young man who certainly had 'It', and indeed he had a small part in the movie of that name. He also played opposite Bow in *Children of Divorce* (1927), was starred with Fay Wray in *The Legion of the Condemned* (1928), and the two were heralded as 'Paramount's Glorious Young Lovers'. But he quickly found his forte in action and middle-America good-guy roles to which he was much better suited. Evidently the moguls dictated that love and sex must be imported and cast their eyes towards Europe.

The great advantage of Silent movies was that they knew no language frontiers. To sell them abroad all you needed to do was translate the titles. This cheap alteration meant that stars could film in any country without having to have the faintest grasp of the language. In addition, there was the advantage that since the First World War the European cinema had been making great strides – particularly in the area of sexual frankness.

While the American commercial film industry was starting on its climb to world domination in Hollywood, the German UFA studios and the Expressionist directors in that country were contributing more to the art of the film than anyone else. Germany was probably the single most influential source of film-making in the 'twenties with a roll-call of great directorial talent in men like G.W. Pabst, Fritz Lang, Ernst Lubitsch, F.W. Murnau and Max Reinhardt.

Their films were typically German in that they dwelt largely on the darker side of human

her passionate, tigerish personality, shown to great effect in films like *Passion* (originally made in German by Ernst Lubitsch as *Madame Dubarry*, 1918), *The Flame* (1920), *Forbidden Paradise* (1924), and *Hotel Imperial* (1927), and in a blazing series of rows with Gloria Swanson (as well as a ridiculous and tastelessly ostentatious period of mourning for Valentino – who she claimed was madly in love with her). These latter episodes showed her to be petulant and prima donna-ish and ultimately helped to make her an object of ridicule.

The male stars – home-grown – were overshadowed by Douglas Fairbanks, who was the ultimate in American manhood. He was dashing, bold, swashbuckling, charming, wholesome, athletic, and the perfect foil for his wife, Mary Pickford, who characterized all the pure femininity beloved by certain sections of the public at the time. Fairbanks was undoubtedly sexy, but his appeal was not entirely based on his sexuality as was – for example – Valentino's.

In contrast to Fairbanks's rather adolescent approach to sex, there was John Barrymore, whose 'great profile' and classic masculine beauty set many hearts a-throb in roles like *Don Juan* (1926), as did an extraordinarily nature, in a twilight world that was handed down from German legend. But they also dealt with realism and with the mind-play of the subconscious. Their films were generally angular and shadowed, dark in content, intent and mood, peopled frequently by ghouls, freaks, predators, madmen, magicians and debauchees. They were post-Freudian, fascinated by dreams and the half-world between reality and fantasy. And they were full of suggested, hinted, covert imagery; of open, frank sexuality. Symbolism hung on every costume and set. For constricted eroticism and stifling carnality they were unsurpassed. Even lesser directors – working under a largely censor-free system and encouraged to use their imagination – depicted nudity, perversion, lust, fetishism, homosexuality and transvestism, often and overtly.

They produced masterpieces like *The Cabinet of Dr Caligari* (1919), *Nosferatu* (1922), *The Hands of Orlac* (1924), *Waxworks* (1924), *Variety* (1925), *The Joyless Street* (1925), *Metropolis* (1926), and others in an astonishing explosion

Elinor Glyn – authoress and inventor of 'It' – on the set of one of her story adaptations, *The Only Thing* (Jack Conway, 1925).

Clara Bow attempted more mature roles when the Talkies arrived, including this one of a half-caste in *Call Her Savage* (John Francis Dillon, 1932).

43

Above: Joan Crawford in a publicity-pose imitation of the Venus de Milo.

Right: Petulant Polish actress Pola Negri was the first in a long line of exotic European stars imported by Hollywood. She became Gloria Swanson's nearest rival as the 'twenties' most passionate sex star, though she spent more time generating bad publicity than making good movies.

of film-making in the 'twenties. Most were marked with a neurosis that was disturbing. Even the thrillers – particularly those of Fritz Lang – were imbued with an aberrant sexuality that motivated the villains.

Frequently foreign audiences never saw the more explicit scenes which gave these films their extraordinary reputation. They were cut by censors long before they reached the cinemas, but a great deal of the symbolism and the suggestion (as in von Stroheim's butchered works) crept by unnoticed or misunderstood. Nude members of the harem were cut from the Arabian Nights extravaganza *Sumurum* (1920, which starred Pola Negri), while supposedly 'careful' editing would turn a mistress into a wife and destroy the point of a film. As the writer of one film so mutilated pointed out: 'I get the feeling that the censor, like certain rather ingenuous girls, must think that you can catch a baby from a kiss. For one copy shows the chemist's assistant giving Thymiane (the heroine) a kiss, and in the next image she is seen cuddling a baby!'[24]

If the public did not see the original versions of these German classics it must be supposed that some of the moguls did, because the list of the talent – both acting and directorial – they plundered from Germany was comprehensive and impressive. Directors like Lubitsch, von Sternberg, Murnau, Lang, Billy Wilder, Robert Siodmak, Karl Freund, Richard Oswald and William Dieterle, and actors of the order of Conrad Veidt, Peter Lorre, Oscar Homolka and Sig Arno all travelled from Berlin to Hollywood in the late 'twenties and early 'thirties and made subsequent impressions on the course of movie history.

Two European actresses who were to be among the biggest stars in movie history had appeared together in Pabst's *The Joyless Street* – the best of several films of the period which dealt realistically with the post-war German Depression and the effects that it had on the lives of the population; it was so forthright in its depiction of prostitution that there was scarcely a country in which it was not severely cut. They were Greta Garbo – as a young girl tempted into brothel life – and Marlene Dietrich, in a one-line bit part. This pair, so different in temperament and sexual allure, were to set new trends in sexual glamour.

The traffic in talent was not simply one way.

Gloria Swanson, Queen of Hollywood throughout the 'twenties, won an Oscar nomination for *Sadie Thompson* (Raoul Walsh, 1928), adapted from Somerset Maugham's 'Rain' (a story considered so notorious that the Hays Office forbade the use of the original title), about the tart who corrupts a minister (Lionel Barrymore).

Douglas Fairbanks — dashing, charming, athletic, the ideal American male — at the peak of his popularity in *The Thief of Bagdad* (Raoul Walsh, 1924).

The Germans recruited foreign actors as well (for instance, Lillian Harvey from England) and their biggest catch was Louise Brooks. An American girl whose Hollywood career had been ordinary at best, she was spotted by Pabst in Howard Hawks's *A Girl in Every Port* (1928). He saw in her everything that he needed for Lulu, the nymphomaniac, in his classic *Pandora's Box* (1929). Brooks's beauty was unique. Her angular features set off by the severest of haircuts, she had the ambivalent man/girl quality which was so appealing to Continental audiences and so right for the insatiable but naïve girl who preys on every sensual experience. This film, together with *Diary of a Lost Girl* (1930), remains a testament to her astonishing, timeless beauty and superb acting abilities. In many respects she led the way for the great trans-sexual appeal of Dietrich.

In France and Italy the tradition of nudity

Left: Gary Cooper was rapidly recognized as one of Hollywood's most beautiful male stars, and at the start of his career was groomed as a screen lover of some potential. But he sensibly saw himself as 'Mr Average Joe American' and settled for good-guy action roles.

John Barrymore ('The Great Profile'), though well into his forties, was regarded as a great screen lover of the 'twenties, at his most ardent and physically arresting in *The Tempest* (Sam Taylor, 1928) with Camilla Horn.

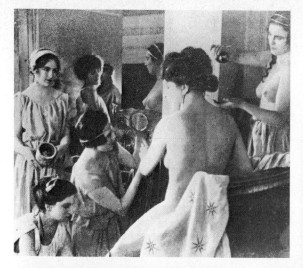

Right: Wege zu Kraft und Schönheit (*Ways to Health and Beauty*) — best known of the German UFA company's supposedly educational *Kulturfilme* series — put on a generous display of nudity with its restaging of Roman bath scenes and Greek gymnastics in praise of sports and personal hygiene.

Far right: Beautiful but unsung Paramount star Louise Brooks (*centre*) reversed a trend by going to Germany to play the nymphomaniac, Lulu, in *Pandora's Box* (1929), most famous of G.W. Pabst's classic cycle of shadowy psychological sex dramas. As a result she found lasting fame and recognition as an actress. Also in this scene — Alice Roberts and Fritz Kortner.

Greta Garbo as a young girl tempted by prostitution in *The Joyless Street* (1925), Pabst's celebrated study of moral and social disintegration in post-war Germany.

and plots spiced with sexuality continued. *Casanova* (1927) was packed with nubile, unclad ladies willing to surrender to the arms of the legendary lover, and the by now almost obligatory historical epic that was Italy's major contribution to the cinema reached its vulgar heights in 1924 with a remake of *Quo Vadis?* which missed at the box-office despite graphic orgy scenes. However, in France there was a new period of experimentation with film, as the avant-garde and particularly the Surrealists saw it as a medium offering great freedom of expression. Sex and violence were mingled teasingly in their films – most notably the Dali-Buñuel *Un Chien Andalou* (1928) and *L'Age d'Or* (1930), and Cocteau's *Le Sang d'un Poète* (1930). Incidentally, it was Cocteau who reveal-

ingly described the cinema as 'that temple of sex with its goddesses, its guardians and its victims'.

The stuff of these Surrealist dreams – or nightmares – was thought altogether too puzzling by the censors, who either cut them drastically or suppressed them altogether. Germaine Dulac's *The Seashell and the Clergyman* (1926) – 'a surrealist fantasy filled with sexual symbols . . . justly cited as the cinema's furthest excursion into the avant garde'[25] – elicited the British Board of Film Censors' disapproval and was banned because – in the Board's own classic words – 'This film is apparently meaningless. If there is any meaning it is doubtless objectionable'!

The Surrealists had little effect on mainstream film-making and, while European films continued to be sexier than those of Hollywood, the West Coast moguls preferred to follow their own path and bring over Continental talent not for the contribution it could make to progress but in a misguided attempt to appear more cultural and to add an extra lustrous scalp to their belts. Most of the creative talents who found themselves in the film capital soon learnt that they had to bend to their masters' will. Some could not stand it and returned quickly to the refuge of their home studios; some compromised and made largely routine movies which did not match their previous best work, or settled for one outstanding achievement (frequently slipped in under the noses of producers) among the dross they were largely saddled with. As Louis B. Mayer piously said in 1922, 'I will only make pictures that I won't be ashamed to have my children see' – a promise he conspicuously failed to keep (unless he was a very broadminded father) when he saw a method of making money – but such sentiments did put constraints on the more individualistic foreign talents.

In fairness to Mayer, it was this diminutive

A Paramount publicity pose of Louise Brooks from the period when she was 'solid with the jelly bean trade' and (said Variety) her acting was 'one of the things you don't mention'.

breathed life into celluloid. Her beauty was extraordinary: reserved, self-possessed, totally assured. The face was totally secure in itself, needing no artifice to change it, based as it was on a magnificent bone structure. Her body was fluid. Hollywood, the world had never seen a woman like Garbo before.

But Garbo, beautiful, desirable though she was, was never a true sex symbol. Despite Alistair Cooke's affirmation that she was 'every man's fantasy mistress. She gave you the impression that, if your imagination had to sin, it could at least congratulate itself on its impeccable taste', Garbo always appealed more to women than to men. Women admired her air of impending tragedy. As an MGM executive put it: 'Garbo was the only one we could kill off. The Shearer and Crawford pictures had to end in a church, but the public seemed to enjoy watching Garbo die.' She was too remote, too unworldly for men. Even when playing a slut, that huge reservoir of self-possession kept her out of the lustier imaginings of male fantasies. Critic Kenneth Tynan put it well when he said: 'What when drunk one sees in other women, one sees in Garbo sober.'

dictator who brought one of the greatest European talents to Hollywood – Greta Garbo. And perhaps he wouldn't have been ashamed to take his children to see *Flesh and the Devil* (1927), which contained one of the most torrid *horizontal* (an important distinction) love scenes up to that date between the enigmatic Garbo and John Gilbert, complete with open-mouthed kissing and much heady passion.

Garbo arrived in Hollywood in 1925 with films in Sweden and Germany behind her. At that point she was no one's idea of a sex goddess and MGM didn't quite know what to do with her. They put her in *Torrent* (1926) and after glimpsing only a few feet of the rushes realized that here was a woman the camera adored. She

Dietrich, the other great import, was a different matter entirely. She *did* appeal to men. But Dietrich properly belongs to another era – an era which Garbo came to reluctantly: the era of Sound.

Sound Effects

The Jazz Singer opened in New York on 6 October, 1927, and by 1930 Silent movies were a thing of the past. In the wake of this revolution some careers were cut short and others

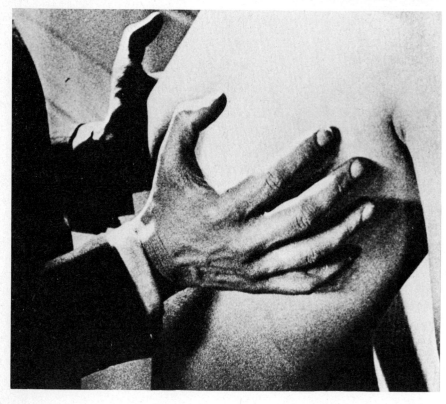

opened up. Musicals became the rage. It was a whole new world. And an important part of it was censorship and Will Hays. 'It was the coming of sound, with its added possibilities of verbal offence, and the tremendous influx of new writers unaccustomed to and unwilling to accept the prohibitions many Hollywood hacks took for granted, that brought into being the so-called "Hays Office Code",' said Philip French in 'The Movie Moguls'. What actors and actresses had been accustomed to doing with their eyes and faces to denote passion, they could now achieve with the suggestiveness, *double entendres* and even verbal frankness put into their mouths by dialogue writers.

This is not to say that the Silents had been totally immune from verbal outrage. In actor Conrad Nagel's obituary published in The New York Times in 1970, the following was reported: 'In a letter . . . (Nagel) denounced as a "hoary myth" a much-quoted story about a silent film in which he lifted a girl and carried her to a bed. According to the story the girl looked at him tenderly but actually said: "If you drop me, you bastard, I'll kill you."

'Mr Nagel recounted that the silent pictures were a source of great joy to many thousands of deaf people and that, being expert lip readers, they would have deluged Hollywood with letters of protest. However, he conceded that there was a basis in fact for the story. He said

A woman sucking the toe of a marble statue is presented as a symbol of sexual frustration in Dali and Buñuel's second joint venture, *L'Age d'Or* (1930), a fierce attack on bourgeois repressions.

that, during rehearsal, another actor – who was suffering from a hangover – had to lift an actress from the floor. She told him, "Use your breath, that's strong enough to do the job!" '[26]

Profanities picked up by lip-readers – real or imagined – were no longer a problem. What was now concerning the censorship lobby was the possibility of unloosed tongues and the havoc they could create. Will Hays – the Czar – went into action. The Code that took his name was not actually drawn up by him. It was drafted in 1929 by two Roman Catholics and formally adopted in 1930. Although all the studio bosses agreed to abide by the Code, it was broken with such regularity and the outcry from outside bodies – particularly the Catholic Church – became so clamorous that independent action was inevitable.

At a time of declining attendances (in 1933 Paramount was nearly bankrupt, while both RKO and Universal were in the hands of receivers) and when 25 per cent of the population was Catholic, the Church was in a powerful position to exert pressure. Although films dealing with sex and other 'sensational' topics were popular – one writer estimated that the 25 per cent of pictures of this nature 'was paying for the industry's losses on the clean 75 per cent which nobody seemed to support' – the industry was clearly vulnerable to a well-organized boycott.

In 1933 the National Legion of Catholic Decency was formed on the instigation of Father Daniel Lord, Martin Quigley, Joseph Breen and a host of Catholic bishops. Protestant groups added their support to the announcement of a plan to order Catholics to boycott films that violated the Code. By June, 1934, some ten million Catholics had pledged to 'rid the country of its greatest menace – the salacious motion picture'. In Philadelphia the Cardinal even ordered Catholics to stay away from all films. Overall business dropped by 10 per cent. The Legion of Decency harassed Hollywood, yapping and nipping at its heels for thirty years and becoming so influential a pressure group that film-makers crossed it at their peril. It drew up a system of classification which dubbed films according to their content in a grade which ranged from A-1 for 'Morally Unobjectionable for General Patronage' down to C for 'Condemned'. Lists of these ratings were regularly sent to Catholic communities

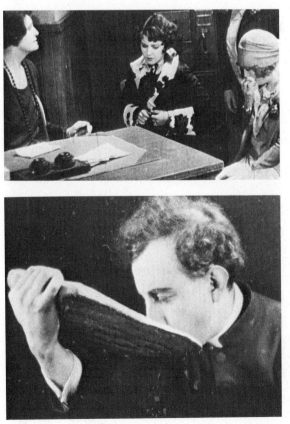

Road to Ruin (Norton S. Parker, 1928) was a typical American morality tale of the late 'twenties; its traumatic plot is neatly summarized by The American Film Institute Catalog: 'Lack of parental guidance leads Sally Canfield (played by Helen Foster) down the ruinous road. Exposed to liquor and cigarettes, she succumbs to their effects and drifts through a series of love affairs with older, worldlier men. Apprehended by the police one evening during a strip poker game, Sally is reprimanded and sent home. She discovers several weeks later that she is pregnant, submits to an illegal abortion, and dies of shock the next evening after unwittingly being paired off with her father in a bawdy house.'

The first Surrealist experiment on film was Germaine Dulac's *The Seashell and the Clergyman* (1926), which reproduced the erotic dream imagery of a frustrated celibate clergyman (Alex Allin).

49

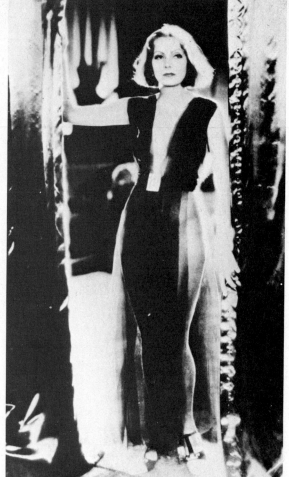

Above: Greta Garbo and John Gilbert in *Flesh and the Devil* (Clarence Brown, 1927), notable for the intensity of its love-making scenes. 'I'm a woman,' said Garbo enigmatically, 'who's unfaithful to a million men.'

Right: Garbo as *Mata Hari* (George Fitzmaurice, 1932), belying the famous description of her that 'boiled down to essentials, she is a plain mortal girl with large feet'.

Opposite: Jane Russell as William Bradford Huie's cabaret dance-hostess in *The Revolt of Mamie Stover* (Raoul Walsh, 1956).

throughout the world and much business could be lost on a C classification.

The strength of its influence may be judged by the fact that between 1936 and 1943 not one condemned film was issued by the MPPDA companies. The six major studio products that were C rated in this period were all revised with the specific aim of meriting reclassification. Indeed, right up until the 'sixties the Legion was able to ensure that substantial changes were made in numerous films under the threat of condemnation. As Richard Corliss has noted, 'The Legion's very existence and demonstrable power have kept many projects from being released or even considered. Other potential film-projects have been abandoned because it was feared that the Legion *might* object to some portion.'

This had the effect of forcing the Motion Picture Producers and Distributors of America to harden up the often ignored Production Code in such a way as to make it binding upon its members and to ensure that if a member purposely broke the Code he would suffer as a result. To this end the Production Code Administration (PCA) was set up within the Hays Office under the direction of Joseph Breen and was empowered to issue a seal of approval to those films that abided by the conditions of the Code. In 1938 Hays estimated that 98 per cent of all films shown in America in the previous year had been approved by his organization. Breen's presence in the Administration and the continued activity of the Legion of Decency ensured that the Code was interpreted in a way guaranteed to satisfy the Catholic pressure groups. Any film that failed to come up to requirements was not issued a seal and if the studio persisted in trying to release a film without official approval it could be fined $25,000. In effect, no picture could get a showing without a seal as all the major distributors and exhibitors were members of the MPPDA.

The Code was thus honoured – at least on the

surface – and it changed the face of the Hollywood film and, most significantly, the attitudes towards sex. The first of three general principles sums up the tone and intent of the document. 'No picture shall be produced,' it reads, 'which will lower the moral standards of those who see it. Hence the sympathy of the audience shall never be thrown to the side of crime, wrongdoing, evil or sin.' And by sin it meant sexual sin.

This principle was to be particularly applied in twelve listed sections, including Sex, Vulgarity, Obscenity, Profanity, Costume and the comprehensive heading Repellent Subjects. But sex was at the core of it all. 'Sex perversion or any reference of it is forbidden', as was white slavery, miscegenation (sexual intercourse between members of different races but here intended to mean whites and blacks specifically), abortion, scenes of 'actual childbirth' and the exposure of children's sex organs. Scenes of passion were considered to have a particularly harmful effect on 'the young and *criminal classes*' (the Code's own italics). It went to particular lengths to make the distinction between *pure* and *impure* love and defined impure love as 'the love which society has always regarded as wrong and which has been banned by divine law'. It then took pains to point out several important matters to note about such a love and its treatment. It must not, in brief, *be detailed* in manner and method, and to underline the fact it should not be presented in such a way as to appear *attractive* and

50

beautiful, comic or laugh-provoking, passion or morbid-curiosity arousing or *right and permissible*.

What sort of love, therefore, was outside the 'divine law'? Presumably any sort of love outside marriage. Homosexuality and incest were obviously taboo and, by extension, so were infidelity and pre-marital sex. The very meat and drink of the film-makers' industry! The challenge for them now was to find loopholes in, ways around, and methods of bending their own Code. And the film-makers were nothing if not ingenious men.

The Hays Code was not, in fact, a populist document drawn up because the majority wanted to call 'Stay!' It was the work of a highly vocal minority who found enough muscle to force their opinions on the general public. At best the Code was an honest if misguided attempt to improve standards. At worst it was a petty-minded, repressive and prudish charter foisted on an admittedly acquiescent public by bigots and reactionaries.

It was most seriously at fault in its total inability to grasp the realities of adult life and attitudes, as exemplified by its strictures about 'The treatment of bedrooms' which must 'be governed by good taste and delicacy' because 'certain places are so closely and thoroughly associated with sexual life and with sexual sin that their use must be carefully limited'. The applications of this were patently absurd and led to the banning of double beds, the introduction into happy marital homes of single divans, and the fact that a husband must not sit on his wife's bed without both feet being placed firmly on the ground. In this respect and many others the Code was more divorced from real life than even the Victorians. Nudity and semi-nudity were, of course, completely banned – their effect 'upon the normal man or woman, and much more upon the young and upon immature persons, has been honestly recognized by all law-makers and moralists'.

The extraordinary thing is that the Code was adopted and, on the surface at least, observed. It seems that not a voice was raised in protest, even though it smashed away any pretence of artistic freedom. No voice, that is, in public. In private, and among the worldly, cynical artists who made up the new Hollywood milieu, particularly writers, the whole business was treated as a bad joke.

Wits like Gene Fowler lampooned Hays and the Code mercilessly. Two of Fowler's 'Ten Commandments for the Motion Picture Industry', written in 1936, read:

'THIRD: Thou shalt not photograph the wiggling belly, the gleaming thigh or the winking navel, especially to music, as goings-on of this ilk sorely troubleth the little boys of our land and so crammeth the theatre with adolescence that papa cannot find a seat.

'FOURTH: Have not thy little dramas in the house of prostitution, the bawdy house or the place of call, for thou givest thereby free advertising to another industry and wilt, anyway, find thyself in the clutch of the law.'[27]

Fowler's satire was pungent and well directed. Even more, it was all true. Fowler battled gamely against the restrictions of the Code and tried to rally support. In a castigating, acid attack in The Hollywood Reporter in 1934, he struck at those who stood and looked on as the Code was put into action. 'Presumably,' he wrote, 'the producers won't, or can't, do anything about it. Armed with the greatest publicity weapon of all time – the picture – the moguls do not realize what opportunity is theirs in the field of militant propaganda and for sound causes.'

But the fact is that good films *were* made despite the restraints put on creative talents. Indeed, the introduction of the Code and the revolution of Sound coincided with the most glorious decade of commercial film-making in Hollywood. But the Code and its conditions were to mould the course of the industry, the subjects it handled and the way it handled them. As one anonymous wit put it: 'Hollywood buys a good story about a bad girl and has to change it to a bad story about a good girl.' Some of the cavalier, anything-goes days were gone. No longer could a producer like Hunt Stromberg shout, as he did in 1928, 'Boys! I gotta great idea! Let's fill the screen with tits!' when taking over the production of Robert Flaherty's *White Shadows in the South Seas*, and maybe even get away with it under the excuse of making a documentary.

The principles and guidelines for future production were carefully laid down and, like it or not, they had to be followed. Herman Mankiewicz (who wrote the script of *Citizen Kane*) said with a deal of truth: 'In a novel the hero can lay ten gals and marry a virgin for the finish. In a movie this is not allowed: the hero as well as the heroine has to be a virgin. The villain can lay anyone he wants, have as much fun as he likes getting rich and cheating the servants. But you have to shoot him in the end.'

For all that, writers and directors conspired to turn out good, even great movies, through the 'thirties and, furthermore, to create the most lustrous, popular, successful and enduring stars the world has ever seen. Stars like Harlow, Gable, Mae West, Dietrich and many others started in the 'thirties, and they created new concepts of sexuality to meet an age of austerity.

Marilyn Monroe and Don Murray in *Bus Stop* (Joshua Logan, 1956).

Now you see it, now you don't

Four views of censorship

Most of Telly Savalas's mixed bath scene (*right*) was cut from the completed version of *Genghis Khan* (Henry Levin, 1965). Sean Connery and Jean Seberg's bathtime romp in *A Fine Madness* (Irvin Kershner, 1966) survived the censor's scissors (*far right*), but curiously some of the publicity stills were doctored – white 'shorts' being painted over Connery's thighs. Walt Disney planned to have bare-breasted 'centaurettes' in the Pastoral Symphony sequence of *Fantasia* (1940), but the Production Code forced him to add flowery brassières in the final version (*bottom, right and second right*). Fairies in some other scenes, however, remained topless. Britain learned in the 'fifties to shoot two versions of risqué scenes – one for domestic eyes, the other for Continental consumption. In *My Wife's Lodger* (*bottom, third right and far right*), Diana Dors had two outfits for one scene: British audiences saw only the former version (Maurice Elvey, 1952).

THE THIRTIES
Hollywood's Hays Days

The King and the Queens

The 'thirties was the decade of the great stars – 'More stars than there are in heaven,' boasted MGM – but amid all of them one stood head and shoulders above the rest, Clark Gable. 'Men could identify with him. For women he was a promise of powerful, earthy sexuality that could hopefully be found at the Woolworth's counter. A regular guy who could be so roughly sweet to fallen women and working girls, as well as disrespectful to highfalutin' ladies. He let the men know that he wasn't hoodwinked by the heroine's pretensions. He let the women know that those puritanical plots might defang but never castrate the randy tomcat he played. Time and again he was reformed at the end by the strictures of the Hays Office and the censoring code. Time and again there was the subliminal wink implying he didn't really mean it.'[28]

Gable, to use the much overused word of the 'seventies, had *machismo*. He was a man, a real man, and, despite his own assertion that 'many disappointed young ladies will tell you that I'm a lousy lay', he came over very strong on film. 'There was a constant aura of sex about him and the plots of his movies often suggested that a night with Gable was a very special experience for the girl involved.'[29] There wasn't a woman in the audience who didn't believe it. One biographer put it more strongly: 'The screen Gable insinuated he had a power to give orgasms, even to a generation of women who still were not too sure whether they were supposed to have them.'[30]

As a result, throughout the 'thirties and, indeed, until his death in 1960, Gable was The King of Hollywood. He was the first of the new breed of lovers. And he was an American lover. Totally different from the effete posturings of Valentino or the suavity of John Gilbert; he could be rough, he would not hesitate to slap a woman around and yet, one realized, he could be tender and controlled. 'He could be a man among men, even a beast with women, but he could also act like a gentleman.' And when Judy Garland sang 'You Made Me Love You' as a birthday tribute to Gable, she might have been speaking for a whole generation of women who had suffered the Depression that bit hard and deep into the heart of America. Valentino and his ilk of the decade before were purely fantasy lovers, but women felt that Gable could, did, exist in real life.

Strangely Gable objected to almost all his great roles and tried to turn them down. He rebelled against the MGM hierarchy in 1933 because he would not accept another of what he termed 'gigolo roles'. He didn't want to play opposite Harlow in *Red Dust* (1932) because he thought it vulgar, and, most extraordinary of all, he never wanted to play Rhett Butler in *Gone With the Wind* (1939). Fortunately, circumstances or pressure forced him to change his mind and, almost from the very start of the decade, he was an immense star.

Against tramps he was superb, against haughty ladies – like Norma Shearer in *A Free Soul* (1931) – he was dominant. This film, as one historian has put it, was 'really about erotic awakening'. Madame Shearer, against her better judgment, has an affair with Gable and hates herself for allowing her cool reserve to break to his bullish sexuality. 'But she loves it, too, as the first of the screen women who were liberated by orgasm in Gable's career as Metro's prize stud.'[31]

He was teamed with a great variety of women in his career – from Vivien Leigh (whom he virtually rapes in *Gone With the Wind*) to Marilyn Monroe (in *The Misfits*, 1960); from Greer Garson (in *Adventure*, 1945) to Grace Kelly (in *Mogambo*, the 1953 remake of *Red Dust*) – but he was at his best opposite tough, wise-cracking cookies like Jean Harlow.

The Harlow/Gable partnership was inspired. After *Red Dust* they played together in *Hold Your Man* (1933), *China Seas* (1935), *Wife Vs. Secretary* (1936) and *Saratoga* (1937; although Harlow tragically died during the shooting and a double was used in many scenes). *Red Dust* was the prototype, and the best, with Gable caught between the charms of Harlow's prostitute-on-the-run and Mary Astor's coolly adulterous lady of class. The basis of the Harlow/Gable matching was the suggestion always that Harlow had a past and Gable had had class but had become a social renegade, dropping out and losing some of his honour but none of his dignity. They knew each other well, this tramp and the slumming man she meets. In *China Seas*, in which Harlow as China Doll is also a prostitute and Gable is the man of good breeding who now skippers a rust-tub steamer, he tells her, 'Anywhere else we'd both be a little soiled.'

The tough, world-weary Gable and the flinty, good-time Harlow struck sexual sparks off each other. Their great appeal lay in the fact that they were both totally at home with their own sexuality; both understood thoroughly their appeal to the opposite sex and neither tried to score acting points off the other. In *Red Dust* 'the two sex symbols clashed and clanged, making beautiful music together. Their screen personalities dovetailed so precisely that it became a high point in the history of movie

The most triumphant teaming of Clark Gable and Jean Harlow was in *Red Dust* (Victor Fleming, 1932), despite Gable's reluctance to do the film on the grounds that he found it vulgar.

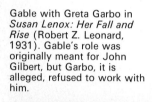
Clark Gable — a man who 'slapped women around with one hand and defended them with the other' (John Kobal).

Gable with Greta Garbo in *Susan Lenox: Her Fall and Rise* (Robert Z. Leonard, 1931). Gable's role was originally meant for John Gilbert, but Garbo, it is alleged, refused to work with him.

erotica, exactly epitomizing 'thirties style.'

Much of this was due to the incandescence of Harlow's personality. Her radiant platinum blonde hair, her tight, hard little body, her unbeautiful face with its odd angles, and her extraordinary ability to be both sensual and an accomplished comedienne, all conspired to make her quite magnetic. She didn't have a lot, physically, but what she had she used and she knew that it pays to advertise.

Harlow is generally credited with shifting the emphasis of male erotic interest from the legs (much displayed by flappers) to the breasts (flattened by Bow and others with a bandeau). She went bra-less, street-walking through her pictures, with her nipples in a seemingly constant state of tumescence (aided, the story runs, by ever-handy ice cubes with which she stimulated them).

Her gowns were invariably clinging, low-cut and backless (dating from her stunning starring debut in Howard Hughes's 1930 *Hell's Angels* in which she says to hero Ben Lyon: 'Excuse me while I slip into something more comfortable'), exhibiting her assets to the fullest. In *China Seas* her satin gown is so *décolleté* that, during a tussle with villain Wallace Beery, it slips down one arm and all but exposes her right breast. She catches it back so fluidly that one can only suppose that it was unrehearsed and the shot kept in by director Tay Garnett as an example of deliciously uncontrived titillation. In the next scene she has weathered the fury of a typhoon and been drenched by the seas washing the decks, and the gown, soaked and dripping, clings so tightly to her body that it clearly shows she's not wearing a stitch of underwear.

Harlow's hip-swinging, gum-chewing, slangy, wise-cracking characterizations were a delight. She perfectly understood the roles she invariably played (even to the point of asking her agent, when he phoned with a new part, 'What kinda whore am I this time?') and she brightened every picture she was in. She knew what she was, the audience knew what she was (and revelled in her), even the censor knew what she was, but she got away with it all because she had immense humour, treated sex as fun and could tell the public all they wanted to know about the character she played without ever needing to resort to heavy-handed verbal explanations.

One of the most delightful of many quotable lines in her sadly brief career was an exchange in *Dinner At Eight* (1933). As the dumb-blonde mistress of a man trying to impress his guests, she strives to make polite, intelligent conversation as they go in to eat. 'Do you know,' she says, 'I read somewhere that machinery is going to take the place of every profession?' Marie Dressler, with scalding disdain, replies, 'Oh, my dear, that's something *you* never need to worry about.'

Her luminescence brightened the post-Hays screen and showed the moguls that, despite the Code's strictures, sex could still be powerfully portrayed on screen if they were imaginative

enough to find ways of interpreting it. Spencer Tracy supplied her epitaph when he said, 'A square shooter if ever there was one'.

Comedy and sex – as shown by Harlow – was a new mixture possible only with Sound. Could a sex symbol make fun of herself, sex and men and get away with it? Would the public accept a travesty of the sex star? Would the censor allow it? Mae West – 'the finest woman ever to walk the streets' – showed exactly what could be done.

By the time she reached Hollywood in 1932 she was already famous and notorious on Broadway for her play 'Sex' which, after a run of three hundred-plus performances, was closed down by the police and the writer/star charged and convicted of obscenity and given a ten-day prison sentence. West's verbal humour was absolutely right for Sound and Paramount gave her a contract to appear in a version of her own play, 'Diamond Lil', but cautiously changed the title to *She Done Him Wrong* (1933). The author of such lines as 'Is that a gun in your pocket or are you just pleased to see me?' and 'It's not the men in my life that count but the life in my men' took movies by storm and in her first film, *Night After Night* (1932), her co-star, George Raft, said, 'She stole everything but the camera.'

Mae West's appeal lay in her statuesque figure – she looked and moved like a galleon under full sail – and her *double entendres*. She summed it up cogently herself: 'It isn't what I do, but how I do it. It isn't what I say, but how I say it. And how I look when I do it and say it.' She was a living exaggeration, with impossibly full figure, heavy in the breast and hips, ludicrously over-vamping with her slashed

mouth and drooping eyelids weighed down with mascara. She was Theda Bara blown up and she knew exactly what she was doing.

She Done Him Wrong, in which she seduced Cary Grant and *didn't* say 'Come up and see me sometime', was an enormous success and virtually saved Paramount from bankruptcy. The fact that it was a hit staved off for a while

Above: Ben Lyon and Jean Harlow in *Hell's Angels* (Howard Hughes, 1930).

Right: Off-screen, Harlow's life seemed as scandalous as the one she portrayed in her movies. Her second husband, MGM producer Paul Bern, allegedly impotent, committed suicide after two months. She divorced her third, cinematographer Hal Rosson, in less than a year, because, she said, he 'read in bed'!

the increasing clamour of the Puritans who loathed her for her cavalier attitude to sex and the fact that she lampooned them as viciously as she relished assaulting Grant's chastity as a Salvation Army officer (he wasn't really, of course, but then things were never as they at first seemed in West's films). The Hays Office watched her like a rabbit watches a snake. Her film *I'm No Angel* presented a particular challenge to censorship, and Quigley, one of the co-draughtsmen of the Code, disapproved in no uncertain terms: 'A vehicle for a notorious characterization of a scarlet woman whose amatory instincts are confined exclusively to the physical. There is no more pretence here of romance than on a stud farm.' In 1934 the Office insisted that *It Ain't No Sin* be changed to *Belle of the Nineties* and that certain lines and scenes be altered, and interfered again with the script of *Klondike Annie* (1936).

By now the bluenoses were in full howl, claiming that she 'pollutes homes'. They could not stand her jokey attitude to the things they held to be most dear or even most obnoxious and, with the Hays Office hounding her, virulent press attacks and even sermons against her from pulpits, her scripts mutilated, her characterization stripped of its humour and her essential earthiness and warm-hearted persona reduced to shreds, her popularity at the box-office waned. She became too hot to handle, her films became husks and she went into a sad decline. Eventually, she was so emasculated by the studio and the censor that she retired from films. She left, however, some of the most glorious sexual parodies ever created and a list of quotable lines almost to rival Oscar Wilde.

She returned in 1970 to steal *Myra Breckinridge* and be the only thing worth seeing in the sorry mess, as well as adding two great gags to the dictionaries of quotations. As an agent, she is met by a bevy of handsome, virile young hopefuls. 'I'm feeling a little tired today,' she says. 'One of those fellows'll have to go home.'

Mae West – 'a great clown who could put more innuendo in the flicker of an eyelash than seemed possible' (David Shipman).

60

And when interviewing a prospective candidate she asks:

'How tall are you, son?'

'Ma'am, I'm six feet seven inches.'

'Forget about the six feet. Let's talk about the seven inches.'

– a line that would never have got past the Hays Office!

Sound faced the censor with a dilemma. The West-type dialogue meant that the belly-laugh was in the mind of the beholder; a total innocent might not even realize the full import of what had been said. The Code laid down certain words (twenty-eight in all) which could not be used under any circumstances, including 'Gawd', 'hot' (applied to women) and 'whore'. 'Damn' and 'hell' could only be uttered 'where essential and required for portrayal in proper historical context'. In other words, a full-blooded male of the type beloved by Hollywood could not swear, or, if he did, he could use only milksop words. The Hays Office raised a huge fuss over Gable's great line in *Gone With the Wind* when he tells Scarlett: 'Frankly, my dear, I don't give a damn', before eventually allowing it.

'With the advent of sound,' wrote Herman G. Weinberg, 'the censor had not only to look frantically for sophistication, but also to listen for it.'[32] He relates that Warner's made a short about Primo Carnera in which 'a trainer was boasting to a crowd of spectators of the big Italian's dimensions: "His hand is three times bigger than any man's hand! His chest is three times bigger than any man's chest! His feet are three times bigger than any man's feet. . . ." At which point, one girl leans over and whispers something in her girl friend's ear which causes them both to break out into a spasm of uncontrolled giggling.'[33]

The word 'bastard' was *verboten* and Laurence Olivier ran into problems over it in his 1945 version of *Henry V*, even though the Code laid down that certain objectionable words could be used 'for the presentation in proper context'. Shakespeare, it seems, was not immune. A subtle treatment of this word occurred in Frank Capra's 1936 *Mr Deeds Goes to Town*, where a bearlike editor has finished upbraiding his staff for not getting the dirt on Deeds. As he leaves the room a young reporter mutters something. 'What did you say?' bawls the editor. Pointing to the ceiling the miscreant blandly says: 'I said you got dirty plaster!'

Directors generally got over the swear-word problem by 'bleeping' it out with some other sound – the slam of a door, the blast of a motor horn, the crash of breaking glass. But to convey a plot detail they had to be subtle. Marlene Dietrich couldn't blatantly refer to her past and her profession in *Shanghai Express* (1932), but she could tell Clive Brook: 'It took more than one man to change my name to Shanghai Lily.'

Whores, harlots, women of the night and shady ladies were a great vogue in the 'thirties. They naturally couldn't be introduced as such but the increasingly sophisticated audience

Above: Marlene Dietrich – the queen of drag.

Left: Dietrich as the faithless Lola in *The Blue Angel* (Josef von Sternberg, 1930).

could spot them a mile away. The contrast to Harlow's brassy hooker with a heart of gold was Dietrich's veiled lady with a mysterious past. By the use of astonishingly subtle lighting, incredible sets and exotic settings, director Josef von Sternberg created for his Trilby a mystique which teased and titillated audiences.

Dietrich in *Blonde Venus*
(von Sternberg, 1932).

of the legion of lost women' in *Morocco* (1930), the nymphomaniacal Catherine of Russia in *The Scarlet Empress* (1934) 'running riot through the phallic symbols and as nightmarish a collection of candelabra and gargoyles as the exotic mind of von Sternberg could devise'.[34]

She was a *femme fatale* and her greatest appeal in these early films was her 'cool disdain', the quality which first attracted von Sternberg to her. She didn't give a damn. She didn't need to because even dressed in drag, evening dress complete with monocle, she was still a woman of potent sexuality. Sternberg didn't undress her, he overdressed her; concealing all those physical delights, masking her face in veils, hiding those legs in trousers, losing those breasts in feathers. It worked triumphantly (women started wearing slacks more frequently as a result of her mannish transvestism).

And when von Sternberg's career was ruined by studio intolerance of his extravagance and the fact that their films together were failing at the box-office, she became Frenchie in *Destry Rides Again* (1939) and showed a brilliant talent for comedy which picked her career up and pushed her forward to new triumphs. Dietrich's appeal was, as many have pointed out, her timelessness. She seemed to come from nowhere, belong to no one but herself. She used men and abused them. She may have sold them her body but they could never buy her soul. She was a riddle and an enigma and she was the darker face of sex.

Perhaps it was because she was so puzzling, because she never took off clothes, swore or paraded her sex that she was acceptable to the censor. More mundanely, the censor probably just could not understand what she was about and how she could convey all the sex in the world with the raising of an eyebrow or the merest suggestion of a wink. To a man who was desperately looking for an inch too much cleavage or a 'naughty' word such subtlety must have passed totally unnoticed.

She was 'the Bitch Goddess', the tantalizing hoyden, the woman who dressed in men's clothes and taunted all preconceptions of sexual identity. That incredible face, those superb legs, that husky voice created on screen an image of reserved wantonness, of forbidden pleasures. She was extraordinarily feminine and yet partly lesbian. As soon as you thought you had pinned down her appeal, she'd changed.

Lola-Lola – the sadistic, tormentingly sexual *chanteuse* who ruins elderly schoolmaster Emil Jannings in *The Blue Angel* (1930) – made her and von Sternberg the rage of Talkies. Posturing, playing on male fetishist fantasies with suspender-held stockings encasing her gleaming thighs and those glorious legs, she teased. She personified the sexuality which exists only in erotic dreams; she was sexual perversity draped in its taboo trimmings, offering herself and snatching back at the last moment.

Her films with von Sternberg were pungent with a heady sensual atmosphere. She was sadistic in *The Devil Is a Woman* (1935), 'one

Music Hath Charms

Although Dietrich sang she didn't make musicals, and it was this genre which really came into its own in the 'thirties. After Jolson had sung in *The Jazz Singer*, there was a period in which hardly a film was made without some sort of musical content. Musicals, of course, meant girls and girls meant sex. Outrageously over- and under-costumed, involved in teasing dance, the showgirls of the chorus lines feasted the eye with their supple bodies.

The very start of the decade saw *King of Jazz* (1930), which was in experimental colour and broke ground for the Busby Berkeley spectaculars to follow. Hung around Paul Whiteman and his band, it was really little more than a revue committed to film, the production numbers interspersed with sketches. The barely-clad lovelies were in attendance, of course, but this

movie, being made before the tightening up of the code, got away with some – for the era – quite extraordinary dialogue.

One skit shows Slim Summerville as a suitor asking a father for his daughter's hand. Father enquires about his financial status:

S.S.: Sixty-five dollars a week should be enough to support two.
Dad: But if there should be children?
S.S.: We don't intend to have children.
Dad: Nevertheless, there might be a baby.
S.S.: Well, we've been pretty lucky so far!

But before long there appeared a man who was to revolutionize the musical, placing the entire erotic emphasis in his films on visual spectacle. In his history of the musical – 'Gotta Sing Gotta Dance' – John Kobal quotes some lines from a song in *Dames* (1934):

'What do you go for?
Go to see a show for?
TELL THE TRUTH
YOU GO TO SEE THOSE BEAUTIFUL DAMES.'
Busby Berkeley knew that and he exploited it in a series of incredible set-pieces in some of the best musicals of the 'thirties and early 'forties. He virtually invented choreography for the camera. Frequently his 'dancers' stood still (often totally unable to move anyway under the massive props he dressed them in) while the camera swooped on them, now high in the roof, now shooting up through the floor, now lasciviously tracking between opened thighs.

If anyone ever treated women as sexual objects, Berkeley did. He dressed them down to nothing but diaphanous wisps and dressed them up as enormous coins or musical instruments (one celebrated mother crashed her way on to a Berkeley set, grabbed her daughter who was extravagantly made up as a piece of the orchestra, and declared: 'Mr Berkeley, I did not raise my daughter to be a human harp!'), and then manoeuvred them into tortuous patterns. He laid them on their backs and synchronized their legs to open and close; he froze them into tableaux, turning them into human statuary, complete, as often as not, with gushing fountains; he paraded and drilled and dehumanized them. He made them all look like his favourite chorine, Toby Wing, and then he let his camera run amok among them, tracking into close-ups of smiles, breasts, thighs, plummeting down amid their surrendered bodies, and all but raping them in its voyeuristic quest.

Berkeley's girls were mere props in the production numbers, and the vastness and opulence of his stages, the mind-numbing profligacy with which he dressed his sets, the lavishness with which he peopled his routines, and the perpetual emphasis on luxury and wealth struck a vicarious chord in the depressed and downtrodden populace, suffering deeply from the effects of the Wall Street Crash.

But Berkeley didn't, like so many other film-makers of the time, simply try to ignore the Depression. Like the 'street' films which had emerged in the wake of the post-war German Depression, he realized that extreme times mean that some must take extreme methods to survive. Instead of making grim dramas like *Joyless Street*, he invented the 'Gold Diggers'. 'All women on Broadway are chisellers, parasites – or, as we call them, gold diggers,' says Guy Kibbee to a friend in *Gold Diggers of 1933*, the first of the series. The gold diggers were the Broadway show-girls and hoofers immortalized in back-stage musical romances, of which *42nd Street* (1933) was the prototype.

In *Gold Diggers of 1933*, the show is in danger of closing and the girls of being thrown out of work and into the soup queues. Things are desperate. 'They'll do things I wouldn't want on my conscience,' Aline McMahon tells Dick Powell (who, with Ruby Keeler, was a stalwart of Berkeley movies). McMahon, Blondell and Rogers resort to sex-blackmail by operating a

The innocent eroticism of many early musicals was exemplified by the all-star revue, *Paramount on Parade* (Victor Schertzinger, 1930), which, said a contemporary review, had 'more ingenuity and good taste and far more humour than most things of its kind.'

Lorraine Marshall daringly under-dressed for *Footlight Parade* (Lloyd Bacon, choreo. Busby Berkeley, 1933).

63

'sting' on a stuffed-shirt lawyer (Warren Williams), planting him in Joan Blondell's bed after he has passed out from too much drink and relieving him of $10,000. Thus do gold diggers operate. However, the girls aren't just after gold, they also have hearts made of the stuff, and all's well that ends well with a mysterious backer putting up enough loot to save the show. And some show!

Berkeley was seldom more salacious than in his treatment of the 'Pettin' in the Park' number, dressing his chorines in transparent skirts and silk, suspendered stockings. The girls and their beaux walk in the park and spoon. The boys lay the girls down on the grass in such a way that the Peeping Tom camera shoots right up their already negligible skirts. Then comes a rain storm in which the girls get soaked, so, naturally, they run to the cover of nearby screens to step out of their wet things. The screens, however, have strong back-lighting and the girls are seen, quite naked, in silhouette; in fact, so revealing is it that the screens could easily have been dispensed with. They emerge to rejoin the fellows clad, mischievously, in armour-plated bathing suits! Do these tin chastity belts faze the lads? Of course not. On runs a baby clutching a can-opener and, as the scene fades, Dick Powell gets to work on Ruby's hardware!

'Spin a Little Web of Dreams' – the ostrich-feather fantasy, complete with semi-naked figurehead, from *Fashions of 1934* (William Dieterle, choreo. Berkeley).

The number from *Fashions of 1934* which inspired the motherly remark, 'Mr Berkeley, I did not raise my daughter to be a human harp!'

'We're in the Money' — the gold diggers' song from *Gold Diggers of 1933*, with Ginger Rogers sporting some unconscious symbolism.

How Busby Berkeley got away with such blatant flouting of the Code is a mystery, but he managed it time and again. All-but-naked girls (the human harps) in *Fashions of 1934*; slave girls, naked except for cascading wigs carefully positioned, supervised by a sadistic slave-master bearing a bull-whip in *Roman Scandals* (1933); and, perhaps most outrageous of all, a regiment of lovelies manipulating enormous bananas (the symbolism surely cannot have escaped the censor) in Carmen Miranda's famous 'Brazil' number in *The Gang's All Here* (1943). This last, incidentally, bears strong echoes of an even more ingeniously erotic number in one of the earliest film musicals, *Sunny Side Up* (1929), whose climax is a frantic all-girl extravaganza in which palm trees shoot up from holes in the stage with bananas sprouting and swelling pneumatically on the branches.

Perhaps it was because his images were so very blatant; perhaps because the times demanded such ostentation; perhaps because there was a certain Ziegfeld/Broadway tradition for it – whatever the cause, Berkeley must have broken the Code more often, more successfully throughout those repressive days than any other film-maker.

Musicals, it seems, could get away with being sexier than other kinds of films, and two other directors in this genre knew exactly what to do and how far to go. Ernst Lubitsch and Rouben Mamoulian, two European émigrés, brought to Hollywood the lightness of touch which has often marked the handling of love, romance and sex in the Continental cinema. Even a bluenose as hard-line as John Wayne has said of Lubitsch,

Jeanette MacDonald, as the Princess, and Maurice Chevalier, as the tailor posing as a baron, enjoy some suggestive by-play with a tape measure in *Love Me Tonight* (Rouben Mamoulian, 1932).

when comparing him with directors of sexual themes in the 'seventies, that his work was on so many levels that all could see it and enjoy it and take from it what they wanted; and Lubitsch said of his own films and the sexual sophistication they contain, 'I let the audience use their imagination. Can I help it if they misconstrue my suggestion?'

Lubitsch's musicals, like his domestic sex comedies, had a unique erotic charm, full of wit and innuendo. *The Love Parade* (1929), his first Sound film, was a serene send-up of European operetta, introducing Jeanette MacDonald, in transparent negligee, as a Ruritanian queen moping for a man fit to be king and satisfy her romantic desires. The film's one flaw was Maurice Chevalier, as Jeanette's eventual consort: popular though he was, his supposed Gallic charm and man-about-town attractions come across now more as randy adolescence, an impression reinforced by his physique. MacDonald and Chevalier were teamed again by Lubitsch in *The Merry Widow* (1934); it was still a far-from-perfect match, in spite of the film's – and Jeanette's – stunning looks. The suave Jack Buchanan

made a far more manly lover in the much-revered *Monte Carlo* (1930).

Rouben Mamoulian's coupling of MacDonald and Chevalier in his delightful fairy-tale musical *Love Me Tonight* (1932) was more acceptable. 'Throughout the film,' said John Kobal, 'one relishes the happy, carefree attitudes towards sex treated with the lightness of touch that was the envy even of Lubitsch.' The story includes a beautiful sub-nymphomaniacal countess (Myrna Loy) who craves men.

'Don't you ever think of anything but men, dear?' asks the innocent MacDonald.

'Oh yes!' answers Loy.

'Oh, of what?'

'Of schoolboys.'

The whipped-cream levity of the 'thirties musicals relied heavily on dancing and there were no two greater exponents than Fred Astaire and Ginger Rogers. 'He gives her class and she gives him sex,' said Katharine Hepburn of their partnership. The fluidity of their movements, the pert prettiness of Ginger and the tight-bodiced, flowing-skirted gowns she wore, and the way the pair melted into each other had an artistic eroticism all its own.

Mobsters and Molls

The other great genre of the 'thirties was the gangster movie, with its triumvirate of stars – James Cagney, George Raft and Edward G. Robinson. The sexual appeal of such movies was evident. In times of disaster, when men are emasculated by lack of work they look to those who get what they want, no matter what the means. Certainly the big-time gangsters were

charismatic in real life as well as on the screen. They were rich when there was no money, they were powerful when the individual had become an unemployment statistic. And they treated their women rough, very rough.

There was no pretence at conventional sexual morality. These men had molls, women kept around purely for their decorative qualities

66

and sexual uses. When they became tiresome they were cast aside. And how they could be abused! The films were laden with sado-masochism. When Cagney ground a grapefruit into Mae Clarke's face over the breakfast table in *Public Enemy* (1931) the public enjoyed it so much that he was obliged to outdo himself in *Lady Killer* (1934) by dragging her across the room by her hair.

When the mobster wanted diversion he just shipped the women in. *Bullets or Ballots* (1936) had a scene where an elevator boy invests a dollar in the numbers racket. The runner who takes it is amazed – a whole dollar – and asks where he got it. 'I just brought a couple of blondes up to the seventh floor,' is the reply. Perhaps the significance escaped the censor.

But were the gangsters portrayed on the screen as virile as the audience liked to believe? French author Ado Kyrou ('Amour-Erotisme et Cinéma') has his doubts. He alleges that Paul Muni's character (a thinly disguised Al Capone) in Howard Hawks's *Scarface* (1932) is marked by 'son impuissance sexuelle et son amour incestueux pour sa sœur'. Not only impotent but in love with his sister! And that Edward G. Robinson is more at home in *Little Caesar* (1930) ordering his men around than he is trying to convince Miriam Hopkins and Glenda Farrell that he's a real man. 'Weren't the tough guys,' the author asks, 'really a product of their own insufficient sexuality or puniness?' Perhaps with the aid of hindsight such analyses can be made – certainly there are those commentators who claim that the masculine world of the gangsters on screen was larded with hints of homosexuality. But to the audience of the day the cocky, swaggering Cagney and his colleagues were simply 'all man'.

A new kind of tough-guy hero grew out of James Cagney's rough treatment of Mae Clarke in *Public Enemy* (William Wellman, 1931). The Assistant Attorney General, disturbed by the gangster-movie trend, questioned 'the right of movie-makers to make films of degenerate modes of living. Many makers of modern movies are catering to a taste for immorality.' But oddly, he was worried only about the films' realistic attitude to sex, not their violence.

67

Beauty and the beast motif from De Mille's *The Sign of the Cross* (1932), a Romans v. Christians epic which hit upon the perfect religio-sexual blend.

Opposite: Elizabeth Taylor as the frustrated Maggie in Tennessee Williams's *Cat on a Hot Tin Roof* (Richard Brooks, 1958).

'Thirties Themes

'When you get a sex story in biblical garb,' said Darryl Zanuck of MGM, 'you can open your own mint.' In the 'thirties De Mille found the philosopher's stone. 'Having attended to the underclothes, bathrooms and matrimonial irregularities of his fellow citizens,' brother William remarked, 'he now began to consider their salvation.'

Although De Mille may have fancied himself God's envoy to Hollywood, he had a very realistic understanding of what his films were about. 'It's just a damn good hot tale,' he would tell his scriptwriters, 'so don't get a lot of thees, thous and thums on your mind.' He started his evangelical mission with *The Ten Commandments* in 1923 and followed with *King of Kings* in 1927. Two more were to come in the following decade. And while he modestly admitted that 'I

didn't write the Bible and I didn't invent sin' he made absolutely sure that the latter was inextricably related in the public's mind to the former.

The Sign of the Cross, made in 1932, was set in decadent Rome in the times of Nero and the rise of Christianity. Laughton played the despot and Claudette Colbert was Poppaea, a thoroughly nasty piece of work. This time De Mille outdid himself in his bathing scene. Colbert's ablutions were performed in an enormous bath of asses' milk which, being thick, had a deliciously titillating effect in covering her breasts and yet putting a tantalizing gleam on them. The sight of the willowy Miss Colbert thus immersed was sensational and De Mille approached her for his next epic.

'How would you like to be the wickedest

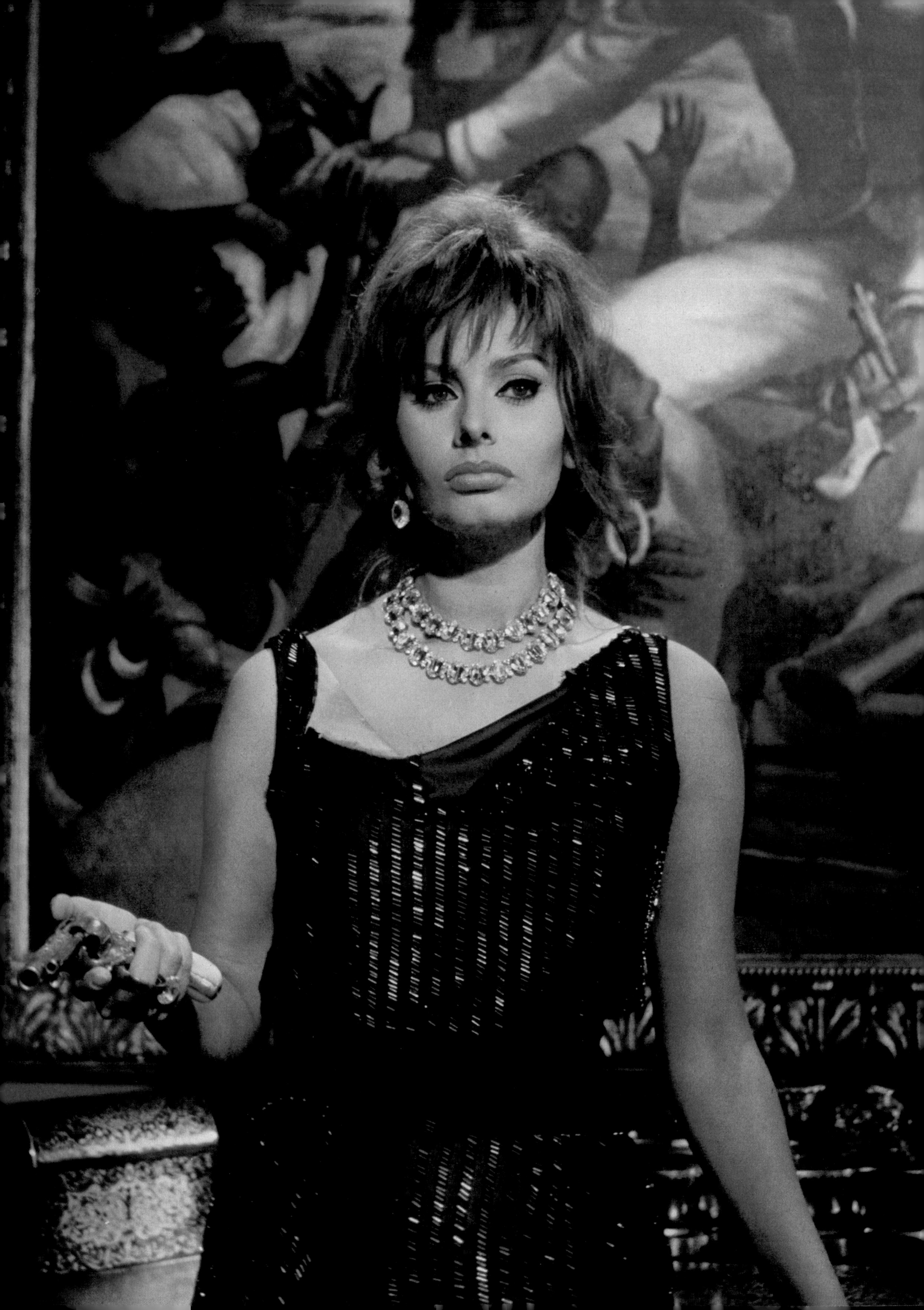

woman in history?' he asked the star. The thought must have appealed, for she was cast in the title role of *Cleopatra* (1934).

De Mille's magic formula for sex coupled with religious themes – perhaps one of the most blatant hypocrisies ever perpetrated in movies – allowed him to bend the Code brilliantly. He undoubtedly had a strong religious background – his father studied to be an Episcopalian minister, but was never ordained, and De Mille himself kept close ties with friends in the clergy – but his commercial instincts were so well developed that his spectacles became by-words in the industry for clever circumvention of the Code's rulings.

The Code affected every area of film-making and profoundly altered the shape of the industry in the 'thirties. Sophisticated comedy became very popular as bright young writers arrived from the East to satisfy the American desire for snappy, crackling dialogue.

The comedy hit of the decade was, undoubtedly, *It Happened One Night* (1934), in which Gable and Colbert played opposite each other as a runaway heiress and footloose journalist. Perhaps the most famous scene is the one that epitomizes the Code's influence. The two are forced to share a room for the night. Remembering the Code's stricture that 'the treatment of bedrooms must be governed by good taste and delicacy', Gable, seeing that the situation could lead to complications, automatically contrives a screen – blankets laid

Left: 'How would you like to be the wickedest woman in history?' De Mille with Claudette Colbert.

Opposite: Sophia Loren as *The Millionairess* (Anthony Asquith, 1960).

Inoffensive bath scene from De Mille's *Cleopatra* (1934). 'Mr De Mille depicts a surprisingly moral life in the Roman and Egyptian courts,' said The Motion Picture Herald.

71

Claudette Colbert and Clark Gable in Frank Capra's *It Happened One Night* (1934). When Gable removed his shirt to reveal a bare chest (allegedly shaven), American undervest sales reportedly slumped by more than half.

over a string bisecting the room – between the two single beds. This is an excellent example of the Code being used to great ironic effect in a film, and the success of the plot can be measured by the fact that the movie won five Oscars, including one for each of the stars.

One of the most popular comedy teams was William Powell and Myrna Loy in *The Thin Man* series. Nick and Nora Charles – the husband and wife detectives – were super-sophisticates. They were rich, smart and flip. In the first movie in which they appeared, an adaptation of Dashiell Hammett's *The Thin Man* (1934), directed by W.S. Van Dyke, they registered perfectly as a couple who were warmly sexual in their relationship ('the first time a sophisticated, affectionate marriage had been realistically portrayed on the screen'[35]), but despite

William Powell, Myrna Loy, and Asta in *Song of the Thin Man* (Edward Buzzell, 1947). Despite the urbanity of the *Thin Man* series and the leading couple's deeply affectionate marital relationship, the Hays Code kept them apart at night.

their obvious and open attraction for each other, they were consigned to single beds with only their dog Asta bridging the gap. It says something for their performances that the credibility of their sexuality is maintained despite this barrier.

The dialogue matches the deftness of the leading players and must surely have raised a censorial eyebrow. Myrna Loy is awoken in the early hours of the morning by a man searching her wardrobe. 'What's that man doing in my drawers?' she asks and Powell's reaction is proof that the pun is not unintentional. During the same eventful night Powell is shot once and superficially wounded. The next day Myrna Loy is reading an account of the incident in the newspapers. She looks up and tells Powell: 'It says you were shot twice in the tabloids.' 'Nonsense,' he replies. 'The man never came near my tabloids!' The delightful craziness of the films and the beautifully mannered acting of the stars proved that good commercial films with an adult attitude to sex could still be made without the heavy hand of the Hays Office marring their gloss.

While some areas of movie-making got more sophisticated, others were tending towards the primitive. The Robert Flaherty documentaries of the 'twenties had provoked an interest in secluded societies. *Nanook of the North* (1920) initiated the public's fascination and was followed by two Polynesian idylls – *Moana* (1926) and *White Shadows of the South Seas* (1928), the movie which inspired Stromberg's 'Let's fill the screen with tits!' remark. Naked native breasts had been seen as acceptable – a number of exploitation movies were subsequently shot which included bosoms of varying tints – although by the 'thirties and Frank Lloyd's *Mutiny on the Bounty* (1935, starring Gable and Charles Laughton) the native girls, played by Movita and Mamo, were very modestly covered. (This film proved, incidentally, that the dictates in the Code against miscegenation were aimed primarily at sex – or even romance – between blacks and whites; Gable's love for a Polynesian girl was passed – she was presumably racially acceptable.)

All these excursions into the primitive life rekindled the popularity of Tarzan, and the casting of the part's most famous interpreter – ex-Olympic swimming champion Johnny Weissmuller – caused the series to become an immense box-office attraction: 'the only man in Hollywood,' said the publicity, 'who is natural in the flesh and can act without clothes.' Maureen O'Sullivan as Jane added to the attraction. Both started the series in the briefest of costumes and Weissmuller's loincloth – slashed down both sides to reveal his upper thigh – was little more than a sop to modesty. The noble savage appeal that his impressive physique and strong facial features so perfectly fitted made him a potent sexual attraction to women, while O'Sullivan's immensely appealing, tomboy/wild-girl beauty found great favour among the males.

From its first manifestation, the Tarzan film

had suffered frequent fluctuations both in its potentially sensual theme and in the garb of its leading players, and continued to do so into the 'seventies when the handsome ape man appeared chiefly on television. The Tarzan-Jane relationship was ambiguous from the start, reaching its erotic zenith in the Weissmuller/O'Sullivan films. This pair were never formally married and maintained a veritable love-nest in their jungle tree-top.

Of all the primitives, none could compare with the biggest of them all – King Kong. Made immortal in Merian Cooper and Ernest Shoedsack's pioneering animation horror movie of 1932, the giant Kong starred in the greatest beauty-and-beast film ever. Can one blame him for falling in love with Fay Wray? Can one blame the makers for taking full advantage of his giant clutches gradually to rend Miss Wray's skimpy clothing from her as she struggles to be free of his monstrous grip?

The mixture of horror and sexual titillation worked magnificently. But can one ignore the implications of the monster/beauty relation-

The acceptability of native bare breasts in natural settings was exploited in a number of films, including the lyrical documentary, *Time in the Sun* (1939), whose topless siesta shots were salvaged from Sergei Eisenstein's abortive epic study of the Mexican people, *Que Viva Mexico!*

Trader Horn (W.S. Van Dyke, 1931), with Harry Carey and Edwina Booth, typified a return to primitive themes in the late 'twenties and 'thirties.

ship? 'An infantile rape image occurs, not on the screen, but in the audience's mind, during *King Kong*, where the immensely sympathetic 60-yard-tall gorilla falls in love with the screaming Fay Wray, who is just about five-and-a-half feet tall.'[36] *King Kong* underlines the fact that fear and sex are very closely linked and that – at some stage – horror movies generally throw the audience's sympathies on to the side of the monster.

In *The Hunchback of Notre Dame* both Lon Chaney (1923) and Charles Laughton (1939) are suitably grotesque and, initially at least, horrifying, but one is manipulated into feeling enormous pity for Quasimodo in his hopeless love for the lovely Esmeralda. And it was in *The Seven Year Itch* (1955) that Marilyn Monroe left a cinema feeling for the much-maligned *Creature from the Black Lagoon* (1954).

The two most enduring horror heroes (if such they can be called) are Frankenstein's monster and Dracula. Frankenstein's monster is the

After *Tarzan and His Mate* (Cedric Gibbons and Jack Conway, 1934), Johnny Weissmuller and Maureen O'Sullivan acceded to the censor's request for a more modest amount of cover-up.

Fay Wray in a publicity pose for *King Kong* (Merian C. Cooper and Ernest B. Schoedsack, 1932).

more sympathetic, but Raymond Durgnat claims that James Whale's original classic version of 1931 is bristling with sexuality, from the phallic imagery of the tower in which the monster is created to what he terms 'necrololitaphilia' – a morbid sexual fascination for dead young girls. As a father carries back to his village the body of his dead daughter – murdered by the monster in an horrific scene cut from the released version – 'a strip of thigh showing white against her thick black stockings sexualizes the corpse of an underage girl'.[37]

Dracula, too, if we are to believe those who tend to seek out sexuality in everything, is an erotic fantasy figure. The sinking of his fangs into the heroine's jugular vein has been compared on different occasions to cunnilingus; to a reprisal against women for the emasculation fear some men have of the woman's vagina; and 'a memory, perhaps, of the infantile desire to suck, cannibalistically, mother's breast to death. Milk becomes blood'![38] Whatever sym-

Love at first sight. . . . The giant gorilla about to abduct Fay Wray in *King Kong*.

bolism the two monsters may have, it should also be noted that film-makers went to great pains to provide both with brides; whether for reasons of continuing commercial success or because the producers were just mushy sentimentalists is for the individual to decide!

Foreign Parts

Europe, as ever, was far less concerned with censorship than America. Individual countries had their own sets of taboos, but none – with the exception of Britain's – was as sweeping and restrictive as the Hays Code. The head of the British Board of Film Censors, Lord Tyrrell, said in 1936 that 'the cinema needs continual repression of controversy to stave off disaster', but it's interesting to note that the US censor cut a scene from the wholly innocuous 1937 Sabu vehicle, *Elephant Boy*, because a temple statue was seen complete with penis which passed uncommented on or unnoticed in England. By and large the British cinema was sexually tame, although its 'thirties fad of

chronicling the love lives of its lustier monarchs – most notably *Nell Gwynn* (1934) and *The Private Life of Henry VIII* (for which Laughton won an Oscar in 1933) – was thought by some to be rather daring.

The Continentals were too versed in the ways of love to allow themselves to be hoodwinked, like the American public, into believing that what the Code allowed to be portrayed on the screen was right and normal and what it banned was wrong and unnatural. To say that there was 'impure' love – in the form of pre- or extramarital sexual activity – was ludicrous and they portrayed it regularly. Nor were they to be shooed out of the bedroom. To them the bedroom

Charles Laughton as lusty King Hal and Wendy Barrie as third spouse Jane Seymour in *The Private Life of Henry VIII* (Alexander Korda, 1933).

75

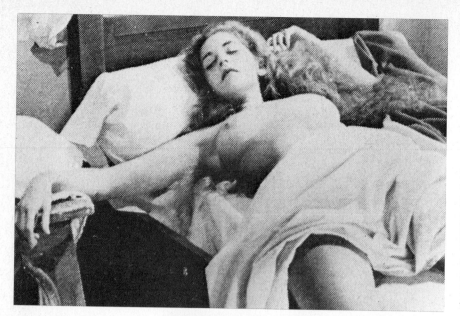

and the bed were the heart of the matter. No single beds, either; couples married, unmarried and adulterous were shown in the boudoir and, not infrequently, in states of undress and even semi-nudity. Breasts were occasionally glimpsed (as in *Lac aux Dames*, a 1934 film starring Simone Simon before she went to Hollywood), and even became a focal point of an orgy in *La Tour de Nesle*, an uncostume drama of 1937.

Germany continued its strong tradition of realism, neither shunning nor excising controversial subjects. Fritz Lang's *M* (1931) is a harrowing story of a sexually aberrant child-murderer, with Peter Lorre giving a stunning performance as the tortured, depraved killer. Hollywood shunned such themes. 'The Children's Hour' – the story of a pair of lesbian school-teachers – was filmed as *These Three* in 1936, but its homosexual theme was so muted as to be unrecognizable, and the subject remained

French director Abel Gance was the most accomplished and least inhibited of the European epic film-makers of the 'thirties, and his style and daring survived into the 'fifties. His remake of *La Tour de Nesle* (1954) — an orgiastic spectacular about Marguerite de Bourgogne, a dissolute and murderous queen of fourteenth-century France — contained far too much nudity for British eyes and was heavily cut in America.

The erotic revels and topless dance scenes in Gance's *Lucrèce Borgia* (1935) were also 'lost in translation', to a degree which caused one American critic to call the diminished film 'a dreary and unsatisfactory entertainment'.

untouched in Hollywood until the film was re-made under its original title in 1961 (retitled *The Loudest Whisper* in the UK). In Germany, however, films like *Mädchen In Uniform* (1931) conveyed lesbianism subtly but unequivocally. Here it was depicted as being inherent in a strict boarding school (during one sequence a girl is stripped by her dormitory mates in an initiation ceremony) and the audience was expected to recognize it as such. 'The rather troubled atmosphere of close friendship between young adolescents, whose senses have still to come to rest on an object different from their own sex, is evoked throughout,' says historian of the German cinema Lotte Eisner.[39]

Abel Gance, the distinguished French director, was quite explicit in his depiction of certain subjects, particularly orgies. The French and Italians used orgy scenes quite regularly but, as Ado Kyrou points out, 'they had a reputation

of bad quality because they were always limited in their expression, impoverished in imagination and denuded of eroticism'.[40] Gance featured an orgy in *La Fin du Monde* (1931) and a much more stirring one in *Lucrèce Borgia* (the liveliest of several versions of the story, 1935) which climaxed with a dinner-guest feasting off a woman's bare breast. Such scenes were, unsurprisingly, cut from prints for circulation in America, although Kyrou states that such orgies were admired in Hollywood, which timidly attempted to imitate the genre by adapting *Le Père Goriot*, retitling it *Paris à Minuit* 'and cramming it with decently dressed women sitting on the knees of mustachioed men'! Evidently, Gance's orgies lost something in translation.

The foreign film which caused the greatest stir in America was, however, not French, Italian or German, but Czechoslovakian; a film which was 'the forerunner of all erotic films and, after more than thirty years, still the most beautiful, the most poetic, still the model of its kind', according to critic Herman G. Weinberg.[41]

The film was *Extase – Ecstasy* hereinafter – made in 1933 by Gustav Machaty and starring Hedy Lamarr. The film caused a sensation from the start because of the sequence in which Lamarr (then Hedwig Kiesler), as the young girl who has left her impotent husband, runs through the woods and bathes naked, and then has a passionate coupling with a young engineer in a hut.

Lamarr's millionaire husband was outraged at the thought of his wife showing off her attractions, bigger than life-size, on the screen before other men and tried to suppress the film by buying up all the prints. In this he failed and a copy found its way to the States. It got through customs and met with no problems in three major cities – Washington, Newark and Boston.

This is doubly surprising because even Paris – so a contemporary report has it – was shocked. A German newspaper report of the time noted a little later that 'the New York State Board of Regents Censorship Commission has rejected an application to show *Ecstasy* on the grounds

Peter Lorre as the sexually disturbed child-murderer, and Inge Landgut as one of his victims, in Fritz Lang's *M* (1931).

Feet first

Recurring images of
erotic cinema: 1

Noel Coward's *The Vortex*
(*right*), with Ivor Novello
(Adrian Brunel, 1927).
Ernest Hemingway's *A
Farewell to Arms* (*centre,
right*), with Adolphe
Menjou and Gary Cooper
(Frank Borzage, 1932).
The Graduate (*far right*),
with Dustin Hoffman
(Mike Nichols, 1967).
*Glissements Progressifs du
Plaisir* (*bottom, right*), with
Anicée Alvina and Michel
Lonsdale (Alain Robbe-
Grillet, 1973). Vladimir
Nabokov's *Lolita* (*far right,
centre*), with James Mason
and Sue Lyon (Stanley
Kubrick, 1962). *Nell Gwynn*
(*far right, bottom*), with
Anna Neagle and Sir
Cedric Hardwicke
(Herbert Wilcox, 1934).

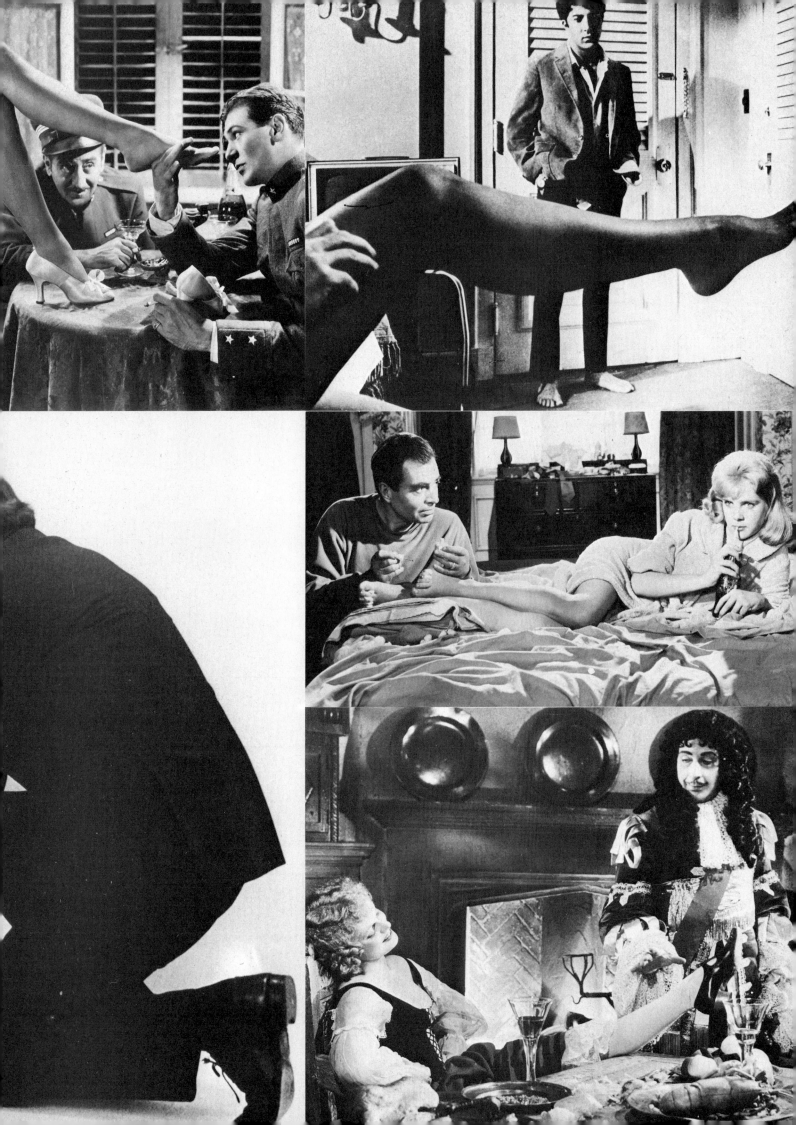

The theme of *Dante's Inferno* continued to attract ambitious film-makers in the 'thirties. This Fox version of 1935 was directed by Harry Lachman and starred Spencer Tracy.

that it is indecent, immoral and tends to corrupt youth'. Significantly, the objections were not primarily to the nude bathing scene or (in Lamarr's own words) 'the sequence of my fanny twinkling through the woods, but the close-up of my *face*, in that cabin sequence where the camera records the reactions of a love-starved bride in the act of sexual intercourse'.[42] In fact, this is, for the time, a remarkably frank portrayal of a woman in orgasm.

The film was taken into America in November, 1934, and adjudged to be obscene by the Trea-sury Department in January, 1935. In July the same year the print was destroyed. The importing company, Eureka, brought a second print into the States and decided to fight the issue. They took the case to the Circuit Court of Appeals where, after debate, Judge Learned Hand decided: 'I saw nothing in any sense immoral. . . .'

However, most exhibitors had been frightened off by the publicity and New York State and others opposed its showing strongly (this, it should be remembered, was only a few years

permissive in their rulings about the powers of the censors. As a result many films were banned in certain areas. The phrasing of the various state laws on film censorship clearly indicate that sex was a primary concern. Nearly all are in terms similar to those of Pennsylvania, the first state to pass such a law, which had ordered its censors to disapprove of films which were 'sacrilegious, obscene, indecent or immoral, or such as tend to corrupt morals'. The situation remained unchanged throughout the 'thirties and 'forties. It wasn't until 1948 and Rossellini's *The Miracle* that a radical change was effected.

Although adverse publicity killed *Ecstasy*, it did exactly the opposite for Lamarr's career. Deserting her millionaire husband she made for London and contrived to meet Louis B. Mayer. He was very dubious about her appeal to the kind of audience he fancied watched his pictures. 'You'll never get away with that stuff in Hollywood,' he told her. 'A woman's ass is for her husband, not theatregoers. You're lovely but I prefer the family point of view. I don't like what people would think about a girl who flits bare-assed around the screen. We have an obligation to the audience – millions of families.' He added with pious paternalism: 'We make clean pictures.'[43] (This preachy pomposity is rather at odds with another piece of advice she says he gave her: 'You'd be surprised how tits figure in a girl's career'!)

Nothing daunted, Lamarr contrived to be on the 'Normandie' – the ship on which Mayer was returning to the States – and, by the end of the voyage, had somehow persuaded him to change his mind. But, having signed her, he wasn't sure how to use her and he loaned her to Walter Wanger to play opposite Charles Boyer's Pepe Le Moko in *Algiers*.

According to Lamarr, Mayer warned her that Wanger might want her to do a nude scene in the movie. 'I found out later,' she records, 'that Mayer had slyly suggested to Wanger I do a nude scene. He probably thought it was fine as long as I didn't do it for MGM.' (If this story is true, it's a glorious example of a mogul's hypocrisy in matters of sex on the screen. Certainly Mayer had a strong Puritan streak – despite the fact that he was one of Hollywood's greatest womanizers – and was heard once to screech in horror: 'Don't show the natural functions!')

There was, of course, no nude scene in *Algiers* (1938) and, despite her undoubted beauty, Lamarr's on-screen career was a great deal less remarkable than her off-screen antics and, particularly, her six divorces.

The moguls' attitude to the Hays Code was equivocal during the 'thirties. They publicly upheld it because to fly in its face would mean that the film in question wouldn't get a showing. At the same time they racked their brains for ways round it and frequently took to horse-trading with the censor. The Hays Office could be capable of crass stupidity in its decisions. (A classic came when the script for the 1939 film *Zaza* was returned to the studio. It called for a scene in which the heroine shouts at the villain:

after the Chicago Chief of Police had publicly stated: 'Any film that isn't fit to be shown to my youngest child isn't fit to be shown to anybody') with the result that over a period of twenty years it was only seen in about four hundred cinemas across the entire continent.

Evidence enough that ever since the Mutual Film case of 1915 local censorship had been rampant. Although that decision had made clear the right of courts to overrule the opinions of local censors, this right was repeatedly overlooked and the courts had become increasingly

Hedwig Kiesler's famous
nude scene in *Ecstasy*
(Gustav Machaty, 1933).
Hedi went to Hollywood and
became Hedy Lamarr.

'Pig! Pig! Pig! Pig! Pig!' A note in the margin
said: 'Delete two pigs.') The famous fight that
was waged to retain Gable's 'Frankly, my dear,
I don't give a damn' was won only at the cost
of 'I've never held fidelity to be a virtue'. In
Destry Rides Again (1939) Marlene Dietrich –
as Frenchie, the soiled saloon queen – was
permitted to tuck money down her cleavage but
not to say 'There's gold in them thar hills!'

Against such inexplicable judgments the
moguls were sometimes just bewildered. 'What
critics call dirty in our movies,' said Billy
Wilder, 'they call lusty in foreign films.' Most
presented their faces to the public as home-
loving family men (the family, of course, extend-
ing to cover all in their employ) and most went
along with, and oft reiterated, Sam Goldwyn's
dicta: 'Motion pictures should never embarrass
a man when he brings his wife to the theatre'
and 'I seriously object to seeing on the screen
what belongs in the bedroom'. But in matters of
box-office business, those dirty hands were still
teaching the cinema to walk.

When a set director once approached Harry
Cohn – head of Columbia and an ogre even by
mogul standards – for his approval of more
expenditure on a set in which the two leads were

to play a major love scene, he said: 'Lemme
tell you something. If in this whole damn
country, when we show that scene, there's one
person who'll be looking at the wall – then
we're in trouble.' On another occasion he
gathered together his writers and shouted:
'Lemme tell you what this business is about. It's
cunt and horses!'

The moguls thought commercially, which
meant that they thought in terms of sex. Despite
morals clauses, scandals and whitewash jobs,
they lived and operated in a milieu of carnality,

where the casting couch was a route to the top. In this environment, it was second nature to those in power to try to bend the Code. The moguls are traditionally pictured as philistinic vulgarians, barely able to read or write, who exercised omnipotent sway over their studios. Certainly they were despotic and some were nearly illiterate (except when it came to the small print in contracts), and if they thought they could make several fast bucks by running around the Hays Office then they wouldn't hesitate.

Hollywood in this decade was a schizophrenic place. Early in the 'thirties the moguls had agreed to abide by a Code – high-minded in its principles – and thereinafter they attempted to short-circuit it. But despite all the restrictions placed on movies by the Hays Office, this was the Golden Age of movies. The studios expanded as the industry became one of the biggest in America. The people flocked to the cinemas and helped to create some of the biggest, most enduring stars the world has ever known. These actors and actresses, who rose to unprece-

Victor Mature and Hedy Lamarr as *Samson and Delilah* (Cecil B. De Mille, 1949), which had 'more chariots, more temples, more peacock plumes, more animals, more pillows, more spear-carriers, more beards, and more sex than ever before' (Bosley Crowther, New York Times).

dented heights of fame at the time, are still the household names they were then. And it is to those audiences, those moguls and, indirectly, to the Hays Office, whose strictures forced producers to find stars with inherent and lasting sex appeal or acting ability (and preferably both) rather than a mere transient ability to walk sexily or look good in rumpled sheets, that we must look with gratitude.

Golden Girls and Boys

Cary Grant, who described himself as 'the longest lasting young man about town'.

Seldom in the history of the cinema has such a range of entertainment been consistently offered to the public by the major studios as weekly hit the screens from 1930 to 1939. Musicals, gangster and crime movies, westerns, social, sophisticated and crazy comedies, horror films, weepies, swashbucklers, biblical epics, romantic dramas: all these and others poured from Hollywood in a commercial torrent. And each genre had its specialist stars.

The actual chemistry which makes a particular actor or actress a big star is, perhaps fortunately, indefinable. That being said, there are certain broad fundamentals which most (though not all) of the great stars shared. These have been defined as looks, personality and talent. Many of the great stars consistently denied their talent ('He's a very bad actor but he absolutely loves doing it' – David Niven of

Ronald Colman, whose Times obituary said: 'His good looks and cultured manners made him an impressive hero of the classic English school.'

himself). Some have denied their own looks ('I have eyes like those of a dead pig' – Brando), but very few denied they had personality. An actor didn't have to have all three to get to the top (and, conversely, some who had all three in abundance never made it at all); some perhaps had none of them and still made it, but by-and-large you had to have one or more to be a star. In addition, or perhaps it was the amalgam of these, there was sex appeal.

Sex appeal, again, is indefinable. Elinor Glyn's adage about 'It' will serve us as well as any to describe sex appeal (although, in fairness, she vehemently denied that the two were synonymous). 'A strange magnetism,' she said, 'which attracts both sexes . . . there must be physical attraction but beauty is unnecessary.' She went on to conclude that 'even a priest could have "It"'.

Lon Chaney was a star without having much sex appeal, or even a personality he could call his own. George Arliss was a star mainly because he was considered a great actor. Rin Tin Tin was a star without being noticeably endowed with any of the physical fundamentals!

But sex appeal counted for a lot. It took different forms, of course, and attracted different sections of the public. For example, Cary Grant and Spencer Tracy both had sex appeal but both were of a unique type; so did Jean Harlow and Greta Garbo. Sex appeal wasn't obligatory but it was extremely important.

The moguls prided themselves on being able to spot star quality. It is to their credit that they succeeded so triumphantly so often, but they also had their failures. Sam Goldwyn, despite devoting huge amounts of money, energy and time to the task, never made Anna Sten the star he thought she could be, and Louis Mayer never fulfilled his promise of making Hedy Lamarr the greatest motion-picture star that there had ever been. The enormous Hollywood publicity machine could and did drum up enthusiasm for its players, but the final word was left with the audience. 'Producers don't make stars,' said Goldwyn. 'God makes stars, and the public recognizes his handiwork.'

The stars often fell into broad categories according to the types of movies they played. For example, there was the typical American hero played so successfully by Henry Fonda, James Stewart, and Gary Cooper; Cary Grant cornered light comedy; Charles Boyer was the unsurpassed Continental lover; Tracy and Fredric March were solid and dramatic; Ronald Colman and Leslie Howard played suave and appealingly fey Englishmen.

Women tended to be simply sexy in a delightful variety of ways. Lovely Carole Lombard captured not only the world's heart with her radiance but also Gable's; Vivien Leigh's mercurial bitchiness as Scarlett O'Hara epitomized the kind of woman Joan Crawford and Bette Davis had already made their own; Lupe Velez – the Mexican Spitfire – captured the imagination with her firebrand Latin hot-bloodedness in films whose titles usually promised more than they delivered – *Lady of the Pavements* (1929), *The Half-Naked Truth* (1932), *Strictly Dynamite* (1934) (though she did manage to electrify audiences in *The Morals of Marcus* with a scene in which she bends forward to the camera to tie her shoe and, in the words of a contemporary critic, 'practically spills out all over the first three rows'); Myrna Loy, cool, sophisticated, was voted 'Queen of Hollywood' in a nationwide poll and thus became Gable's publicity consort; it was said of Madeleine Carroll that she was 'the most beautiful woman in the world'; Norma Shearer got knocked around by Clark Gable in *A Free Soul* (1931) and specialized, for a time, as the over-sexed woman. These and many others made up the pantheon of Hollywood fame.

Right in the middle of the decade came a male star who, through his on-screen portrayals and his off-screen shenanigans, became synonymous with sex – Errol Flynn. Jack Warner made a brave decision to cast him when unknown in the part of *Captain Blood* (1935) after Robert Donat turned the role down. Flynn and the picture clicked, and the young actor was cast in the swashbuckling mould of Douglas Fairbanks. But he brought something to these parts that the clean-cut Fairbanks had lacked – powerful sex appeal. In a series of 'thirties pictures from *Blood* through *The Charge of the Light Brigade* (1936), *The Adventures of Robin Hood* (1937), *Dawn Patrol* (1938), *Elizabeth and Essex* (1939) to *The Sea Hawk* (1940) he became the hero of men and the fantasy action-man lover of women.

He was impudently attractive, with a boyish gleam in his eye which, matched with a good deal of obvious athleticism, made him an instant success as a sex symbol. The stories, whispers, rumours and scandals which surrounded him only added fuel to his sex appeal. Mysteriously, he thought himself a bad screen lover and in his autobiography (which candidly admits to many, varied and sensational amorous adventures) he commented: 'Screen loving is such a self-conscious thing for me that I find myself drawing back, growing cold. In fact, I can think of only two, John Barrymore and John Gilbert – not Flynn – who could actually give a literal sexual feeling to a scene with a woman without being self-conscious about it. As for me, there is something in such a private scene that I cannot get myself to do even with the most delightful leading ladies.'[44] Millions who flocked to see him play opposite women like Olivia de Havilland (to whom he admitted being deeply attracted and with whom, according to Bette Davis, 'he was deeply in love' but who managed to elude him), Joan Blondell in *The Perfect Specimen* (1937), Rosalind Russell in *Four's a Crowd* (1938), Bette Davis (with whom he fought) in *The Sisters* (1938) and *The Private Lives of Elizabeth and Essex* (1939), probably would not agree with this uncharacteristically modest statement.

Whether he was fighting with his wives – particularly French actress Lili Damita – living it up with David Niven (who affectionately referred to him as 'a magnificent specimen of the rampant male') and other hell-raising chums, feuding with studio bosses, or cutting a swathe through the compliant womanhood of California, Flynn was, in the public mind, everything that a movie star should be. A roisterer, a carouser with soiled madonnas, a boyo; 'in like Flynn' was the expression.

The 'thirties was his greatest era but in the early 'forties 'The Headhunters' (his own description) were after him. In 1942 he was arrested for statutory rape, charged with having had sexual intercourse with an under-age girl called Betty Hanson. The case against Flynn was weak and (according to him) the District Attorney's office 'dug up' another girl called Peggy Satterlee and levelled a second charge against him. When the facts of his arrest were known they caused an international furore.

The case went before the Grand Jury who

Charles Boyer, the supreme Continental lover, who 'knew how to create an atmosphere of tenderness very simply and without any sentimentality' (Aldous Huxley).

Leslie Howard, the phlegmatic Englishman – 'a man of great personal charm which increased with the years' (C.A. Lejeune).

David Niven, successor to Colman and Howard as Hollywood's resident romantic Englishman.

Carole Lombard —
unstintingly adored by the
public, her colleagues and
husband Clark Gable.

Gina Lollobrigida in *Solomon and Sheba* (King Vidor, 1959).

Carroll Baker in *The Carpetbaggers* (Edward Dmytryk, 1964).

87

Jane Fonda as *Barbarella*
(Roger Vadim, 1968).

decided there was no charge to answer and Flynn was freed. Within the week, however, the DA decided to override that decision and press for a conviction. Things drifted on for months – 'five months that shook the world's glands' was how Flynn described it – keeping the headlines busy with postponement after postponement, until the case finally got to court.

The girls told their stories; Peggy Satterlee testified that Flynn had had sexual intercourse with her, but *without her consent* on board his yacht 'Sirocco' – 'She was implying a knock-her-down-drag-her-out rape,' Flynn commented. Betty Hanson declared that the event had occurred in Flynn's house. The sordid details were uncovered and many inconsistencies cropped up in their stories (Satterlee, a well-developed girl whose age, it seems, was never

satisfactorily established, turned up in the witness box dressed in bobbysox and pigtails). News of the revelations pushed the war off the front pages and the world seemed to wait with bated breath to hear the jury's verdict. When it came Flynn was totally exonerated and the prosecution discredited.

Why the charges were ever brought is still something of a mystery. Flynn himself darkly hints that there were people in Hollywood out to destroy him. The DA's office seemed to be particularly zealous in the conduct of the affair and it is possible that Flynn was being used as a scapegoat. Whatever the truth, Flynn's career slowly declined from that date (though it may not have been entirely due to the odium that surrounded the event; he was fed up with swashbuckling and his extraordinary rate of

living took a heavy physical toll) and although he continued acting spasmodically until his death in 1959 he never quite reached the sublime heights of his 'thirties magic.

Jack Warner – for whom Flynn worked over many years – said of him: 'He had a mediocre talent, but to all the Walter Mittys of the world he was all the heroes in one magnificent, sexy, animal package. Actor or no actor, he showered an audience with sparks when he laughed, when he fought, or when he loved.'

Errol Flynn was the very essence of what stars and sex symbols of the 'thirties appeared to be. On his death actor Tony Britton telegrammed Trevor Howard: 'Old Errol died laughing. Can you beat that?'

'How'd you like to tussle with Russell?' Thus ran the tag-line to a movie which was to prove quite extraordinary in so many ways. It made an unknown girl a star before the picture was ever shown; it provoked one of the bitterest rows between a film-maker and the Hays Office ever; it took three years from completion before the film went on general release.

The movie was *The Outlaw* (1943), the director was Howard Hughes, and the whole circus was the talk of the 'forties. When he decided to make *The Outlaw*, Hughes had kept away from films for seven years (he had been behind *Hell's Angels* in 1930, *The Front Page* in 1931, and *Scarface* in 1932) and he approached his new project, a story about Billy the Kid, in his own idiosyncratic way.

(A measure of his individuality, especially in dealings with the movie industry, was his decision to buy a controlling share of RKO in 1948 – he bought it outright in the 'fifties – and his deal with the man he made head of the studio. The studio manager was to run the place but Hughes was to have approval of the casting of all leading ladies. Hughes's closest confidant for many years, Noah Dietrich, said that the deal 'aided his libido' and that he was never sure, during the years when Hughes dabbled extravagantly in the industry, whether the films or the furtherance of his sex life was more important to him.)

Dietrich reports that Hughes came to him one day, highly excited. 'Today,' he enthused, 'I saw the most beautiful pair of knockers I've ever seen in my life.' The spectacular mammaries belonged to a young dental receptionist named Jane Russell (the job, the location and, indeed, the discoverer change according to which version you read; the physical attributes do not).

Hughes wanted Russell to play Rio and he got her. He wanted a young unknown to play Billy and he got Jack Buetel (who remained an unknown even after *The Outlaw*). He wanted Howard Hawks – who'd directed *Scarface* (1932) with such success – and this too he accomplished. Within weeks of the start of shooting Hughes's constant interference caused Hawks to quit so the ex-boy wonder and eccentric millionaire took over.

Hughes knew exactly where the film's appeal lay – below Russell's chin and above her waist – 'There are two good reasons why men will go to see her,' he said. Russell's breasts were to be the focus of the movie. He devoted take after take to shots of Russell leaning over the wounded Kid's bed, fussing and fretting, re-shooting, realigning the camera until he got just the right effect. It evidently worked. At the première, as Russell leaned forward, a member of the audience hollered 'Bombs away!'

Magnificent though her assets were, Hughes decided that her chest needed a little more help to produce just the right result. The designer in him came to the fore and, muttering 'This is really just a very simple engineering problem', he retired to the drawing board. The story of how he designed her bra is famous, but a memo he circulated about the treatment of her bosom is not (Noah Dietrich quotes it in his book 'Howard, The Amazing Mr Hughes' and attributes its timing to the making of *Macao* (1952), some years after *The Outlaw*. It shows just how much value the tycoon placed on Russell's frontage and must surely rank as one of the most bizarre memoranda ever circulated in Hollywood):

'I think,' Hughes wrote, 'Russell's wardrobe . . . is Christ awful. It is unrevealing, unbecoming, and just generally terrible. There is one exception, and that is the dress made of metallic cloth. This dress is absolutely terrific and should be used, by all means.

'However, the fit of the dress around her breasts is not good and gives the impression, God forbid, that her breasts are padded or artificial. They just don't appear to be in natural contour. It looks as if she's wearing a brassiere of some very stiff material which does not take the contour of her breasts. Particularly around the nipple, it looks as though some kind of stiff material underneath the dress is forming an artificial and unnatural contour.

'I am not recommending that she go without a brassiere, as I know this is a very necessary piece of equipment for Russell. But I thought, if we could find a half-brassiere which will support her breasts upward and still not be noticeable under the dress. . . .

'Now, it would be extremely valuable if the brassiere, or the dress, incorporated some kind of a point at the nipple because I know this does not ever occur naturally in the case of Jane Russell. Her breasts always appear to be round, or flat, at the point so something artificial here would be extremely desirable if it could be incorporated without destroying the contour of the rest of her breasts . . . (the memo continues by reiterating all the points already made and then goes on) . . .

'However, I want the rest of her wardrobe, wherever possible, to be low-necked (and by that I mean as low as the law allows) so that the customers can get a look at the part of Russell which they pay to see and not covered

Jane Russell in *The Outlaw* (Howard Hughes, 1943). Censor Joseph Breen was driven to despair by Miss Russell's ample chest. 'I have never,' he wrote to his boss, Will Hays, 'seen anything quite so unacceptable as the shots of the breasts of the character of Rio. . . . Throughout almost half the picture, the girl's breasts, which are quite large and prominent, are shockingly uncovered.'

Jane Russell in *Underwater*
(John Sturges, 1955), which
had an underwater première
in Florida.

by cloth, metallic or otherwise.'[45]

Such astonishing, almost obsessional attention to detail had the effect of running up a colossal $3\frac{1}{2}$ million dollar budget for the picture, dragging the shooting on for months and thoroughly alarming the censor. Breen saw the script in 1940 and reacted immediately and without having seen a single frame from the rushes by bombarding Hughes with memos. He wanted robes worn over night-gowns, wondered whether the scene in which Billy rapes Rio could be handled 'in good taste' and warned, 'Care will be needed in this scene with Billy pulling Rio down on the bed and kissing her, to avoid sex suggestiveness'! He must have been near-apoplectic about the sequence in which Doc (Walter Huston) tells Rio to keep the wounded Billy warm, and she does it by climbing in next to him!

Part of the plot centres around a grudge between the older Doc and Billy over ownership of a strawberry-roan horse. When Doc objects to Russell's unusual nursing of the Kid, the latter replies by pointing out that Doc had used his horse and 'A fair exchange is no robbery!' Hughes changed this to 'You borrowed from me, I borrowed from you' which Breen disliked because of its implications. Dietrich records that Hughes was childishly delighted with the

alternative he devised for Billy's riposte – 'Tit for tat'. This upset Hays and the line was changed yet again to something totally innocuous.

The subject of the Russell bosom really raised Breen's ire. There is no doubt that after Harlow's brave lead the Hollywood cinema had become breast-fixated and the censor had found it prudent to institute an exact – to the inch – ruling as to how low a dress could be cut (hence Hughes's reference in his memo 'as low as the law allows') and the extent of cleavage to be shown (even stills to be used in publicity had to be submitted to the censor and could be suppressed or ordered to be changed; one was returned to the company annotated: 'Lift the bra an inch, take out cleavage, tuck in belly button and pull up slacks').

Hughes decided to fight against censorship, but it was more for sound commercial reasons – gaining invaluable press coverage and publicity – than for noble liberal ideals. Breen refused to issue a seal of approval for *The Outlaw* until Hughes had reshot offending passages, and these constituted a great deal of the entire length of the movie. Hughes refused. There was a stalemate but there was also the fact that Breen was about to leave his post, and when he did Hughes cut a very few feet, changed a few lines and got his seal without trouble. However, he wasn't ready to release it.

In the meantime, America had entered the war and Hughes's conglomerate industrial network was much involved in the production of essential supplies, particularly planes. Whether because he became so busy running his factories or because, as he is alleged to have said: 'The longer I wait, the more valuable the picture will be. I'm building up the public's desire to see *The Outlaw*', he decided to hold back the release of the film and stimulate public interest with a tease campaign centred around Russell. It may partly have been due to the fact that the one airing the film did get – in 1943 – resulted in a universal critical panning, and he reasoned that, if cleverly handled, the public would click through the turnstiles to see the star and not the film.

Hughes held it until 1946 before putting it on release. It went out without a seal – a daring venture; that had been withdrawn because of the salacious content of the advertising, pegged on startling and lurid artwork of Russell, which had her half-lying in straw, blouse slipping off shoulder, skirt hitched well up a thigh against which she pressed an extremely phallic revolver. The ballyhoo of Hughes's campaign made Russell one of the most popular pin-ups of the war and a household name before she'd ever been seen on the screen.

Whether the ploy worked is in some doubt. Some accounts say that the picture did barnstorming business and proved that the grip of the censor was slipping, because previously a film without a seal was automatically dead. Dietrich – one of the men closest to Hughes – claims that the years of publicity weren't enough to guarantee success, that the audience laughed in the wrong places (by general consent it's a rotten movie) and that although the people came to see it for its value as a curio it never netted enough to pay back Hughes's investment. The 'Variety Updated All-Time Film Champs' ('Annual and Ongoing Compilation of Features Grossing $4,000,000 And More' in rentals in the US–Canada market up to and including 1973) show that it had taken $5,075,000 (the next film of the same decade above it was *Meet Me In St Louis*, 1944, at $5,200,000; the next below it *Battleground*, 1949, $5,060,000, and the highest listed film of the 'forties was Walt Disney's *Pinocchio*, 1940, at $13,000,000).

Whatever the truth, and with Hughes it's often so difficult to sift truth from legend, *The Outlaw* was important for one reason. It was a

watershed in the development of Hollywood. It proved that the Code could be flouted, that a movie could do business without a seal and that the 'forties audience, made more sophisticated by the rigours of war just as it had been after the First World War, could and would still pay money to see sex and now wanted a more adult treatment of it from Hollywood.

The single most influential event concerning Hollywood in this decade was, of course, the war. The war meant that millions of men were separated from their women, and that they – and those they left behind – needed their morale maintained. They needed escape, they needed pin-ups, they needed sex. And if they couldn't get the real thing then (in the word of the day) the ersatz would do. No entertainment medium was better able to supply this than the movies.

During the 'forties the stranglehold of censorship began gradually to weaken, for, just as morals generally changed to suit the desperate circumstances, so did the celluloid mirror need to reflect them. People facing daily dangers tend to resort to the arms of the opposite sex for comfort. Live today for you never know what tomorrow may hold was the philosophy, and casual affairs, brief, desperate moments of relief, became much more common. Obviously, Hollywood could no longer stick rigidly to a stress on marriage and a pretence that no other form of sexual activity took place.

Allied fighting men in all the theatres of war could pin up a picture of a pretty girl on their lockers, but Hollywood could bring them that same girl, larger than life, walking, talking and loving to fuel their fantasies and enliven their dreams.

America entered the war in December 1941, and, from that point until Japan's surrender in 1945, Hollywood turned its incredible resources towards the war effort. It made information films, it made propaganda films, it boosted morale, it brought smiles. Perhaps Betty Grable's legs did as much for American morale as Capra's *Why We Fight* series; certainly both played their part in the victory push. Would Gable have contributed more by staying in Hollywood and winning the war alongside John Wayne and Errol Flynn than by flying bomber missions over Germany to shoot training films? Whatever the answer, while the men fought on celluloid or foreign soil, the women in Hollywood weren't making socks, they were making films.

The start of the decade saw a new fashion in cinema sex. Having explored most of the erotic possibilities of showing breasts without actually showing breasts, they hit on a new formula. Actually, it came from a well-developed sixteen-year-old girl who walked through a 1937 film – *They Won't Forget* – wearing a sweater a couple of sizes too small for her.

Lana Turner arrived – breasts jiggling – in the manner she was to continue. And she caused a revolution in the knitwear industry. The logic of the too-tight sweater is unbeatable. Who could object to a woolly? It has no plunging neckline, no slashes down it, it shows

'Howdya like to be in movies?' Sweater-girl Lana Turner (*on the left*) in her first film, *They Won't Forget* (Mervyn Le Roy, 1937).

Clash of symbols

Recurring images of erotic cinema: 2

Victoria Vetri (*right*) in *When Dinosaurs Ruled the Earth* (**Val Guest, 1969**). The 'Brazil' number (*centre, right*) from *The Gang's All Here* (**Busby Berkeley, 1943**). Erotic fantasy (*far right*) from *Juliet of the Spirits* (**Frederico Fellini, 1965**). *Cobra* (*bottom, centre*), a risible Rudolph Valentino vehicle (**Joseph Henabery, 1925**). Martine Beswick (*bottom, far right*) in *Slave Girls* (**Michael Carreras, 1966**).

Ann Sheridan – the 'Oomph Girl', a tag she despised.

no cleavage. Nothing is less sexually arousing than a sweater . . . depending, of course, on who wears it and how. Turner wore it like a burlesque dancer wears sequins. It showed nothing and everything. The Sweater Girl had arrived. And it must have come as no surprise to anyone that in her first film this teenage tease is raped and murdered.

The way Turner was discovered is pure Hollywood hokum. There she was, a peach ready for the plucking, leaning those lovely breasts over the counter of Schwab's drugstore drinking a soda, when this big-time journalist – Bob Wilkerson, publisher of The Hollywood Reporter – walked in, took one unbelieving look, and said: 'Howdya like to be in movies?'

By 1940 she was getting established. She nearly wrecked her career by scandalizing the studio in a runaway marriage to bandleader Artie Shaw, which probably puzzled the newly-weds as much as the match did Betty Grable, who was seeing a lot of Shaw, and Greg Bautzer, well-known lawyer, to whom Turner was engaged and with whom she supposedly had a date the evening of the wedding. She was still only nineteen, after all!

However, a girl who provokes the censor's wrath can't be all bad and the studio forgave her magnanimously. Breen, with his seeming obsession about exposure of breasts, had at last tumbled the fact that sweaters weren't the sole prerogative of spinster librarians and tooth-braced high-school bobbysoxers, and in 1940 decreed that 'sweater shots' which obviously accentuated the contours of breasts would be rejected out of hand.

The 'forties had their own equivalent of the It Girl. Carole Landis was given the inexplicable soubriquet of The Ping Girl. Why Ping? Why, indeed. She was also described as a 'bureau with the top drawer pulled out'! Ann Sheridan

was The Oomph Girl. And what was Oomph? Sheridan herself described it as 'the sound a fat man makes when he bends over to tie his laces in a phone booth'. Which is less than romantic and one must suppose that she had become sick of the term when she said this. She certainly knew exactly what it meant during the decade, because she wrote an autograph to one of Errol Flynn's friends – whom she disliked – with the following inscription: 'I'm the Oomph Girl. Oomph you'!

However, the emphasis of the 'forties was on glamour girls, decorative pin-ups who posed for countless stills and publicity shots. Veronica Lake, with her 'peek-a-boo' hairstyle falling over one eye, was one of the most glamorous, the contemporary cousin to the Mata Hari seductress. Marie McDonald was 'The Body' – which is self-explanatory – and, from the evidence of her films, she had little more to recommend her.

But the greatest of all the pin-ups was undoubtedly Betty Grable. She was the 'Gam Girl', on account of her fabulous legs – insured by Twentieth Century-Fox for $1,000,000 (more even than Astaire's). She appeared in 'one of the most famous pin-ups of all time' (asserts

Veronica Lake in her 'peek-a-boo' period. She agreed to change her hairstyle when wartime factory girls imitated it and got their tresses caught in the machines.

Mark Gabor, historian of the genre), helped to fix the word – unknown before the decade – into the language and feasted the eyes of hundreds of thousands of fighting men. 'The classic pose – the one-piece swimming suit, high heels, and delicate ankle bracelet – seemed to say, "Follow me home, boys. I'm what you're fighting for."'[46]

Grable's appeal is difficult to understand today. She wasn't a siren, she certainly wasn't a goddess, she wasn't even particularly erotic. She was, as Richard Schickel puts it in 'The Stars', 'a sort of great American floozie'. He continues: 'Miss Grable's beauty – if that is the word for it – was of the common sort. Nor did she offer much in the way of character or maturity. Her appeal to lonely GIs was surely that of every hash-house waitress with whom they ever flirted.' She was a warm-hearted hoyden with an ever-ready shoulder to cry on, a brash, slightly vulgar attraction, and a homeliness, a feeling of being real, that the other pin-ups never had.

The guy in his bunk at sea, on watch in some jungle outpost, or waiting on stand-by through long nights to fly the next mission, could look at Grable and those legs and feel that, given the chance, he could find solace with this brand of sympathetic, almost maternal woman. He didn't have a hope in hell of making it with Sheridan or the others, but Grable, he felt, could be had. Grable described herself as 'strictly an enlisted man's girl'. The others, in Kyrou's words, were 'lifeless erotic machines'. He said, 'The pin-up is a stereotyped beauty, big, well-developed, smiling, provocative. She is the contradiction of the sophisticated woman; in her presence a man has no problems because she holds no mystery. She is a head and a body, ever smiling, perfectly wholesome, a hopelessly stupid creature.'[47]

Grable was different; she had life. Certainly she was not sophisticated, but she seemed *sympatico* and she looked a 'good sort', the type of girl who would listen to one's problems, boost one's ego, and send one on one's way, refreshed and re-affirmed in one's belief in human nature.

She specialized in her films as 'The girl on the make', an updated gold digger – epitomized in her 1953 outing with Marilyn Monroe and Lauren Bacall in *How To Marry a Millionaire* – who eventually realized her limitations and surrendered her ambitions for the poor man who captured her heart. If anyone in films had gold beating beneath her bosom it was Betty Grable.

Turner and Grable typified the way in which producers, directors and writers in the early 'forties, with the Hays Office still vigilantly watching for deviations, injected sex into movies. Ken Englund – writer of *The Secret Life of Walter Mitty* (1948) – wrote a satirical guide to such ploys which, like all satire, contains a deal of truth. He isolated three plot devices which recurred with monotonous regularity (the piece was entitled 'Quick! Boil Some Hot Clichés') and described them thus:

Betty Grable – 'a sort of great American floozie'.

'THE OUTDOOR OR AIN'T-NATURE-GRAND SCENE:
The girl in a tight white sweater takes a deep breath and looks around at the other wonders of nature and exclaims (after much coaching): "Oh, Timothy, isn't it beautiful!"

'Timothy takes a look at her heaving sweater and exclaims back significantly: "Sure is!" and his meaning isn't lost on anyone.
'THE BACKSTAGE MUSICAL: (a Grable speciality)
Can't we do something about the circular iron ladder backstage and that typical shot of chorines descending? I know it's a dandy way to catch the backs of girls' legs, but can't we repaint the ladder or something, or twist the iron the other way?
'EPICS, RESTORATION DRAMAS, PERIOD PIECES:
The leading lady is taking a bath in a tub or rain barrel – a maidservant pouring in hot water. The bather looks up, shocked to find that George Sanders has taken the maid's place and is now pouring. There must be another way to show Paulette Goddard's pretty shoulders in relation to history without always resorting to this prairies bubble bath.'[48]

The Hays Office still held sway in the early 'forties and, after nearly ten years of its rule, it seemed that movie-makers, who had found uncounted ways of getting round the rules, were by now rather barren of ideas. The Code's continuing lack of reality in its attitude to human life and relationships was a severely hampering constraint. Fritz Lang complained of the censor's interference on *Man Hunt* (1940): 'The Hays Office warned us that we couldn't show the heroine as a prostitute. We had to put a sewing machine in her apartment, so in that way she was not a whore but a seamstress.'

Even more extraordinary was the office's decision to bring decency to Walt Disney! *Fantasia* (1940) contained an idyllic sequence in which pretty little female centaurs cavorted with their budding breasts bared. Hays stepped in and garlands were introduced to cover the offending parts.

However, the strictures on 'impure' love were relaxing. To try to ignore adult sexual relationships – particularly pre- and extra-marital sex –

Barbara Stanwyck as the homicidal adulteress in Billy Wilder's *Double Indemnity* (1944).

was becoming an increasingly ridiculous aim. In the first years of the decade came Garbo's last movie, *Two-Faced Woman* (1941). The plot centred around stodgy ski-instructress Garbo's play for Melvyn Douglas, their affair and, because she believes that he is bored with her and yearns for someone more frivolous, her pretence to be her own, prettier, more flirtatious and sexy twin sister, with whom he falls in love.

To avoid any censorial complications, MGM married the pair in the opening reel so that Garbo would only be in competition with herself to keep her husband's affections. The Hays Office seemed to have no objections to this, but the Catholic, ultra-conservative Legion of Decency raised a howl because, if Melvyn Douglas *was* duped by his wife's impersonation and chased the sister with amorous intent, the implication was that he wanted to bed her and that constituted adultery! MGM withdrew the movie and spliced in a scene in which he receives a 'phone call telling him of Garbo's deception, which means that, when he goes after the 'twin', he is really only playing along with his own wife. This twist not only nullified the piquant point of the film, it also killed the movie stone dead at the box-office.

A few years later such petty-minded meddling was to be all but stifled. By 1944 and *Double Indemnity*, adulterous relationships were portrayed, if not explicitly, at least comprehensibly. The audience was never left in any doubt as to the prime motivation of Fred MacMurray's fatal involvement in Barbara Stanwyck's plot to murder her husband and claim the insurance. From their first meeting there is an aura of strong sexuality in their relationship. MacMurray is besotted with Stanwyck; they react to each other in a physical manner which, by the way the principals play it, depicts a stifling lust. MacMurray allows himself to be corrupted not so much to get the money but to get Stanwyck, and we are left in no doubt as to the fact that even before the murder is accomplished, the deadly pair have relieved their carnality.

Perhaps the adultery became more acceptable in the eyes of the censor because it was inextricably intertwined with crime and evil and both got their come-uppance in the end. Much the same circumstances surround the torrid lustfulness of Lana Turner and John Garfield in *The Postman Always Rings Twice* (1946). Garfield falls under Turner's sluttish, ruttish spell and, because of her overwhelming physical attraction for him, is induced to murder her husband.

Deadly dames who worked their wiles through their sexuality littered movies of the period. 'They could simulate love to worm a secret, steal a compromising paper or deliver a stab in the back,' says Kyrou. There was a string of them, from Barbara Stanwyck and Turner's steamy Cora, through Lisbeth Scott's attempt to deter Bogart's investigation of his missing wartime buddy (and her fiancé) in *Dead Reckoning* (1947), and Rita Hayworth's treacherous *Lady From Shanghai* (1948), to

Betty Grable's famous wartime pin-up pose. She was known as the 'Gam Girl' and her legs were insured for a million dollars.

Claire Trevor in *Murder, My Sweet* (*Farewell My Lovely* in the UK, 1944).

One of the very best was Mary Astor's nefarious Brigid O'Shaughnessy in John Huston's brilliant *The Maltese Falcon* (1941). By playing on her beauty she not only manages to lure Sam Spade's partner to his death, she also leads Spade (Bogart) a merry dance through the many convolutions of the plot. At the end, Spade deduces that much of the mayhem is directly traceable to her, and she makes a final play to the worse side of his nature, enticing him so that he won't hand her over to the police. The atmosphere is tense with longing and Astor's powerful sexual aura contests with Bogart's ethical code as a private eye.

She's gambling that his lust for her will be a big enough bribe to overcome his professional duty. But, unlike MacMurray in *Double Indemnity*, professionalism and a sense of masculine dignity are dominant. He won't surrender to her. 'I won't because all of me wants to, regardless of consequences, and because you've counted on that with me, the same as you counted on that with all the others . . . I won't play the sap for you.' They clinch and kiss fiercely, hungrily, and Bogart is in danger of weakening when the bell sounds and the police arrive.

The body-bribe is a strong element in the movies of the time; without it many of the best 'forties films would have been rendered meaningless. (Incidentally, *The Maltese Falcon* also alludes to other taboo topics. Peter Lorre's portrayal of the dapper little crook Joel Cairo hints subtly at the character's homosexuality, which is far more evident in the original Dashiell Hammett book, as is the nature – subdued but obvious in the movie – of Spade's sexual relationship with his partner's wife. However, one scene from the book is omitted, that in which the Astor character has to strip and be searched.)

Although censorship was loosening (mostly as a result of Joseph Breen's resignation early in the decade to take up an appointment at RKO for a year before returning and finding that things had altered), it was still in evidence. In the 'thirties Jean Renoir's *La Chienne* (*The Bitch*, 1931) had been banned completely in the States because of its story of a bank clerk who falls in love with a prostitute, steals large sums from his employers to squander on her and finally murders her because she has been unfaithful with her pimp. In 1945 Fritz Lang considered the climate right to remake the picture as *The Scarlet Street* with Edward G. Robinson as the clerk, Joan Bennett as the hooker and Dan Duryea as her pimp. The plot was much the same, but the action pivoted on the fact that the pimp is accused, convicted and executed for the murder while Robinson keeps silent. There was an outcry – this was probably the first time in a movie that a character had got away scot free with a murder even though the burden of his guilt weighs Robinson down and he spends the final portion trying to make the police believe his confessions – and the New York censor rejected it, calling the film 'indecent and immoral'. Notwithstanding, adultery and prostitution were now being plainly suggested in movies and the industry was breaking free, little by little, from the straitjacket of censorship.

The cult of the naughty lady reached its peak with *Gilda* (1946). 'There Never Was a Woman Like Gilda!' the posters screamed, and with the incandescent Rita Hayworth in the role they were very nearly right. Hayworth was the woman who confirmed men's suspicions that girls with red hair had a tempestuous nature to match. *Gilda* made Hayworth one of the biggest stars and sex symbols of the decade, remembered forever for her rendering of 'Put the Blame on Mame' and her super-erotic not-quite-striptease. In the public's mind Gilda and Rita became synonymous. 'Every man I knew,' she later said, 'had fallen in love with Gilda and wakened with me.'

Hayworth's strip in *Gilda* revealed the wildcat beneath the black velvet gown, even though she removed nothing but her glove. Hair tumbling to her shoulders, mouth wide open, high on the reaction she's working on all those watching her, the dance became her hallmark. She virtually repeated it in *Pal Joey* (1957), again taking off nothing but a glove and again kindling in the minds of the audience an image far more erotic than if she'd stripped to

Mary Astor and Humphrey Bogart in *The Maltese Falcon* (John Huston, 1941).

a G-string. The most erotic of all her routines was 'The Heat is On' number in *Miss Sadie Thompson* (1954), based on Somerset Maugham's 'Rain', in which she performs before an audience of island-locked, sex-starved marines. Her dance is a bump-and-grind travesty of the sexual act, and it is little wonder that the beer the soldiers are swilling erupts from their glasses in a frothy flow of symbolic ejaculation. Hayworth summed up her own

attitude as neatly as anyone could: 'A girl is . . . a girl. It's nice to be told you're successful at it.'

And, in the 'forties, a man was a man, and *the* man was Humphrey Bogart. *The Maltese Falcon* at the very start of the decade brought him to stardom and a fame he was not to lose, even after his death. Bogart was not a heart-throb; he was not even particularly handsome. But he was totally at home with his own masculinity, assured and confident in it. His beat-up face, with its scarred lip and deep lines, and his amused cynicism earned him roles which appealed to an audience in times of crisis and war. He looked strong, mentally and physically; he looked as if he could cope and, while he obviously knew fear, he was able to face it. As Sam Spade and Philip Marlowe (in *The Maltese Falcon* and *The Big Sleep*, 1946), as Rick in *Casablanca* (1943), and Steve in *To Have and Have Not* (1945) he portrayed a man who lived by his own rules, who might break the law of society (for good reason) but never broke his own law, who might be a little soiled but who had dignity, and who was, no matter what might befall, true to himself.

Such a man, of course, ignores normal sexual morality and such a man could not exist, on screen, under the rules of the 'thirties. The 'forties relaxed these rules and Bogart's hero muscled into the public consciousness. In *Casablanca* ('the best bad film ever made') Bogie loves Ingrid Bergman. In happier days before the war, in Paris, they have had an affair, a real sexual affair, no watered-down, holding-hands, one-day-we'll-be-married sop to sensibilities. Bergman disappears with the coming of the Nazis; Rick, who 'puts his neck out for nobody', runs a café in neutral Casablanca, a place where no questions are asked and a haven for refugees. Bergman turns up with husband, thought dead but found to be alive, looking for help. Rough, tough Rick, of course, selflessly gives it, to the accompaniment of 'As Time Goes By' – *their* song. The part established Bogart, up to then a heavy, as a romantic lead, but it wasn't until two years later that his true sexuality was given full expression.

To Have and Have Not was an almost un-recognizable adaptation of the Hemingway novel. The Rick character again appears, though with a new name. The film is banal, with a trite plot and frequently laughable dialogue. But it sparks into life when Bogie and the leading lady, with whom he is deeply in love and to whom he will later be married, appear.

The girl is Lauren Bacall, in her first movie. Cool, poised, worldly, she sets the screen alight from her first entrance. James Agee of Time described her thus: 'A javelinlike vitality, a born dancer's eloquence in movement, a fierce female shrewdness and a special sweet-sourness. With these faculties, plus a stone-crushing self-confidence and a trombone voice, she manages to get across the toughest girl a piously regenerate Hollywood has dreamed of in a long, long while. She does a wickedly good job of sizing up male prospects in a low bar, and growls a louche song more suggestively than anyone in cinema has dared since Mae West.'

Opposite Bogart she was atomic. He'd been around, he'd been hurt; she'd been around, she'd been hurt. She had no illusions about herself, she was used to getting by, making out as best she could. She wanted him and she let him know it. She was a new kind of heroine, in a line from Harlow's golden-hearted tramp but a lot less brassy, a lot more classy; less of a tramp, less obvious in her sexuality.

She offers herself to Bogie, boldly and without shame. 'You don't have to do anything. Not a thing.' . . . (Beat) . . . 'Oh, maybe just whistle.' . . . (Beat) . . . 'You know how to whistle, don't you?' . . . (Longer beat) . . . 'You just put your lips together' . . . (Long, heady, electric pause) . . . 'and blow.' That wicked, wanton mouth; those confident eyes – it's one of the most blatant – and yet beautifully allusive – sexual propositions on film. 'My idea of sex,' she said, 'is that it is mostly in the face.'

The chemistry of Bogie and Bacall – the self-assured male and the coolly confident female – showered sparks in *The Big Sleep*; *Dark Passage* (1947), in which she harbours him – an escaped convict trying to prove his innocence – in her bachelor-girl flat and allusion is made to her affairs; and *Key Largo* (1948). Seldom have two people so effectively carried the genuine love and desire they felt for each other in life over to their encounters on screen.

Bogart's co-star in *Casablanca* was Ingrid Bergman. Her career in America was guaranteed by her appearance, first in Sweden and then opposite Leslie Howard, in *Intermezzo* (also known as *Escape to Happiness*, 1938 and 1939) in which she played the mistress of a married violinist. Her stately, almost glacial beauty typecast her, for Hollywood liked its women to be of certain types (whores, for instance, were generally the preserve of Claire Trevor – in films like *Stagecoach*, 1939, and *Key Largo* – for which she won an Oscar; classy ladies went to Greer Garson, as in *Mrs Miniver*, 1942, and so on).

'I came to Hollywood,' she said, 'when all the other actresses were very artificial; they had tremendous hairdos that never blew in the wind, they got out of bed with perfect make-up, and whatever they did they looked as glamorous as they could. I refused to look glamorous. I dressed in simple clothes and the audience could identify with me.' She added with more modesty than accuracy, 'I was never considered a great beauty, a *femme fatale* or sexy; I was just a simple girl, the refugee and the good girl.'

This seemed to suit her perfectly for roles like the nun in *The Bells of St Mary's* (1945) and the Maid in *Joan of Arc* (1948), but she had ambitions elsewhere. 'I got very, very tired of being good and when we did *Dr Jekyll and Mr Hyde* (1941) I was given the part of Dr Jekyll's fiancée who was a very good girl and Lana Turner was a barmaid of . . . light virtue. I was

terribly envious of Lana Turner's part and I thought she might like mine, so I persuaded the director to switch the parts, which he did. And that was one of my greatest triumphs!'

This break with typecasting gave her a chance to tackle a wider range of roles, including two which flew in the face of the Code. 'We were very restricted with love scenes in those days,' she remembered. 'In *Notorious* (1946), Hitchcock wanted very much to have a long kiss but that was forbidden; they stood over us with a watch and allowed us to kiss for a precise period – a very few seconds – before they told us to break it off.' Hitchcock, however, was determined to circumvent this ruling and he approached it with the ingenuity with which he approached his tricky plots. He contrived a scene in which Cary Grant and Bergman start their kiss on a balcony and continue, with breaks and nuzzles and endearments, across the length of a room to a ringing telephone, and in between a rather garbled conversation she holds. 'Talk, kiss, talk, kiss,' she remembered, and the scene seems to last forever. 'The censor couldn't cut it,' she said happily. Hitch had cocked a snook triumphantly at the bluenoses.

In the previous year another attempt to break down the barriers hadn't succeeded quite so well. Bergman was teamed opposite Gary Cooper in a version (sometimes rather remote) of Hemingway's *For Whom the Bell Tolls*. The highpoint was to be the scene in which Coop and Bergman share a sleeping bag. If double beds were taboo for married couples it can be imagined what reaction a sleeping bag for unmarried lovers would generate. This love was to be cataclysmic – 'Did you not feel the earth moving?' Coop says famously after one amorous scene. The effect, however, was less

The Killers (Robert Siodmak, 1946) helped to establish Ava Gardner as a leading Hollywood glamour-girl in the 'forties. Said Bogart, echoing Elinor Glyn: 'Whatever it is, whether you're born with it, or catch it from a public drinking cup, she's got it, and the people with the money in their hands put her there.'

'My idea of sex is that it is mostly in the face.' Lauren Bacall – *above*, with husband Humphrey Bogart in *The Big Sleep* (Howard Hawks, 1946), and *right*.

Opposite, top: Cary Grant and Ingrid Bergman's censor-snubbing telephone love-in in Alfred Hitchcock's *Notorious* (1946).

Opposite, bottom: Eddie Bracken and Betty Hutton in *The Miracle of Morgan's Creek* (Preston Sturges, 1943), an outrageous satire on wartime morals which somehow escaped the censor's scissors.

than earth-shattering. Murky lighting made the bag and its occupants difficult to discern – 'You couldn't see if it was two people in one sleeping bag, or two bags,' said one commentator; and Bergman commented, 'It was a very, very clean scene – all we did was talk! Love scenes in those days were never allowed to be horizontal and so when we had that lovely scene with the kiss and the sweet line "Where do the noses go?" it had to be done standing up – we weren't allowed to shoot it in the sleeping bag.'

In 1945 Bergman was perhaps the biggest female star in Hollywood, but despite her success in shady lady roles the public preferred her in more angelic parts (her blushing coyness when Bing Crosby as Father O'Malley in *Bells of St Mary's* winks at her touched the public more than her supposed earth-moving abilities in a bag) and after playing a prostitute in *Arch of Triumph* (1948) her career declined somewhat. It was very nearly killed completely by a hysterical and wholly hypocritical public outcry against her love for director Roberto Rossellini.

They were both married; they made a film together called *Stromboli* (1949); they fell in love, they lived together and Bergman carried his baby. It was as if Father O'Malley had put Sister Ingrid in the club! She was denounced as 'Hollywood's apostle of degradation' in the US Senate, her movies were not shown and she couldn't film in Hollywood. Even after she and Rossellini regularized the union by divorcing their respective spouses, marrying and having twins to add to the first boy it looked as if

Ingrid Bergman's film career outside Europe was finished forever. It wasn't until after the marriage had broken up and she made *Anastasia* seven years later in 1956 that she could find acceptance again (in typical Hollywood style with an Oscar!). What the 'forties audience would accept on the screen, they wouldn't condone in their idols when they were off it.

This double standard that the public – or at least certain vociferous sections of it – seemed to hold in relation to their screen idols found perhaps its strangest manifestation when the press, apparently fuelled by certain vested interests, turned against one of the world's best-loved stars – Charlie Chaplin. The outcome of a series of almost inexplicable charges against him resulted in an even odder censorship row over a film he made in answer to his persecutors.

Chaplin took a stand in the early years of America's involvement in the war, demanding a second front in Europe, greater support for her ally, Russia, and for what he termed 'peace-mongering'. This had made him very unpopular with some interests within the country because of the deep suspicions they held against Russia (which led to the McCarthy witchhunts) and because Chaplin was not a citizen of the country.

In 1943, Joan Barry, a young woman who had had an affair with Chaplin, filed a paternity

suit against the actor. Chaplin willingly submitted to a blood test and the results clearly showed that he could not possibly be the father. Meanwhile, more trouble was looming.

Chaplin apparently had a tip-off from a friend – a judge at the Supreme Court – that there was a political cabal out 'to get' him. He was charged under the Mann Act, which could be invoked to indict any man transporting any woman who was not his wife over a state boundary and then having intercourse with her. The charge accused Chaplin of taking Joan Barry from Los Angeles to New York for this purpose. In fact, the charge did not hold water and Chaplin was cleared. Again things seemed to be in his favour; again there was a further twist.

In 1946 the paternity case was reopened and, despite the evidence of the blood test, the second hearing (the first resulted in a hung jury) found against him and he was forced to support the child.

These vicissitudes in his fortunes made Chaplin's resolve to complete a pet project the more determined. Orson Welles had previously approached him with the idea of doing a documentary on the famous French murderer, Bluebeard Landru. The documentary had fallen through, but Chaplin was much taken with the idea of creating a comedy out of the bones of the

Left: Burt Lancaster, in his sub-Fairbanks beefcake days, as *The Crimson Pirate* (Robert Siodmak, 1952).

Opposite top: Linda Darnell and Richard Haydn in *Forever Amber* (Otto Preminger, 1947), a tame adaptation of the steamy novel by Kathleen Winsor.

Opposite bottom: Gregory Peck and Jennifer Jones as the fiery, antagonistic lovers in King Vidor's *Duel in the Sun* (1946).

Right: Tony Curtis as *The Prince Who Was a Thief*, directed by Rudolph Maté in 1951, when Curtis's haircut was taken more seriously than his acting.

Far right: Durable, sleepy-eyed tough-guy Robert Mitchum: 'Every two or three years I knock off for a while. That way I'm always the new girl in the whorehouse.'

story and calling it *Monsieur Verdoux* (1947). The hero is a bank clerk who is thrown out of work by the Depression. Although he is married to a bedridden wife and has a son, he decides to earn his living by marrying rich spinsters and murdering them for their money. The writing took two years and when the script was complete he sent it to the Hays Office for approval; he shortly received an answer – it was to be banned in its entirety.

Chaplin met with Breen to discuss his objections. Changes were agreed and made. There was a showing of the final edited version and it received a seal.

By the time it was released in 1947 Chaplin had become a favourite target for several pressure groups who saw him as a traitor. The New Jersey Catholic Legion picketed the film and the American Legion threatened theatre owners across the country with a year-long boycott by its members if the film was shown. In the face of such antagonism Chaplin was forced to withdraw the movie, although it did respectable business in those cinemas which actually got to exhibit it. Chaplin had become a scapegoat. In the early 'fifties – and hounded by McCarthy-ites – he left America, reportedly for ever, and only returned in 1973 to be awarded a special Oscar for his unique contribution to film art.

Chaplin's exchange with the Hays Office shows that, on occasion, a certain amount of middle-ground between movie-maker and censor could be found. Certainly, there was some horse-trading in which both sides were prepared to give a little for the sake of compromise. (The haggling over Rhett Butler's

lines in *Gone With the Wind* was a prime example.) To give themselves some elbow-room in these negotiations, writers would frequently insert gratuitous scenes that they knew would meet with censorial disapproval to create a smoke-screen and help them slip something past the hawk-eyes of the Code that they really wanted retained.

Distinguished critic Pauline Kael in an introductory note to 'The Citizen Kane Book' cites the case of the scene set in a bordello that was included in Herman J. Mankiewicz's shooting script submitted to the Hays Office in 1941 but which was omitted from the final version. The script elicited this reply from Breen:

'. . . we are pleased to advise you that the material, except as noted hereinafter, is acceptable under the provisions of the Production Code and suggests no danger from the standpoint of political censorship.

'There is one important detail in the story at hand which is quite definitely in violation of the Production Code and, consequently, cannot be approved. This is the locale, set down for scene 64, which is, inescapably, a brothel. Please have in mind that there is a specific regulation in the Production Code which prohibits the exhibition of brothels. . . .

'Page 83: There should be nothing about this scene which indicates that Georgie is a "madam", or that the girls brought into the party are prostitutes. This flavour should be very carefully guarded against.'[49]

In the final script both the character of Georgie and the bordello were eliminated – neither Mankiewicz nor Welles probably ever intended that they get through – and a substitute scene of dancing girls appearing at a celebration in Kane's newspaper office was inserted.

Whether the inclusion of the scenes was in order to allow other things through or whether – as Pauline Kael suggests – it was a matter of honour to the writer that he should make the gesture of challenging the censor, is difficult to assess. Certainly some of the subject matter in the film should at the time have raised a censorial eyebrow. Kane, a married man, takes a mistress and there is a confrontation scene between his wife and the other woman. Throughout, the girl tries to protest the innocence of their relationship – she seems always to be cut off in mid-sentence – but no one watching seriously believes that the involvement is not adulterous or about to become so.

In addition, Kane was closely modelled on newspaper tycoon W.R. Hearst, and Kane's insistence on his protégée, Susan Alexander, becoming an operatic star by using the considerable publicity muscle of his newspaper chain, was a direct analogy to Hearst's own attempt to make his mistress, Marion Davies, a top movie star. The subject matter was politically extremely sensitive and Mankiewicz's bluff with the bordello may have been an attempt to blunt the impact of the Hearst analogy; whether this is true or not the comment in the Breen letter about 'no danger from the standpoint of political censorship' may be worth noting.

The war created its own hysteria within Hollywood. For a time its propaganda machine sought to show how beastly the Hun really was and how brutal the Japs. Most of the films were of little worth, and indeed were crude attempts to agitate hatred by playing on common stereotypes and fears. Much was made of

A British film which caused rare controversy in the 'forties (*bottom*) was *The Blue Lagoon* (Frank Launder, 1949), about shipwrecked youngsters (Donald Houston and Jean Simmons) discovering love. An earlier version (*left*), shot in Africa in 1923, starred Arthur Pusey and Molly Adair.

atrocities against women and children, though after the war the horrors of Auschwitz or the Burma railway far outweighed the histrionic imaginings of movie-makers. This, of course, is not to say that all films of the period dealing with the war were so contrived. The work of Capra, Huston and Ford – especially in the area of documentary – was admirable.

The male sex symbols who remained in Hollywood were, almost to a man, winning their own theatres of war virtually single-handed. Indeed, the Hollywood version of Errol Flynn's exploits in *Objective Burma* (1945) very nearly caused a rift between the British and the Americans, the former objecting to the fact that, while their men had been waging a long, dispiriting, bloody and terrible campaign in Burma, Flynn and the Americans came out with all the credit!

Hollywood women were seen in uniform on screen doing their bit too. They also ran the Hollywood Canteen, where they waited on servicemen. The ramifications of the war were, of course, treated with care. Too many men were receiving 'Dear John' letters for a realistic portrayal of what wives and sweethearts might be up to while they endured the sexless priva-

tions of their loved-ones' prolonged and enforced absence. If a woman was seen to err she was generally depicted as a thoroughly bad lot, anyway, without whom the wronged GI was better off. The all-American virtues of love of country, motherhood, sanctity of marriage and the rest were treated with reverence, devotion and awe by everyone except Preston Sturges.

Sturges made brilliant, irreverent and terribly funny comedies. In 1943 he had taken a glorious side-swipe at marriage in *Palm Beach Story*, which starred Claudette Colbert and Joel McCrea, and he followed up the next year with *The Miracle of Morgan's Creek*. Here was a movie which came hilariously closer to the truth than any other made about the home front. Indeed, so biting was the satire and so close to the knuckle was the subject matter that James Agee was prompted to comment: 'The Hays Office has been either hypnotized into a liberality for which it should be thanked, or has been raped in its sleep.'

The Miracle of Morgan's Creek puts into perspective the reality of wartime romance, sex and marriage. Young Trudy Kockenlocker gets drunk at a party and wakes the next morning very hung-over and with the dim memory that she married a soldier during the riotous proceedings of the previous night. Unfortunately, she cannot exactly remember his name; was it Ratskywatsky or Ritzywitsky? Whatever, she cannot now contact him as the troops have pulled out and, horror upon horror, her night of alcoholic love has left her with the time-honoured soldier's farewell – a pregnancy.

Small-town morals being what they are, Trudy (Betty Hutton) must find herself a husband and father for the child. Norval Jones – officially unfit for service – is at hand and agrees to the union and to keep Trudy's secret by claiming the child as his own. The typically uproarious and convoluted Sturges plot puts poor Norval (Eddie Bracken) through all manner of misadventures with the military and the law, but all comes right in the end when Trudy delivers not one child but sextuplets – all male! As the supposed father, Norval – thanks to the cult of male virility – becomes a national hero and is made a colonel!

In one comic blow Sturges debunked many a sacred cow and, furthermore, managed through his dexterity not to overstep the mark of good taste. The Hays Office passed it perhaps

because 'prudes could console themselves with the thought that the film made quite a comment on the morals of the nation in time of war'.[50]

The war's end prompted two challenges to the Code that showed movie-makers were finding its restrictions ever more irksome and irrelevant. In 1947, Twentieth Century-Fox decided to handle a property that already had a reputation for its sex emphasis – *Forever Amber*. Breen, naturally, reacted with horror; he did not want it made at all, but in the face of Fox's insistence directed that the title be changed. This, too, Fox refused. However, the film was rather less than sensational; Amber (Linda Darnell) was allowed only a third (four, in fact) of the lovers she romped with in the book and all was weighted to make her out as a totally evil woman. The result caused reasonably sophisticated critics to scorn it for its dilution and, predictably, the Legion of Decency to dub it 'a glorification of immorality and licentiousness'.

Miss Darnell's charms had been more suggestively hinted at, oddly enough, in William Wellman's 1944 *Buffalo Bill*. In this unlikely setting she played an Indian school-teacher in love with Bill Cody and jealous of the fact that he prefers a woman of his own race, Maureen O'Hara. While Bill (Joel McCrea) and O'Hara dine in one room, Darnell steals into O'Hara's bedroom to try on one of her dresses. O'Hara catches her. Darnell strips off the dress and the camera cuts to her feet around which lie layers of discarded petticoats. The implication – and it is forcibly conveyed – is that she wears no underwear under her simple suede shift, which she then grabs and clutches to her naked body as she climbs over the window-sill and disappears.

Sex had come at last to the Western. *The Outlaw* had used Russell's body as a pivotal plot device, and in 1946 there came King Vidor's *Duel in the Sun*, whose steamy plot caused it to be known affectionately as 'Lust in the Dust'. Its theme of passionate, unfettered love between a rake (Gregory Peck) and a fiery half-breed (Jennifer Jones) looks more than a little absurd now, but the film was, in any case, spared an *Outlaw*-type mauling from the censor by its serious intent, superior artfulness, and possibly the fact that the unfortunate casting made for rather feeble erotic fireworks.

While the bitch heroine who used her sexuality to lure men into crime and disaster held sway on the distaff side, the men who emerged in the 'forties tended to be rougher and tougher than the suave lovers of the 'thirties. The primitives had Weissmuller and then Lex Barker as Tarzan. Added to them was 'The Hunk' – Victor Mature – in *One Million BC* (1940), a piece of prehistoric hokum concerning animal-skinned Neanderthals, monsters and a briefly clad Carole Landis. The trend was towards such atavistic heroes, with Burt Lancaster joining the ranks in his debut, *The Killers* (1946), along with droop-eyed Robert Mitchum, who, one felt, would as soon bat a dame as kiss her, and another young man, Kirk

Italian neo-realism added a new dimension to the depiction of sex on the screen. In *Paisà* (Roberto Rossellini, 1946) Maria Michi played a girl forced by war into prostitution whom a client fails to recognize as his former sweetheart.

Douglas, who looked similarly inclined. To contrast with these tough guys, there were the 'pretty' men like Tyrone Power and Robert Taylor, whose appeal – much to their own disappointment – lay more in their faces than their underrated acting ability.

In Germany, the private perversions and predilections of the ruling Nazis were not generally reflected in the cinema, which was purged in the name of purity. However, in 1943 UFA made *Munchhausen*, with a harem scene bedecked with naked girls. It's not at all certain whether the rigorous censorship inside Germany allowed this to pass totally un-checked. There are certainly prints in existence in which the scene is shown *in toto*, but there are also some in which much of the nudity has been excised.

In the post-war years it was in Europe that the greatest changes in sexual attitudes took place. The Continental film industry had either been suppressed or subordinated to the occupy-ing Nazis and was in a very bad state by the Armistice. It recovered quickly, however, and in many countries the harsh grimness of the war years was reflected in a new realism on the screen, a realism that extended to the depiction of sex.

France and Italy remained true to their pre-war traditions and were far less prudish about nudity than their transatlantic cousins. Italy's realism was given a great impetus by the work of Roberto Rossellini, particularly *Rome – Open City* (1945), much of which was filmed under the noses of the Nazis and showed vividly what life was like for those 'conquered' by the Axis powers. The Fascist régime prior to Mussolini's fall had boosted morale with exploitative movies like *Slave Merchants*, which showed human merchandise bared at the breast, but as true cinema Rossellini's contribution was enormous and he dwelt on the predicament of ordinary people forced into extraordinary situations, like Maria Michi's fresh-faced girl turned prostitute in *Paisa* (1946).

Such films began finding a market abroad – although frequently with the more contro-versial scenes cut – and it was probably Giuseppe De Santis' *Bitter Rice* (1949) that did more than any other film to internationalize European products. This story, set in the Po Valley rice fields, with its earth-mother star, Silvana Mangano, set the trend for predatory, full-figured Italian women that was to become such a feature of the 'fifties.

All over Europe the seeds of 'fifties movies were being sown and the shift was away from Hollywood. In France the way was being prepared for the Nouvelle Vague. In Martine Carol there was a hint of Bardot yet to come. And there was a growing acceptance of sex as an integral – and joyful – part of adult life. The film-makers of Europe were to have the pro-foundest effect on the treatment of sex in the next years, and to force the movie industry to grow up at a pace that, had they been able to prognosticate it, would have horrified the censorial lobbies in America.

In *Bitter Rice* (Giuseppe De Santis, 1949) Silvana Mangano set the post-war trend for earthy, voluptuous Italian heroines. The film itself was a strange mixture of sex and socialism.

robably no decade in the history of Hollywood saw such rapid and sweeping change as the 'fifties. Since the 'twenties, Hollywood had been the Mecca for movies, and American standards, tastes and ideals had been culturally imprinted on the consciousness of millions of non-, even anti-Americans throughout the world. But in the 'fifties the entire industry underwent profound internal disturbances which were to affect the course of its future history. Two factors in particular were the cause of Hollywood's decline from the greatest single centre of film-making to what was virtually a ghost town in comparison to its former glory. One was the breakdown of the studio system and the other the astonishing (at least to the movie moguls) rise of television.

The stranglehold of the studios, and the potentates who ruled them, slackened off because post-war audiences and the economic and social climate in which the industry operated had changed. Previously, stars had been, for the most part, pampered puppets; directors and writers – even producers – were minions to be cosseted when successful and ruthlessly discarded at the first hint of failure. Now a constellation of circumstances conspired to make creative people within movies yearn for independence, and new tax laws in the States helped them achieve this. Power devolved away from the conglomerates towards smaller, freelance units.

In addition, television made devastating inroads into the audience which the moguls had considered exclusively theirs. Cinema attendances fell dramatically. So did receipts, and the movie industry – although not unaccustomed to financial hardship – quite quickly found itself needing to make economies. 'Why,' asked Sam Goldwyn, 'should people go out and pay money to see bad films when they can stay at home and see bad television for nothing?' Indeed, they could also see bad movies for free because many studios were desperately off-loading old stock onto the rapacious TV companies to raise cash.

These events were to have a direct influence on movie subjects and the way they were handled. Anti-trust legislation had prohibited the studios – in a further erosion of their power – from block-booking a year's catalogue of films into houses in advance. This, plus the new and entertaining toy of television, meant that the cinema had to move firmly into the market-place and fight with all the acumen, ability and commercial instinct it possessed to woo audiences (who had previously queued for hours to see whatever it pleased Hollywood to show

them) back through the nation's turnstiles.

And at the beginning of the 'fifties came the clash which was to effect radical change in the area of local censorship. Rossellini's *The Miracle* was about a simple-minded peasant who was seduced by a stranger she believed to be St Joseph. It had been licensed by the New York censors but encountered fierce Catholic opposition, headed by Cardinal Spellman who ordered all Catholics to avoid the film – an instruction that exceeded his authority. Many Catholic organizations joined the effort to stop the film being seen and the cinema was picketed and subjected to harassment. The state censorship board revoked its licence, an action that was upheld by the New York courts. The case finally reached the Supreme Court in February, 1952.

The court's finding in favour of the film was a severe blow to the Legion, and forced it to rethink its role. Even more importantly, however, the court completely overturned the Mutual decision of thirty-seven years before and declared that 'it cannot be doubted that motion pictures are a significant medium for the communication of ideas', clearly implying that they were therefore within the free-speech guarantees of the First and Fourteenth Amendments. The whole system of prior restraint was severely undermined by the statement that such limitation was only to be allowed in 'exceptional cases', although no judgment was made on the question of whether prior censorship was constitutional.

The century was half over; people at last had money, had undergone experiences like war which had broadened their attitudes, and were less liable to accept control by small but powerful lobbies. Many within the industry now saw that the time was long overdue for a slackening of moral rigidity in films and an adult approach to adult problems.

The Continental cinema had shown the way and the new decade brought plenty of fresh young talent to flex its muscle and try its ideas. Literature and the theatre led the movement. Young writers – some who had experienced war and its fundamental brutality at first hand – were bursting with important things to say. The way they wanted to say them was different too – more direct, more basic. And joining their ranks was an entirely new breed of actors. Young, unshackled from the great Shakespearean theatrical tradition, they looked and talked like the non-acting members of their own generation.

Brando was the prototype 'fifties male. Moody, broody, with a sullen sexuality. The

Jack Lemmon and Marilyn Monroe in *Some Like It Hot* (Billy Wilder, 1959), which helped to undermine the Production Code in the late 'fifties by satirizing sex.

grim set of his jaw through which his lines emerged as a mumble, the compact energy of his frame, the insolence of his stance, marked him down as a new kind of sexually dominant male. There was no sophistication here, no suavity, no flip and humorous nonchalance. Instead there was an animalism and a fierce intensity which riveted the attention.

Many Hollywood old-timers loathed the Brando-style hero. 'The Brando school are grabbers, not lovers,' said Adolphe Menjou. 'If it wasn't that the script says they get the girl, they wouldn't.' He was wrong, of course, because he didn't understand the nature of the new audience, the high school and college kids in the drive-ins, with wheels beneath them, love on the back seat and a new music – rock & roll – pumping out of the radio.

There was certainly resentment against Brando, Montgomery Clift, Rod Steiger, James Dean and others of that ilk. Bogart was vitriolic about them. 'I came out here with one suit and everybody said I looked like a bum. Twenty years later Marlon Brando comes out with only a sweat-shirt and the town drools over him. That shows how much Hollywood has progressed.' He and others objected to the fact that many of the new stars hadn't had long stock-company and straight theatrical experience; hadn't, as it were, paid their dues. Many, it seemed, came in off the street, were ex-truck drivers or gas-station attendants. 'Shout "gas" around the studio today,' Bogie grouched, 'and half the young male stars will come running.'

If Hollywood did drool over these young lions it was because the town needed them, needed the life-style and attitudes they epitomized. Because they could play – as their predecessors from the previous generation could not – the heroes of contemporary fiction. They reflected the heroes – called anti-heroes – of

Mailer's 'The Naked and the Dead', James Jones's 'From Here to Eternity', Tennessee Williams's 'A Streetcar Named Desire', Arthur Miller's 'Death of a Salesman'.

All these works were to be filmed in the decade and two were to become censorial *causes célèbres* because of the themes they handled. Both *Streetcar* and *From Here to Eternity* were to turn the censorship question upside down, with no little assistance from Williams's *Baby Doll*.

A Streetcar Named Desire (1951) was one of Hollywood's first excursions into truly adult film-making. Williams's strange, sex-pervaded work came West with impeccable credentials. It was an acknowledged *tour de force* on Broadway where such things as the Breen Office and Legion of Decency held no sway. Warners bought it and charged Elia Kazan – who had directed it for the stage – and Williams to turn it into a film. Breen was immediately alerted and warned that extreme care would have to be

The prototype 'fifties male – Marlon Brando with Eva Marie Saint in *On the Waterfront* (Elia Kazan, 1954).

taken with such delicate subject matter.

The work oozed brooding sexuality in its penetrating examination of the relationship between the brutally, aggressively masculine Stanley Kowalski (Brando) and the genteel Blanche DuBois (Vivien Leigh), the suicide of whose homosexually-inclined husband leads her to nymphomania. And the dramatic development called for a climactic rape in which Kowalski brutishly takes his sister-in-law while his wife, Stella, is giving birth to a child. For Hollywood in the very early 'fifties this was strong meat indeed. Predictably, Breen objected. He could not condone overt references to homosexuality, so the dead man became 'unmanly' rather than queer, and he would not tolerate too many offensive words, so a few 'damns' and suchlike were deleted. Breen also insisted on the presence of 'compensating moral value', and the ending was altered – Stella being made to leave Stanley so that the husband appeared to be punished for his behaviour.

Kazan and Williams agreed to these changes but would not countenance any dilution of the scene around which the whole play was balanced – the rape. They fought Breen's every attempt to interfere with it.

The position adopted by author and director to preserve the scene is important, for *Streetcar* was not a cheap exploitation film and the rape was no gimcrack device to set turnstiles clicking. Williams's play was an accredited theatrical

Prelude to rape – Blanche (Vivien Leigh) provokes Stanley (Marlon Brando) into action in *A Streetcar Named Desire* (Elia Kazan, 1951).

Carroll Baker as *Baby Doll* (Kazan, 1956).

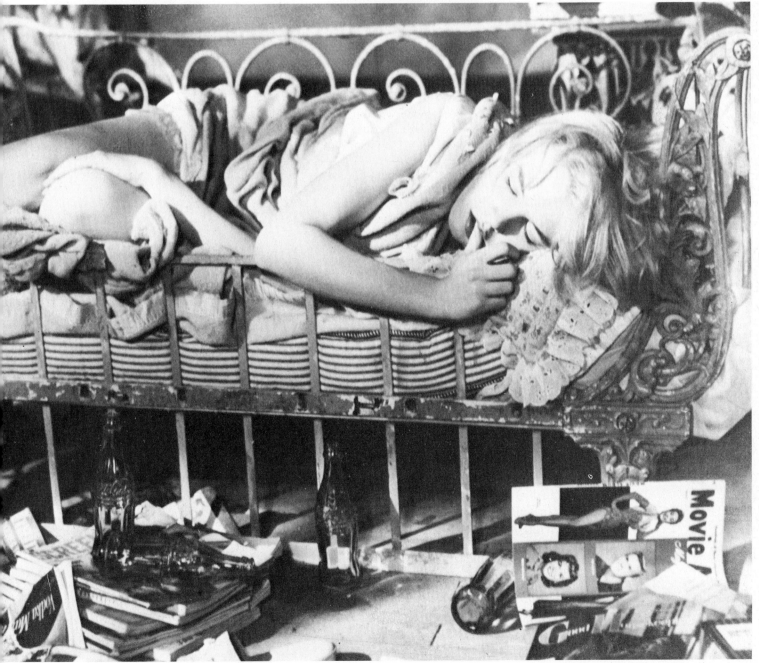

achievement and a work of undoubted integrity. He and Kazan might trade a few 'hells' and play down the homosexuality, but they would not allow the dramatic prop to be knocked out from under the screenplay. Williams wrote to Breen: 'The rape of Blanche by Stanley is a pivotal, integral truth in the play, without which the play loses its meaning.' Eventually Breen stood down over it, but harassed the makers with pettifogging changes, which did nothing to harm the work although it was rather less frank on screen than on stage. The result, however, was good enough to win Vivien Leigh and Kim Hunter (as Kowalski's wife) Oscars.

But the story didn't stop there. Kazan later revealed the part played by the Catholic Legion of Decency in attempting to suppress the movie. Kazan heard that a booking for the film at the New York Radio City Music Hall had been cancelled by Warners and that the cutter who had worked with him on the picture had been sent East. He started making enquiries and, after much evasion by those concerned, discovered that the Legion was intending to give the film a Condemned rating, which would theoretically prohibit all Catholics from seeing it.

Thoroughly rattled and fearing (with some cause) that theatres showing the movie would be boycotted or picketed and that priests would stand in lobbies checking whether their parishioners entered, Warners could see their large investment in the film melting before their eyes. They asked the Legion to specify any changes which would make the movie acceptable and gain it a favourable rating, but the body continually insisted – in what must appear to be a piece of enormous hypocrisy – that it was not a board of censorship and that it just offered

guides to members of its faith. They refused repeatedly to indicate any cuts, but said that if the company wished to re-edit and resubmit the film they would judge the new version on its own merits.

Kazan hastened to New York and there met a Catholic layman who had suggested cuts acceptable to Warners and who 'had striven to bridge the gap between the picture's artistic achievement and "the primacy of the moral order"' as it was interpreted by the Legion. The cuts were, in fact, trivial, amounting to less than five minutes of running time and including a barely credible re-editing of a scene in which Kim Hunter, as Stella, 'comes down the stairway to Stanley after a quarrel'. The Legion wanted the accompanying music and some close-ups deleted because they 'made the girl's relationship to her husband too carnal' – something that must be regarded as a credit to the sensitivity of the actors, composer and director. Despite their protestations to the contrary, the Legion members had shown themselves to be very active censors and it was their interference in so obviously artistic a movie that incensed Kazan to such an extent that he made the facts public.

If the Breen Office was liberalizing its rules, the Legion certainly was not and Kazan ran foul of it again some five years later with another Tennessee Williams piece, *Baby Doll* (1956), of which it said 'this film is morally repellent both in theme and treatment. It dwells almost without variation or relief upon carnal suggestiveness in action, dialogue and costuming. As such it is grievously offensive to Christians and traditional standards of morality and decency.'

The subject matter of the movie was almost bound to incite the wrath of the Legion. Baby

Burt Lancaster and Deborah Kerr's celebrated clinch in *From Here to Eternity* (Fred Zinnemann, 1953).

Marilyn Monroe in her first small break, a co-starring role with Adele Jergens in *Ladies of the Chorus* (Phil Karlson, 1948).

Monroe fights the New York heat and gives pleasure to Tom Ewell in *The Seven Year Itch* (Billy Wilder, 1955).

117

Doll (Carroll Baker) is a nubile, sexually ambivalent creature – a child with a woman's knowingness of her own potent ability to provoke a man's carnality; a woman with a high degree of infantile innocence. She is married to Archie Meigham (Karl Malden), a man many years above her own teenage years, sleeps in a cot wearing the most libidinous yet childlike two-piece nightie (soon to become a fashion rage) and sucking her thumb. The ripeness and taunting desirability of her body are contrasted with her refusal to allow her husband his conjugal rights until she has attained the age of twenty. Their surroundings – the oppressive heat of the Deep South and the decay of Meigham's once-prosperous cotton mill – heighten the overpowering atmosphere of repressed lust, seething sexual tension and gradually mounting frustration. Her husband's desperate craving for her body becomes near-obsessional as he peers at her through a hole in the connecting wall. An unhealthy, suffocating aura is evoked.

Into this milieu comes Vacarro (Eli Wallach), a smart operator who is gradually taking control of the local cotton business and has his eye on what's left of Meigham's assets. Meigham, driven by sexual frustration and facing ruin at Vacarro's hand, commits arson on his rival's property. Vacarro hits back with a determined effort to seduce Baby Doll.

The Legion, possibly incensed by a monster poster depicting a provocatively posed Carroll Baker which had been displayed close to its headquarters, stepped in. Primarily it objected to the Peeping Tom sequence and another equivocal scene in which Vacarro and Baby Doll are indulging in some form of unspecified sexuality. The most probable explanation was that they were masturbating each other, or at

Monroe's nearest rival in the sex-symbol stakes (but still nowhere in sight) was the generously endowed Jayne Mansfield: *above*, with husband number two, muscleman Mickey Hargitay, at a film première; and *right*, with Tom Ewell and symbolically placed (but still milk bottles in *The Girl Can't Help It* (Frank Tashlin, 1956).

Opposite, top: Mamie Van Doren (here in a 1957 publicity still) was the Mansfield of second features.

Opposite, bottom: Brigitte Bardot in *Viva Maria!* (Louis Malle, 1965), in which she was one of two soubrettes (the other was Jeanne Moreau) tangled up in a Mexican revolution.

least enjoying some form of manual foreplay, but this cannot be certain, for the entire scene is shot with the camera concentrated above the actors' waists while they are seated on a swing and making conversation which gives no hint. Baby Doll is, however, clearly registering in her face and breathing an intense sexual excitement, probably leading to orgasm, and the implication which came across to many was that after the fade this piece of sexual play was fully consummated. Kazan denied the adultery, but the Legion was not to be placated even though the Breen Office (actually, now the Shurlock Office as Breen had retired in 1954 and had been succeeded by Geoffrey Shurlock) had taken a liberal view and awarded the film a seal.

Into the fray on the side of the Legion jumped Cardinal Spellman of New York, who utterly condemned the movie from the pulpit of St Patrick's Cathedral, calling its theme 'revolting', its advertising 'brazen' and declaring it so evil that any Catholic attending it was committing a sin. It was later revealed that the Cardinal had not seen *Baby Doll*. This did not, however, deter Catholics from following his exhortation. Exhibitors were still in awe of the power of the Catholic boycott and the film's box-office was affected.

Between Kazan's two controversial movies came *From Here to Eternity* (1953). James Jones's account of army life in Hawaii immediately prior to the Japanese attack on Pearl Harbor had been a runaway best-seller and a target for criticism with its graphic portrayal of barrack-room life, explicit sex and realistic language. When Harry Cohn, head of Columbia, bought the rights, the Breen Office expressed shock. Two plot points particularly worried Breen – the passionate affair between Sergeant Warden (Burt Lancaster) and Karen, the wife of his commanding officer (Deborah Kerr), and the brothel in Honolulu where Prewitt (Montgomery Clift) meets the prostitute Lorene (Donna Reed).

The latter difficulty was quickly overcome by the simple expedient of turning the brothel into a club. Although it was unstated, the audience – unless they were appallingly naïve – must still have understood the nature of the establishment and Lorene's position within it. The adultery, however, was more difficult. As if the extra-marital relationship were not enough, it was between a member of the 'other ranks' and an officer's lady, and it reached the height of its passion on a beach, in the open air, with the principals clad only in bathing suits! Furthermore, neither character seemed to show the slightest remorse about the incident. Director Fred Zinnemann and writer Dan Taradash resisted Breen's suggested changes stoutly. Although they did agree to a sop of a line in which Deborah Kerr recognizes that her relationship with Lancaster is irregular, they refused to have the two dressed in anything more than swimsuits for the climactic love scene.

In fact, they won the battle and the matching

of the gentlewomanly Miss Kerr (who had been typed in demure roles) and the muscular Lancaster created a memorable scene of horizontal sexuality. Audiences were left in no doubt as to the extent of their passion as the camera cut away to show foaming Pacific rollers pounding and surging onto the beach in a fine example of one of the cinema's favourite symbolic orgasm clichés (others have included fireworks starbusting; trains roaring in and out of tunnels; thunder and lightning crashing across the sky; horses rearing; flames leaping; liquids spurting out of bottles; and, if the affair is romantic as well as passionate, the camera wheeling heavenwards through sunlit treetops).

The beach scene in *Eternity* became famous and did much to ensure the film's success. Another great contribution was the fine acting of all the players, particularly Donna Reed and

In Claude Autant-Lara's *En Cas de Malheur* (*Love is My Profession*, 1958) Brigitte Bardot was the *gamine* who blatantly seduces lawyer Jean Gabin by raising her skirt. Most of the scene was cut from the French and American versions.

Opposite, top left: The decadence of Nazi Germany epitomized in Helmut Berger's parody of Dietrich's *Blue Angel* in *The Damned* (Luchino Visconti, 1969).

Opposite, top right: Paul Newman and Robert Redford as *Butch Cassidy and the Sundance Kid* (George Roy Hill, 1969).

Opposite, bottom: The bump-and-grind 'Hey, Big Spender' number from *Sweet Charity* (Bob Fosse, 1968).

Roger Vadim's *Don Juan . . . Or If Don Juan Were a Woman* (1973) was an absurd piece of sexploitation, but at forty Bardot still looked splendid in the buff. Jane Birkin joined her for this lesbian sequence.

Frank Sinatra, who had fought tenaciously for the role of Maggio in the teeth of much opposition. Both won supporting Oscars. In addition, the movie won the Best Film award; Zinnemann and Taradash collared the direction and scenario Oscars; and Burnett Guffey got one for his photography. After such overwhelming acclaim, films like *Eternity*, dealing with adult themes in a realistic manner, were assured of a very much easier passage through the film censor's office on all future occasions.

The Hollywood movie was at last growing up, and receipts for films like *Eternity* proved that the public could and would accept mature themes with a frank sexual approach. However, Hollywood was recognized the world over for its glamour, and this saleable product had by no means been set aside.

In the 'fifties Hollywood created its biggest, best-loved and most potent sex symbol of all –

120

Marilyn Monroe. Little can really be said about this beautiful, vulnerable and finally tragic woman that has not been reiterated time and time again. Her appeal was, perhaps, in her frailty; in that look of wistful innocence and trust; in the longing to be loved; even in the faint clouding which appeared in the eyes and gave birth to a feeling that behind the monstrous publicity, the global adoration and the stupefying success, there was profound fear.

In the early days it didn't matter because, of all the sex symbols, the harsh eye of the camera loved Marilyn the best. That unblinking lens, one felt, could never make her ugly, show her in a bad light, or fail to register her magnetic presence. From the time she shone out of a line of dancing girls in *Ticket to Tomahawk* (1950), strolled on in *All About Eve* (1950) and illuminated a few scenes of *The Asphalt Jungle* (1950), to her dominance in films like *Bus Stop* (1956), *The Seven Year Itch* (1955) – which literally elevated her to impossible heights in a four-storey high poster above Times Square – and *Some Like It Hot* (1959), Monroe conducted a love affair with the camera which gave her a celluloid life she could never match off the screen. The 'fifties belonged to Marilyn, and in that decade it almost seemed as if the world belonged to her also. But by the second year of the 'sixties she was dead – a memory, a source of posthumous analysis, eulogy, sentimentality. She perhaps knew what she was and what she had become. 'A sex symbol becomes a thing,' she is reported as saying. 'I hate being a thing.'

With Monroe's death the old-style female sex symbol died. None ever came after her cast in the same traditional mould. Her death spelled the end of Hollywood razz-a-ma-tazz glamour. No longer was it enough to have a pretty face

and a large bust, and the point was proved by the multiplicity of Monroe-types who tried and failed to make it in her wake. Jayne Mansfield in the States, Diana Dors in Britain and many others in every European country with a film industry, achieved little more than, at best, superior starlet status. Marilyn had been old-fashioned in her own times, but so triumphantly vibrant that she was able to break the rules.

After her fight to be accepted as an actress, *every* girl wanted to be an actress. Even Raquel Welch – perhaps nearest in image to the old-

Marlon Brando in *The Wild One* (Laslo Benedek, 1953), with Mary Murphy as the agent of his moral regeneration.

Opposite: Black-and-white is beautiful. . . . Raquel Welch and Jim Brown enjoying miscegenation in *100 Rifles* (Tom Gries, 1968).

James Dean in *Rebel Without a Cause* (Nicholas Ray, 1955) with Natalie Wood. Dean starred in only three films, yet came to symbolize a whole generation and was as revered as Valentino after his untimely death in a car smash.

style sex star – has worked hard and with partial success to cast aside the cheesecake stigma (but 'Who,' said Peter Fiddick in The Guardian, commenting on a Raquel Welch TV show, 'is this old-fashioned broad who says she wants to be recognized for the singing-dancing-joking talents she undoubtedly has, but insists on coming on like Son of Jane Russell?'). It became accepted that sex symbolism could no longer be an end in itself, that modern film-making demanded something more. Monroe desired this fulfilment perhaps more than anyone else: 'The best way for me to prove myself as a person,' she once commented, 'is to prove myself as an actress.'

The new woman was coming not from Hollywood but from Europe. She was young and she was nearer the spirit of post-war youth. Her name was Brigitte Bardot, and she had a wanton wilfulness about her, a kittenish but ultimately totally feminine appeal which made the big breasts and silvered hair redundant. This French girl/woman with her pout, her firm, lean flesh and her natural, unglamorized looks, was much closer to the image of Brando and Dean than that of Monroe and Hayworth. She portrayed the newly discovered teenager, the rebel against strict bourgeois upbringing, the woman who takes her pleasure with whom she chooses, and follows her own inclinations and desires. It was a part, moreover, which she carried into life. It really mattered little that her films were undistinguished (undistinguished, that is, except for the alacrity with which she seemed ready to shed her upper garments and expose her delightful breasts – at least for home-consumption in France; these were the days of the double-standard, when often two versions of a scene were shot, one for Anglo-Saxon and the other for Continental markets, the former calling for at least bra and pants, and, at bath-times, a decently high water-line).

Bardot's life-style, her image of French liberality in matters of love and sex, made more impact on foreign consciousness than did the films (often directed by Roger Vadim, her husband and mentor in her early days) which displayed them. Bardot was a precursor of the confident, liberated, self-sufficient stars of the 'sixties and 'seventies like Jane Fonda and Julie Christie, though she has herself clung to her original screen image. At forty, over twenty years after she began in movies, she is still stripping off for ex-spouse Vadim (in *Don Juan, or If Don Juan Were a Woman*, 1974) – and, one should add, proving that she still has the equipment to justify doing so.

Youth, of the kind represented by the younger Bardot, was a movie preoccupation in the 'fifties. There was a good deal of adult fear about such modern manifestations of the youth culture as violence, juvenile delinquency and, of course, the concomitant sexual amorality. Films spotlighting the evils of being young were rushed out, including *The Blackboard Jungle* (1955), which had a 'new' type of music by an unknown singer as its theme and which – as rock & roll – sparked off a cultural revolution. Bill Haley and his song, 'Rock Around the Clock', allied to the delinquency theme of the film, helped to impress upon the adult and official mind the threat from the young. Two years previously the 'brutish' Brando had seared an image of violent youth in *The Wild*

Otto Preminger challenged the American censors over the candid sexual terminology and explicit examination of rape in his courtroom drama, *Anatomy of a Murder* (1959) – and won. In this scene defence counsel James Stewart produces exhibit A – Lee Remick's torn panties.

One (1953) as Johnny, the brooding leader of a motorcycle gang. So startling was the film, and Brando's portrayal, that Britain banned it; and, although it looks fairly innocuous now, it remained unseen in the UK for well over a decade and a half.

This was, perhaps, one of the most controversial films of the decade, its sexual content muted but strongly in evidence. There is a clear, if not overt, relationship drawn between the violence of the gang and sex. Britches (Yvonne Doughty) is a gang girl, breasts pushing temptingly against a sweater three times too small and legs encased in tight jeans. She has a yen for Johnny and pushes herself on him, stopping him in the street of the small town the gang terrorizes, and referring to their first meeting at a motorbike scramble. The nature of that meeting is plain, not so much from what she says as the way in which she says it: 'We were really on the Christmas tree that night, remember? Boy was I green . . . was I green. . . ? I had a guy.' It is evident that she lost her virginity to the forceful, callous Johnny and that he dumped her soon after, leaving her to become gang property.

Brando is attracted to Kathie (Mary Murphy), the girl who works in the town's café, but she rejects him at first because he is rude to her father – the weak law officer who allows feelings between the townspeople and the gang to run high and eventually get out of hand. Later, however, Brando rescues her from other members of the gang who are riding around her on their bikes taunting her. Johnny rides up, a knight in black leather, lifts her onto the back of his bike and drives off into the country. As she rides pillion, the surging power between her legs obviously affects her and her distressed face softens into pleasure. When they stop Brando stumbles towards her and grabs her in a violent embrace. She, however, pushes him away and instead sinks to the ground and turns to his bike which she caresses. 'I've never ridden on a motorcycle before. It's fast . . . it scared me. . . . It felt good.' The atmosphere is tense – will Brando rape her or will she submit to his rough advances? Neither happens and the film eventually opts for a more prosaic, unsatisfactory beauty-and-beast, badman-finds-redemption ending.

The great youth symbol of the 'fifties was James Dean. In a mere three films – *East of Eden* (1954), *Rebel Without a Cause* (1955) and *Giant* (1955) – he was imprinted on the consciousness of youth as a symbol of revolt, unrest, brooding unpredictability, discontent and unspoken yearnings. On screen and off he epitomized the Crazy Mixed-up Kid, at odds with parents, authority and the world. The fact that he literally drove himself to self-destruction set the seal on his persona and he was elevated by a generation to the status of near-martyr.

In *East of Eden* he discovers that his mother, whom he believes dead, is in fact running a local brothel; in *Rebel* he is the middle-class kid who, despite having everything, inexplicably goes off the rails. In *Giant* he becomes the poor boy determined to make good and, on inheriting a plot of Texas land rich in oil, goes money-mad; despite his near monomania and debauched life he is enormously appealing to Rock Hudson's daughter, who very nearly falls into his bed.

By releasing his mildly risqué comedy *The Moon is Blue* (1953, with Maggie McNamara and William Holden) without a seal, Otto Preminger demonstrated that the Production Code was not sacrosanct.

In *Suddenly Last Summer* (Joseph L. Mankiewicz, 1959) Elizabeth Taylor played a willing Tennessee Williams heroine who wastes her allure on a homosexual.

'Breast or leg?' The suggestive picnic scene from Alfred Hitchcock's *To Catch a Thief* (1955), with Grace Kelly and Cary Grant.

Giant also starred an actress of potent sexuality – Elizabeth Taylor. Hudson and Taylor stepped out of their traditional moulds in this movie, playing members of a rich, powerful cattle family who age, graciously and well, during the course of the story. Another controversial element is introduced when their son falls in love with and marries a Mexican girl. This hedged round the miscegenation issue in that the girl wasn't actually black and she had the advantage of being a doctor – a foreshadow, no doubt, of Sidney Poitier (the first authentic black star) as the enormously acceptable bourgeois black man who loves white Katharine Houghton in *Guess Who's Coming to Dinner* in 1967.

Some of Hollywood's attempts to tackle controversial themes in the 'fifties look rather tame in retrospect, and many of the stands taken by committed film-makers look faintly ludicrous with the passing of the years. *The Moon is Blue*

(1953) is a case in point. Otto Preminger wanted to film this Broadway comedy about a girl who is described as a 'professional virgin' who won't surrender her charms until she finds her Mr Right, although her attitude to sex and the way she plays off two suitors – and would-be seducers – seems frank. The Production Code Administration objected to the subject matter and, even more strongly, to the use of taboo words like 'virgin'. United Artists pressed on, defied the censor, ignored the fact that the film was refused a seal, resigned from the MPPDA, and issued the film without a seal. The initial investment of $500,000 was transformed into a gross take of $6 million.

While the fight over a word like 'pregnant' seems pathetically trivial in the light of film candour in later years, United Artists' stand and commercial victory were important in that they confirmed that the refusal of a seal did not automatically mean box-office death, and they dealt a blow to the Production Code that in the next decade would become a *coup de grâce* during Sidney Lumet's struggle over *The Pawnbroker*. Preminger was to have another tussle – in 1959 over the language content of *Anatomy of a Murder*, in which precise sexual terminology was unflinchingly used in the courtroom scenes which tried to establish whether or not Lee Remick has been raped.

Despite its flirtation with controversy, Hollywood could and did still turn out the glossy, beautifully made commercial entertainment films that had been its trademark for so long. Many film-makers observed that sex could be treated in a lighthearted and subtle way which slyly poked fun at censorship. Alfred Hitchcock's attitude to screen sex was highly individual, and in his treatment of it he could be compared to Ernst Lubitsch for subtlety and good humour. When asked why he had a seemingly infallible ability to cast unknown and very beautiful actresses in his films who later became big stars, he replied, 'I suppose it's because I was born with two crystal balls.'

In 1955 he made a light thriller called *To Catch a Thief*, about a series of jewel robberies in the south of France. Grace Kelly and Cary Grant were the protagonists – he, a successful thief suspected of robberies he has not committed setting out to catch the real miscreant, falling for rich-girl Kelly, and allaying her suspicions. One of the highlights is a picnic in which the food and ambiance are used to heighten the sexual attraction that is developing between the pair: 'Breast or leg?' asks Grace Kelly, making it clear by her tone of voice that there may be more to the offer than the piece of chicken she is holding in her hand.

Hitchcock's philosophy of sex is consistent with the rest of his approach to film-making: 'Sex on the screen should be suspenseful,' he explained in an interview with François Truffaut[51]. 'If sex is too blatant or obvious, there's no suspense.' In the same conversation he stated why his heroines were the blonde, cool, lady-like types epitomized by Grace Kelly and other look-alikes he subsequently used. 'We're after the drawing-room type, the real ladies who become whores once they're in the bedroom. Poor Marilyn Monroe had sex written all over her face, and Brigitte Bardot isn't very subtle either.'

An actress who fell broadly into this stereotype was Doris Day. Hitchcock used her in *The Man Who Knew Too Much* (1955) and thereafter she started an extraordinary career as a professional screen virgin of the type objected to in *The Moon is Blue*. She was invariably the prim and proper career girl whose sexual drive is directed into her job until she comes up against an extremely virile male. At first they fight; he sees her as a challenge, she resists stoutly; ultimately they marry. That was more or less the skeleton of the series' plots.

The forerunner was *Teacher's Pet* (1958), in which as a lecturer in journalism she comes up against Clark Gable. The next year the glossy sex comedy of a peculiarly American type that

Many of Europe's female stars appeared topless in the 'fifties, including Martine Carol (*left*) in *Nathalie* (Christian-Jaque, 1957), and Silvana Pampanini, who specialized in neo-Roman romps such as (*below*) *O.K. Nérone* (Mario Soldati, 1951).

127

she was to make her own was crystallized in *Pillow Talk*, where she pits wits and maidenhead against Rock Hudson. The string of successes, though rooted morally in the 'fifties, continued into and reached its peak in the 'sixties, elevating Day to the unusual position of an *anti*-sex symbol.

Doris Day was a strange anomaly in the era of Monroe and Taylor, the latter successfully making the transition from child actor to adult star with her erotic roles in *Cat on a Hot Tin Roof* (1958) and *Suddenly Last Summer* (1959). Both were Tennessee Williams works which dwelt typically on the seamier side of human relationships. Williams dominated the drama of the 'fifties: six of his plays or stories were filmed during the decade; the other four were *The Glass Menagerie*, *A Streetcar Named Desire*, *Baby Doll*, and *The Rose Tattoo* – for which Anna Magnani won an Oscar as the frustrated wife who finds relief with Burt Lancaster. Williams's observation that 'We are all civilized people, which means that we are all savages at heart but observing a few amenities of civilized behaviour'[52] seemed peculiarly apt for the generation that had seen the veneer of civilization stripped brutally aside by war.

As with *Tea and Sympathy* (1956), in which an older woman (Deborah Kerr) seduces a schoolboy to prove he's not queer, *Cat on a Hot Tin Roof* was muted for the screen, the homosexuality of Paul Newman being given less emphasis than the vitriolic disdain of his wife (Taylor). *Suddenly Last Summer* was a much more bizarre affair, of which homosexuality, psychosis and even cannibalism were features. As an indication of the changing climate, they got past both the Production Code Administration and, grudgingly, the Legion of Decency without a fight. *Cat* established both Taylor and Newman as actors of considerable power, as

well as potent sex stars who would find their true *métier* in the more permissive atmosphere of the 'sixties.

By 1959 the moral climate had changed so much that a very funny sex-oriented comedy like *Some Like It Hot* need pull no punches. Transvestism, sexual ambivalence and seduction were openly treated, even though it was strictly for laughs. Jack Lemmon and Tony Curtis, in drag and living with an all-girl band, give rise to any number of sexy misunderstandings, and inspire the most celebrated tag-line in movies ('Dammit,' confesses Lemmon to Joe E. Brown, who is determined to seduce him/her whatever the odds, 'I'm a man.' 'Well,' responds Brown, 'nobody's perfect!').

The steamiest sequence, however, was Monroe's innocent seduction of Curtis. The latter abandons his skirt for blazer, glasses and uproarious Cary Grant accent in order to catch Monroe; pretending to be enormously rich, he lures her out to a yacht and feigns impotence. She, being a big-hearted girl and seemingly unaware of her own desirability, offers to help him over his difficulties. Wearing a dress which allows her breasts to move unrestricted, and throwing herself – physically – into her crusade to restore manhood to Curtis, she reaches perhaps her highest point of on-screen carnality, made the more erotic by her do-gooding ingenuousness and Curtis's increasing difficulty in pretending that her ministrations are having no effect on him (how, indeed, can one believe Curtis's statement at the cessation of filming that kissing Monroe was 'like kissing Hitler'?). Sexual spoofs like *Some Like It Hot* helped to erode the spirit and the letter of the Code and prepare the way for more serious portrayals of sex on the screen.

The challenge of television had, of course, been a major factor in forcing the cinema to become more sophisticated and daring. By 1955 the Legion was finding over a third of all films objectionable in part or whole. The realization soon spread that its negative approach was outdated. Even Pope Pius XII called for a more positive effort 'accompanied by an educational endeavour', and a programme of film education and study was launched. By 1958 the Legion was beginning to announce 'specially recommended films'.

The pioneering work of the European cinema in the late 'forties had had its effect in Hollywood, and by the 'fifties the American industry was even plundering the Continental cinema for some of its greatest stars. Perhaps most notable among them was the beautiful, statuesque Sophia Loren. Under Carlo Ponti's tutelage she had risen from nude extra in 1950 extravaganzas to top billing in such epics as *The Pride and the Passion* (1957). She and Gina Lollobrigida fulfilled the Anglo-Saxon image of the Latin earth mother – big, sensual, full-figured women whose bounteous charms are matched by a full-blooded love-making technique and a hot-headed temperament.

It was a fashionable period for large ladies, and Anita Ekberg from Sweden also achieved

Sophia Loren as the farmer's wife who sleeps with her stepson in *Desire Under the Elms* (Delbert Mann, 1957).

busty prominence, making films in many countries, including *La Dolce Vita* in Italy. This film, a dramatic exposé by Fellini of hedonism and debauchery in modern Rome, caused a sensation in 1959, and its title became an international term for sybaritic living. Ekberg played a mindless Hollywood sex symbol endlessly pursued by Marcello Mastroianni and a ratpack of sensation-seeking photographers. Her finest hour, however, came in a later Fellini film – one of the episodes in *Boccaccio '70* (1962), called *The Temptation of Dr Antonio*, in which she mocked her own image by playing a giant milk-advertising poster that comes to life and plagues an anti-sex campaigner.

As ever, the Continental directors were more daring than their rivals in America and Britain, the candour of their films being typified in France by Roger Vadim's *And God Created Woman* (1956), with Brigitte Bardot. Sweden was breaking out in a strange cult of nudist movies, curiously unerotic travelogues in which the participants wandered around undraped and proved that you need more than a lack of clothes to be sexy. However, a formidable talent was emerging in Ingmar Bergman who, like a cinematic Tennessee Williams, tended to spotlight the more bizarre face of human drives and its manifestation in sexually aberrant or abnormal activity. Indeed, many of the seeds sown on the Continent in the 'fifties through the work of Fellini, Bergman and other filmmakers were to bear fruit in the cultural and behavourial patterns of America and Britain. Their influence was to be considerable, not least in helping, by their artistry, to break down the censorship of serious adult films.

The 'fifties set a trend that was to be fully exploited in the 'sixties. Sex in the movies was no longer to be coyly hinted at, visually and verbally. With the start of a new, brash, artistically and culturally exciting decade, the petty fights, squabbles and restrictions of the 'fifties were to make way for a new and not always welcome mood of licence.

The rapidity with which the legitimate cinema in America, in a decade and a half, shrugged off the shackles of censorship and tested public inhibition to the hilt was, to say the least, spectacular. At the beginning of the 'sixties, in spite of a growing audacity epitomized by the sexual cynicism of (remarkably enough) a British film, Jack Clayton's *Room at the Top* (1958), nudity (except in the censor-snubbing nudist-camp films) was virtually non-existent and normally excised from more liberated foreign imports; themes like homosexuality could only be tackled seriously, obliquely and off-screen (as in Tennessee Williams's *Suddenly Last Summer*); and the biggest scandals were more likely to be caused by language than bare flesh (such as the sexual terminology used freely in Otto Preminger's controversial rape-case courtroom drama, *Anatomy of a Murder*).

Yet in the early 'seventies, exhibitors in New York felt bold enough to show, overtly and to the standard picture-going public, hard-core pornography of the intensity of *Deep Throat* (1972) and *The Devil in Miss Jones* (1973), and – for a while at least – were able to get away with it.

At the same time, full-frontal nudity and explicit sexual activity became so commonplace in the commercial cinema as to make the dirty-mac skin-flick circuit not only redundant but tame by comparison. The entertainment film had finally attained adulthood (and, on occasion, adultery) in the 'fifties after a long, fantasy-ridden adolescence, and these further developments into sexual freedom were the result of a thaw in the moral climate of society which gathered momentum throughout the 'sixties.

The bastions of censorship began to crumble on all fronts. The escalating economics of film-making and the slackening in the dictatorial power of the studios caused the industry to start questioning – and flouting – the limitations of its own Production Code; local censorship bodies were, from time to time, snuffed out in certain areas of the United States on grounds of being unconstitutional; the serious erotic themes of foreign film-makers like Bergman, Fellini and Antonioni were sanctified and shown uncut in art-houses, to be followed by American imitators; and even the Catholic Legion of Decency, it was increasingly realized, could be disregarded without necessarily incurring the loss of one's cinematic soul (i.e. profits).

Censorship bodies, for their part, made some attempt to match the swing in public attitudes. In 1961 the Code was amended to allow 'sex aberrations' to be shown, provided they were handled with 'care, discretion and restraint'. And in 1965 the Legion inaugurated an award system. The latter also introduced a more complex coding system during this period.

Progress was, nevertheless, halting at times. Baths, for instance, made a come-back (if, indeed, they'd ever been away), particularly in such spectaculars as the absurdly over-budgeted *Cleopatra* (1963), but they were still subject to the prurient eye. In *Genghis Khan* (1965), the bath-time cavortings of warrior Telly Savalas with a bunch of Oriental handmaidens were (mercifully, some might feel) severely slashed; while, more oddly, in the publicity stills for *A Fine Madness* (1966), depicting Sean Connery and Jean Seberg enjoying an ablutionary romp, a pair of 'shorts' was carefully painted onto Connery's thighs to promote belief that he and Jean weren't actually bathing in the buff. Later, of course, in such films as *Performance* (1970), *Quiet Days in Clichy* (1969) and, most explicitly, *Superfly* (1972), domestic mixed bathing became a much-used sexual motif.

One welcome step forward in the early 'sixties was the injection of satire and more adult attitudes into the sex comedy, although it had to compete with a phenomenally successful but 'vaguely salacious and completely vacuous'[53] series of *anti*-sex comedies such as *That Touch of Mink* (1962) and *Send Me No Flowers* (1964), in which Doris Day continued to fight to save her ageing honour from the likes of Rock Hudson, Cary Grant, James Garner and Rod Taylor. The grown-up sex comedy had been pioneered by Otto Preminger with *The Moon is Blue*, but the sharpest exponent was Billy Wilder, whose Marilyn Monroe vehicles, *The Seven Year Itch* and *Some Like It Hot*, had demonstrated his healthy lack of reverence for the subject.

In 1960, he made *The Apartment*, a biting send-up of the extra-marital sex-life of the average American business executive, in which Jack Lemmon, as a humble insurance agent, climbs his way up to the executive washroom by lending his apartment to his bosses for their frequent illicit liaisons. Shirley MacLaine is one of the girls involved, driven to near-suicide by the callousness of Fred MacMurray, but eventually loved by Lemmon.

The Apartment was a great success, but Wilder stretched permissiveness a fraction too far in his underrated (and little-seen) *Kiss Me, Stupid* (1964), which mated Dean Martin with Felicia Farr, Ray Walston with Kim Novak, but fell foul of both the Legion of Decency and the box-office. The Legion attacked it as 'a

Felix Franchy and Ruth Gassman as *Michael and Helga* (Erich F. Bender, 1968).

131

Shirley MacLaine and Jack
Lemmon in *The Apartment*
(Billy Wilder, 1960).

thoroughly sordid piece of realism which is
aesthetically as well as morally repulsive.
Crude and suggestive dialogue, a leering treatment of marital and extra-marital sex, a
prurient preoccupation with lechery com-
pound the film's bald condonation of immorality.' Although a bit nudging (it's set in a
town called Climax), *Kiss Me, Stupid* was a
funny and genuinely erotic farce which deserved
better than it got.

Wilder engaged Jack Lemmon again much
later for his overlong but very pleasant *Avanti!*
(1972), which both delighted and surprised
those who saw it by exposing the entire charms
of the plump and primly English Juliet Mills.

More serious sexual themes continued to be
chiefly the preserve of Tennessee Williams,
whose explorations of rape, frustration, homosexuality and cannibalism had already been
seen in 'fifties screen adaptations. Now it was

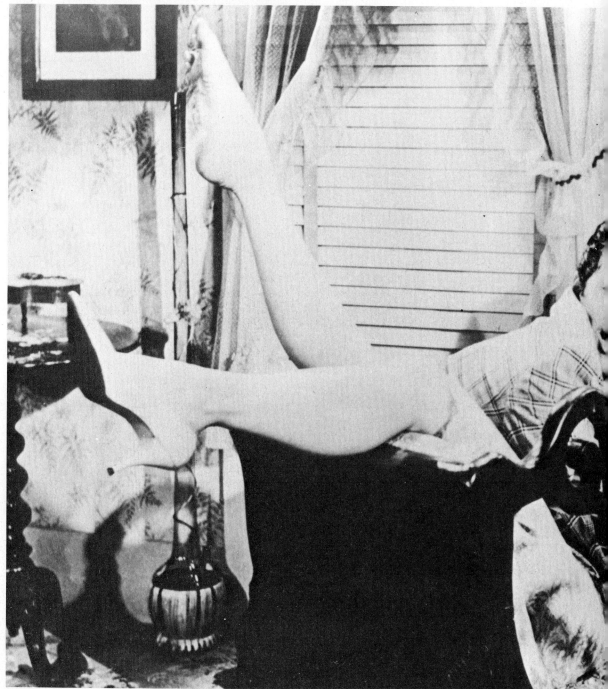

Dean Martin and Kim Novak
in Billy Wilder's unsung sex
comedy, *Kiss Me, Stupid*
(1964).

132

the turn of the gigolo and VD in *Sweet Bird of Youth* (in the play, the character played by Paul Newman was also castrated, but as far as the cinema was concerned, this was still 1962, not 1972); adultery and nymphomania in *The Fugitive Kind* (1960), which brought together Marlon Brando, Anna Magnani and Joanne Woodward; ageing promiscuity in *The Roman Spring of Mrs Stone* (1962), with Vivien Leigh; dormant spinsterish lust in *Summer and Smoke* (1961), with Geraldine Page; and a veritable anthology of erotic desires in *The Night of the Iguana* (1964), with Richard Burton as a reprobate ex-minister.

John O'Hara contributed prostitution to the list of steamy subjects in the adaptation of his novel *Butterfield 8* (1960), which won an ailing Elizabeth Taylor one of her Academy Awards. The oldest profession was a popular theme in 'sixties films, though the boldness of its treat-

ment varied considerably. *The World of Suzie Wong* (1960), for example, about a Hong Kong tart, and the cop-out version of Truman Capote's *Breakfast at Tiffany's* (1961), with a miscast Audrey Hepburn, were hopelessly soft-centred. (A sign of the times and the changing ideals of feminine beauty was Billy Wilder's comment on Audrey Hepburn's lack of mammary super-abundance: 'She's like a salmon swimming upstream. She can do it with very small bazooms. Titism has taken over this country but this girl singlehanded may make bazooms a thing of the past. The director will not have to invent shots where the girl leans way forward for a glass of Scotch and soda!')

Jules Dassin's *Never on Sunday* (1960), on the other hand, was an enjoyably lusty celebration of whoredom, made by the performance of the exuberant Greek actress, Melina Mercouri. Significantly, the Legion condemned it, but it was still a considerable hit at the box-office. *Walk on the Wild Side* (1962), with Laurence Harvey, broke further new ground by being openly set in a brothel, as did *A House is Not a Home* (1964) by failing to condemn the central character, a madam. Even Billy Wilder got in on the act with *Irma la Douce* (1963), another teaming of Lemmon and MacLaine, but the film was accused of dishonesty and sentimentality and did badly.

Contrasting themes were supplied by the glumly seething *The Dark at the Top of the Stairs* (1960), in which Dorothy McGuire is frigid, and *The Chapman Report* (1963), a neo-Kinsey fictionalization about randy, frustrated housewives. The latter had a gang rape scene involving Claire Bloom over which the Legion had some influence, forcing considerable cuts.

The Legion objected (successfully) to a similar scene in Elia Kazan's *Splendour in the Grass* (1961), a rare attempt at this time to question the conventional repression of youthful sexual needs, in which Warren Beatty literally falls sick with unconsummated desire for Natalie Wood, who in turn goes mad. The conventions were also questioned in another

Ava Gardner tries to make Richard Burton's unfrocked priest jealous by frolicking with beach boys in Tennessee Williams's *The Night of the Iguana* (John Huston, 1964).

Natalie Wood movie, this time with Steve McQueen, *Love with the Proper Stranger* (1963), but a promising theme (casual pregnancy) sold out to a romantic ending.

John Huston, meanwhile, bridged the old and new Hollywoods with *The Misfits* (1961) by teaming two golden stars (Clark Gable and Marilyn Monroe) in a love story, then hardening the plot by making them soiled divorcees at odds with each other. Huston it was, too, who chose to put *Freud* (1963) on the screen, a worthy but rather dull dramatized portrait of the great psychoanalyst (played by Montgomery Clift), focusing on Freud's own hangups and a couple of sensational case histories which led to the development of his basic theories and methods.

The most significant inroads into the old order of taboos, however, were made by a newer generation of directors, most notably Stanley Kubrick and Joseph Strick. Kubrick's achievement was to enter the sexual minefield of Vladimir Nabokov's *Lolita* (1962) and emerge unscathed. His screen version of the celebrated

story of Humbert Humbert's obsession with a sexually precocious minor (played in the film by the then fourteen-year-old Sue Lyon) was daring in that he chose to tackle the theme at all. But his skill, good humour and unsensational approach protected the film from a major outcry, and even the Legion of Decency (reassured, no doubt, by the element of retribution in the story) refrained from condemning it. However, Kubrick regretted that, because of the mood of the times, 'it was not possible to portray Humbert Humbert's obsession on the screen with all the eroticism suggested in Nabokov's novel'.[54]

Joseph Strick first made his name with a sardonic short, *Muscle Beach* (1948), which gently mocked exhibitionists and fitness fetishists. He followed this much later with *The Savage Eye* (1959), an abrasive study of the ugly side of life in Los Angeles, as viewed by a disenchanted divorcee, and a hard-working adaptation of Jean Genet's play, *The Balcony* (1964), set in a brothel. Then, with independent backing, he fulfilled an ambition to put James Joyce's *Ulysses* (1967) on the screen, complete with Molly Bloom monologue, four-letter words and all.

This was the first overt attempt to put the language of real life into a film, and the movie ran into immediate trouble, especially in Britain – though not, curiously, in the United States, where its exhibition was carefully and cleverly controlled so as not to offend the Catholic element. The Legion of Decency (now calling itself the National Catholic Office for Motion Pictures) saw and passed it because, as its new executive head, the Rev. Patrick J. Sullivan, told Alexander Walker, 'we felt it would appeal principally to students of James Joyce.'[55] He further pointed out that 'Joyce is mandatory reading in many Catholic schools and colleges. It was not unusual for nuns to escort their English classes to the film.'

The Catholic Office were of the opinion that the film's controversial climactic speech, in which Molly Bloom (Barbara Jefford) sits in bed and gives rein to her erotic fantasies, frustrations and yearnings, was not so much 'dirty talk' as a 'soliloquy of a quasi-classical nature'![56] In Britain, film censor John Trevelyan had other thoughts. A recent celebrated case in which the book 'Last Exit to Brooklyn' had been found to be obscene concerned Trevelyan, who thought that the language in Molly's monologue might constitute grounds for a prosecution. 'The film,' he pointed out in his book 'What the Censor Saw', 'contained dialogue that at this time we believed would generally be regarded as outrageous, offensive and possibly obscene, so we decided to ask for a number of cuts.' Joseph Strick was angry at these deletions and fought a vigorous campaign in the press against them.

The interesting point about Trevelyan's excisions was that all but one were in matters of dialogue and the majority were taken from the one speech by Molly. This is undoubtedly a monologue of great power and it was wedded to rather mundane visual images. Indeed, to hear the speech without watching the film is to experience most of its effect. A few of the deletions concerned four-letter words. In the following passage the excisions are bracketed so that the reader may compare for himself the effect of the Joycean prose with the version which appeared on British screens:

'I wish he was here or somebody to let myself go with (and come again like that I feel all fire inside me or if I could dream it when he made me spend the second time tickling me behind with his finger I was coming for about five minutes with my legs round him) I had to hug him after Oh Lord I wanted to shout out all sorts of things (fuck or shit or anything at all) only I would look ugly all those lines from the strain.' (The lack of punctuation is as it appears in Appendix 2 of 'What the Censor Saw'; the bracketed material was taped from a television showing of the film and has been kept punctuationless.)

Most of the passages deleted were concerned with sexual allusions, innuendo and descriptions. The following are a selection to give a flavour of the censor's objections:

'Yes because he must have come three or four times with that tremendous big red brute of a thing he has though his nose is not so big'; 'What's the idea making us like that with a big hole in the middle of us like a stallion driving it up into you'; 'Always having to lie down for them better for him to put it in from behind the way Mrs Mastiansky told me her husband made her like the dogs do it'; 'Of course compared with what a man looks like with his two bags full and his other thing hanging down out of him or sticking up at you like a hat-rack no wonder they hide it with a cabbage leaf'; 'First I'll look at his shirt or I'll see if he has that French letter still in his pocketbook'.

Molly's discontent stems from the fact that she and Bloom have not had full sexual intercourse for 'ten years, five months and eighteen days – not since five weeks prior to the birth and death of their only male issue, Rudolph Bloom, junior, aged eleven days'. In her fantasies she

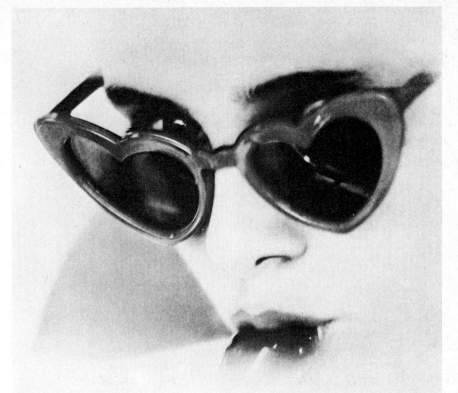

Sue Lyon as *Lolita* (Stanley Kubrick, 1962).

thinks of other men. The longest deletion came in the middle of a passage about young men and must have been demanded because of its specific reference to oral intercourse:

'Those fine young men I could see down in Margaret Strand bathing place from the side of the rock standing up in the sun naked like a god or something and then plunging into the sea with them why aren't all men like that it would be some consolation for a woman like that lovely little statue he bought I could look at him all day long there's real beauty and poetry for you (I often felt I wanted to kiss him all over also his lovely young cock there so simply I wouldn't mind taking him in my mouth if nobody was looking as if it was asking you to suck it so clean and white he looked with his boyish face I would too in half a minute even if

Maurice Roeves and Barbara Jefford (as Molly Bloom) in James Joyce's *Ulysses* (Joseph Strick, 1967).

Nude with guitar . . . Peter Sellers as the accident-prone but intrepid Inspector Clouseau in the nudist-camp sequence from *A Shot in the Dark* (Blake Edwards, 1964).

In Britain, it was finally left to local authorities to decide whether or not to show the film (although ironically, three years later, in 1970, Trevelyan's Board 'felt able to pass the film uncut'; the full version even appeared on British television in 1972, admittedly on the minority channel, BBC2). In Ireland, the source of its inspiration, it was, inevitably, banned, while in New Zealand, it was shown to segregated male and female audiences! The United States thus took on, for the first time in its cinema history, the air of a leader of liberal expression in the movies.

The language barrier was also breached by Shirley Clarke in *The Connection* (1960), a study of drug addicts in which the word 'shit' was used as a euphemism for heroin. By the mid-'seventies, of course, there was hardly a film script without the word scattered liberally throughout it, but in 1960 the New York censors didn't like it and clamped down on *The Connection* for two years. Later, Shirley Clarke made her acclaimed *Portrait of Jason* (1967), a two-hour interview with a Negro male prostitute, whose language is candid to say the least.

The films of Strick and Clarke represented the best of a brief spate of open-minded independent (as opposed to underground) film-making in the United States in the 'sixties. Others, like Leslie Stevens's *Private Property* (1959), gained an overblown reputation based on their low budgets and supposed integrity and realistic handling of sexual themes, but censorship difficulties (*Private Property* attained no certificate in Great Britain) probably boosted their importance to an unjustified degree. Better was Alexander Singer's much admired *A Cold Wind in August* (1962), about an affair between a teenage boy (Scott Marlowe) and a raddled stripper (Lola Albright), which Peter John Dyer thought had 'moments of perception and reality that bring it closer to Kubrick's early work than to such vehicles for personal advancement as Leslie Stevens' *Private Property*. . . . The love scenes, often frankly written and directed, have a genuinely sensual impetus.'[57]

On the other side of the Atlantic, Anthony Harvey made the excellent *Dutchman* (1966), which uses sex (white girl arouses Negro in deserted subway carriage and then stabs him to death) to highlight the race problem. The fact that Harvey had to film and reconstruct his subway in England is an indication that some themes were still too strong for the American authorities.

The factor which most effectively undermined the censorship machinery of 'sixties America was nudity. As late as 1964, total nudity – even briefly glimpsed – was still unacceptable to both the Code and the Legion, and breast exposure was strictly taboo. The few attempts to break the decency barrier ended in compromise or scissor-work, including the bed scene in *Becket* (1964), which had to be reshot in order to reveal less of Peter O'Toole's comely companion; similar sequences in *The Americanization of Emily* (1964) involving James Coburn's bed-

some of it went down what it's only like a gruel or the dew there's no danger besides he'd be so clean compared with those pigs of men I suppose never dream of washing it from one years end to the other the most of them only that what gives the women the moustaches I'm sure) it'll be grand if I could get in with a handsome young poet at my age.'

The excision of these passages undoubtedly reduced the power of the prose, although Barbara Jefford's extraordinarily sensitive rendering of these meandering sentences turned the monologue, cut or complete, into a forceful, accurate and realistic portrayal of a frustrated but normally sexed woman who is beset by desires and lusts on the one hand and revulsion, detestation and the deep-seated repression of her religion on the other. The British Board of Film Censors passed the film with the cuts, but the peculiar system of local licensing allowed it to pass unchallenged in Greater London despite heated attacks from censorial lobbies. A further row blew up at the Cannes Film Festival because some of the sub-titles had been blacked out. Controversy followed the film wherever it went, in fact, and contributed to the good business it recorded.

136

mates; and Barbara Bouchet's swim in Otto Preminger's *In Harm's Way* (1965), originally planned without benefit of bikini but finally shot with the actress adequately clad. One or two commercial movies, such as *The Prize* (1964) and *A Shot in the Dark* (1964), tried to take advantage of the licence enjoyed by the neo-documentary nudist-camp films by throwing in a naturist sequence, but the camerawork was painstakingly discreet.

Curiously, the one notable exception to the nudity taboo involved a rear view rather than a front – to be precise, Elizabeth Taylor's bare buttocks, revealed on a massage slab in *Cleopatra*, a film generally frowned on by the Legion of Decency for its 'immodest costuming'. Another epic, *The Bible* (1966), also got away with bottom exposure in the scenes depicting Adam and Eve, but in this instance (as Arthur Knight and Hollis Alpert so neatly put it) 'the Legion bowed to higher authority for the nude scene – the Bible itself'.[58]

'In itself,' the Legion declared in 1965, 'nudity is not immoral and has long been recognized as a legitimate subject in painting and sculpture. However, in the very different medium of the motion picture, it is never an artistic necessity . . . the temptation for film-makers to exploit the prurient appeal to nudity in this mass medium is so great that any concession to its use, even for otherwise valid reasons of art, would lead to wide abuse. For this reason, the National Legion of Decency will continue to apply the policy of resisting every effort to employ nudity in film production.' At the end of the same year a leading official commented that 'In the last two years, thirty-four films, of which twenty were major American productions, would have been released with

scenes employing nudity had not the producers realized that they would then have been condemned.' Even when the Legion later underwent a mild bout of reform, renaming itself the National Catholic Office for Motion Pictures (or NCOMP) and conceding that some serious and morally worthwhile films could include erotic episodes, it nevertheless retained an especially severe attitude towards nudity on the screen.

However, the crunch came in 1965 when Sidney Lumet's *The Pawnbroker*, an independent American production of intense seriousness, was condemned for showing a scene in which a young Negro prostitute bares her breasts at Rod Steiger. If they allowed this, the Legion argued, nudity would become rampant in movies – 'just as common as blowing your nose' was their rather spurious analogy. The film was also refused a Code seal. Instead of compromising, the producers stuck to their guns and appealed to the Motion Picture Association of America (or MPAA) – tacitly encouraged, as it happened, by the Code's Geoffrey Shurlock, who saw this as the only way to achieve a relaxation of Code policy towards nudity.

The 'objectionable' scene in *The Pawnbroker* was crucial both to the plot and to the motivation of the central character, Nazerman (Rod Steiger). The girlfriend (Thelma Oliver) of Nazerman's assistant Jesus is a whore who goes to the misanthropic survivor of Auschwitz to sell jewellery she's received from private sessions conducted unbeknownst to her pimp. She wants the money to prevent Jesus falling in with a gang planning to rob the pawnshop. Nazerman offers her a sum, but she needs $20 more and offers her body to him. 'I'm good,

Thelma Oliver's attempted seduction of Rod Steiger in *The Pawnbroker* (Sidney Lumet, 1965), which fought to retain its controversial nude scenes, won its case, and caused the Production Code to be completely revised.

137

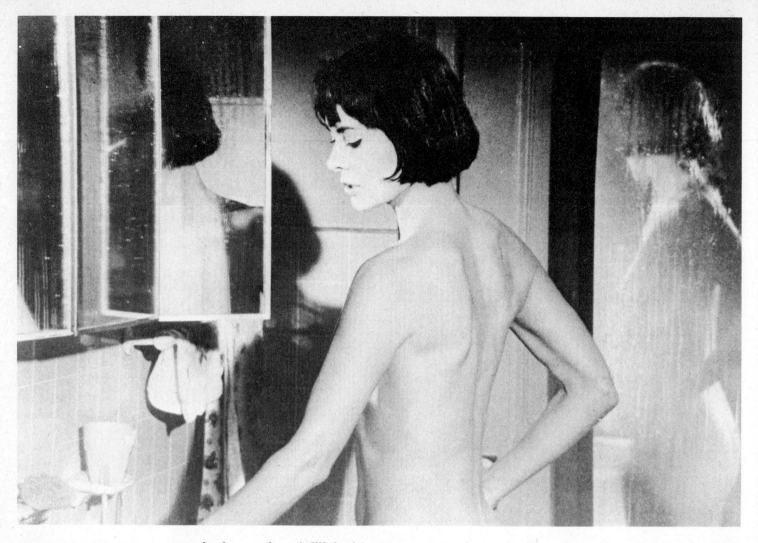

The mirror masturbation
scene from D.H. Lawrence's
The Fox (Mark Rydell, 1968)
with Anne Heywood.

Opposite: Yugoslav heart-
throb Bekim Fehmiu in *The
Adventurers* (Lewis Gilbert,
1970).

pawnbroker, real good. I'll do things you never even dreamed about,' she says pathetically. She strips off her dress to reveal her naked breasts, saying, 'I'll show you how pretty I am. Look, look, look.' The scene quickly flashes between the girl, Steiger and Auschwitz where girls are being forcibly scrubbed for work in the camp brothel. Nazerman sees his own wife sitting naked on a bed as a Nazi officer stands over her. Nazerman's head is smashed through the window as he is forced to look at his wife's humiliation. The girl's voice comes back: 'It don't cost nothing to look. Look. Look.' Disgusted and sick at heart, Nazerman gives the girl her coat and the money, and pushes her out. The sequence has no titillation; instead it is a poignant, moving exposition of two people's desperation.

The MPAA gave *The Pawnbroker* its blessing, much to the chagrin of the Legion (sadly, it was later reissued with cuts and Catholic approval), and Shurlock had his wish. Criticism of the Code over *The Pawnbroker* spurred the new President of the MPAA, Jack Valenti, to revise it completely, and in 1966 all the hoary old Hays restrictions were removed and replaced by a set of 'standards' based, broadly speaking, on 'good taste'.

A brief introduction indicated that the new Code was to be very different from the old. Its opening sentence explained that 'This revised Code is designed to keep in close harmony with the mores, the culture, the moral sense and the expectations of our society. The revised Code can more completely fulfil its objectives, which are:

(1) To encourage artistic expression by expanding creative freedom; and
(2) To assure that the freedom which encourages the artist remains responsible and sensitive to the standards of the larger society.'

The lengthy and detailed restrictions of the old Code were reduced to ten brief paragraphs, three of which refer to sex: 'Indecent or undue exposure of the human body shall not be presented'; 'Illicit sex relationships shall not be justified. Intimate sex scenes violating common standards of decency shall not be portrayed'; and 'Restraint and care shall be exercised in presentations dealing with sex aberrations.'

The new Code made one major innovation, for it said that 'The Administration, in approving a picture under the Code, may recommend that advertising for the picture carry the information line, "Suggested for Mature Audiences". This element of classification ran contrary to all previous policy, for the film industry in America has always been bitterly opposed to anything that might limit audiences. But Warner Brothers had introduced the SMA tag as a way out of the impasse concerning *Who's Afraid of Virginia Woolf?*, the $7½ million film

140

which had originally been rejected by the PCA.

This had been intended as a 'once-only' exception, but it set a precedent that was bound to be followed, and within six weeks *Alfie* was also released in this way, although the abortion scene clearly violated the old Code, which prohibited such a subject. In recompense a number of apparently trivial cuts were made, the studio agreeing to remove the hint of the dogs in the act of sex and leaving only a preliminary shot of them sniffing intimately at each other. It also agreed to take out a shot of Alfie throwing a woman's panties at her, as being too specific. Thirdly, there was a line, tossed by Alfie at Shelley Winters, while he is setting her up for a candid camera shot. Seemingly referring to the camera, but actually on the make for her, he says, 'Well, I've got two positions [for taking pictures] – straight up or sideways, depending on your nationality.' This, they thought, was too pointed.

The new Code thus gave official approval to the restriction of admission to certain films to adults, although use of the SMA was supposed to be cautious. However, Valenti's new Code soon foundered in face of the type of film being made by a declining industry probing new areas in an attempt to attract a different audience from that now served by television. By 1968 over half the films passed by the PCA fell into the SMA category. Interestingly, both *Alfie* and *Virginia Woolf* were rated A4 by the National Catholic Office for Motion Pictures.

Meanwhile local censorship had been dealt a severe blow by the Supreme Court decision in the Freedman Case of 1965 that existing pre-censorship systems were unconstitutional on the grounds that they failed to 'provide adequate safeguards against undue inhibition of expression'. Within months state and city censorship boards were challenged in the courts and found to be procedurally deficient. Many boards disappeared altogether; others were reformed in an attempt to comply with the court decision, but they were relatively toothless as a result.

The relaxation of the Code's stern stance and the decreasing power of the NCOMP and local censorship created an ambivalence within the industry which persisted to a degree thereafter. On the one hand, producers continued to accede to calls for restraint, even in their more lurid offerings. In *The Carpetbaggers* (1964), for instance, Carroll Baker was rephotographed in a black negligée after a nude scene had been objected to; in *Harlow* (1965), also with Carroll Baker, most of the scandalous 'facts' of the platinum blonde's love life were toned down; and in *The Victors* (1963) and *Bonnie and Clyde* (1967) extensive nude shots of (respectively) Elke Sommer and Faye Dunaway were reduced to a few tantalizing glimpses. NCOMP's dilemma was illustrated when a spokesman declared: 'If there was a classification system that worked, we would reconsider our position on nudity.'

On the other hand, many film-makers were beginning to regard the Code as irrelevant and the NCOMP as ineffectual, and increasingly the supposedly sacrosanct injunctions against excessive nudity, 'illicit' sex relationships and sex aberrations were ignored. When the Code refused its seal, films were simply exhibited through subsidiary companies which were not signatories to the Code. (Bob Hope then commented: 'Nowadays when a film is awarded the Production Code Seal, the producer cries, "Where have we failed?"')

The same *Bonnie and Clyde* which worried about Faye Dunaway's flesh thought nothing of implying oral sex, which was also an unmistakable feature of *Hurry Sundown* (1967) and two British films, *Charlie Bubbles* (1967) and *I'll Never Forget Whatsisname* (1967). Both the last two named were rejected by Code officials in 1968 and released through subsidiaries without a seal. However, *Charlie Bubbles* was rated A3 by the NCOMP, probably because its sex was more associated with pain than joy. Another British film, *Alfie* (1966), had as its hero an unrepentant philanderer and contained an abortion sequence. Lesbianism was a motivation in *The Group* (1966) and, more particularly, in *The Fox* (1968), which also included female masturbation. Casual and extra-marital sex was becoming a common plot element in films, most candidly in *Point Blank* (1967), *The Americanization of Emily*, *The Cincinnati Kid* (1965), *The Sandpiper* (1965) and *Two for the Road* (1967), among many others. The hair-trigger theme of miscegenation was tackled (though as inoffensively as one could imagine – the lovers had not had pre-marital sex, at the man's insistence!) in Stanley Kramer's *Guess Who's Coming to Dinner* (1967). And nudity, for some reason still the most

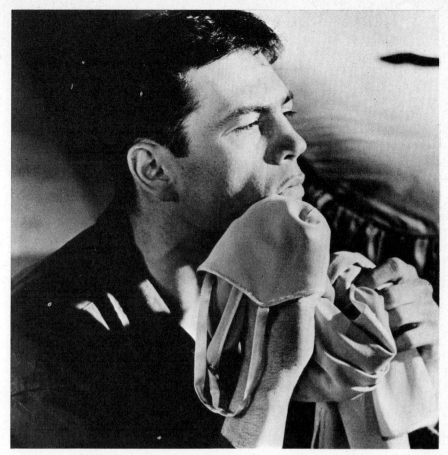

Robert Forster as the soldier in love with Elizabeth Taylor's underwear in *Reflections in a Golden Eye* (John Huston, 1967).

Opposite, top: Marlon Brando and Maria Schneider in the 'Butter Scene' from *Last Tango in Paris* (Bernardo Bertolucci, 1972).

Opposite, bottom: Oliver Reed and Georgina Hale in *The Devils* (Ken Russell, 1971).

resilient bastion, made bolder and more frequent encroachments onto the screen. The native girls in *Hawaii* (1966) no longer wore the flesh-coloured breast-cups which had so amused the dusky extras in *Mutiny on the Bounty* (1962).

Antonioni's British-made film, *Blow-Up* (1967), offered an early swift glimpse of female pubic hair. (*Blow-Up* precipitated a deadlock between the Administration and MGM, who had an enormous investment in a film which the director refused to cut by a single frame. The studio solved the problem by releasing the film through a subsidiary which it owned and which was not a specific signatory to the Code. The film was condemned by the Catholic Office and was a commercial success.) The distinguished male bare bottom positively flourished too, beginning with Anthony Quinn's in *Zorba the Greek* (1964) and continuing with Alan Bates's in *Georgy Girl* (1966), Kirk Douglas's in *The War Wagon* (1967), Paul Newman's in *Cool Hand Luke* (1967), Peter Fonda's in *The Trip* (1967), and Burt Lancaster's in *The Swimmer* (1967).

One film – John Huston's *Reflections in a Golden Eye* (1967) – seemed to incorporate everything. This catalogue of sexual hang-ups has Marlon Brando as a prissy homosexual, Elizabeth Taylor as his randy wife (displaying her rear again, only this time she used a stand-in), male *and* female nudity, voyeurism, knicker fetishism, and a next-door neighbour who has (off-screen, thank God) cut off her nipples with a pair of garden shears.

Two genres in particular seem to sum up the galloping amorality and screen permissiveness of the 'sixties: the low-budget American International pictures inspired by Jack Nicholson and Roger Corman, and the James Bond spy films and their numerous imitators.

American International, a small but enterprising independent company, started out with a successful formula for teenage beach-party films, and then, with a few fine words about 'reflecting the exciting social changes, crises, rationalizations and adjustments of society in our time', launched into a frenetic series of sensational dramatizations of modern delinquency. The most celebrated – and notorious – of these were the motorcycle and psychedelic drug pictures, particularly two directed by

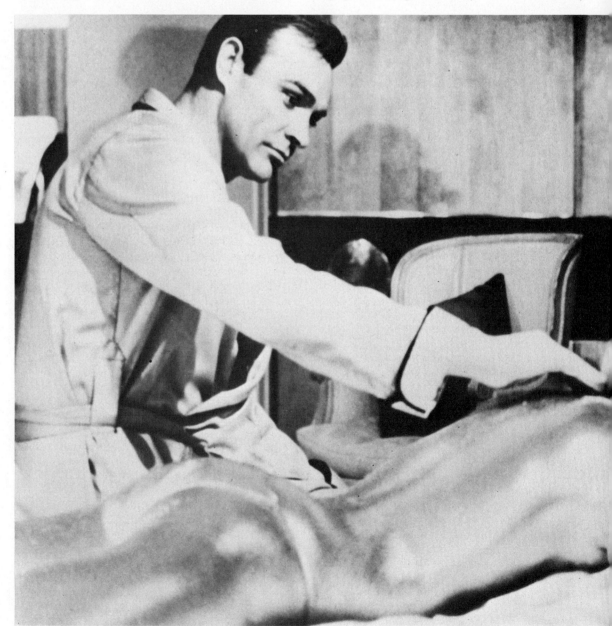

Sean Connery (as James Bond) discovers Shirley Eaton painted to death in *Goldfinger* (Guy Hamilton, 1964).

142

Roger Corman, *The Wild Angels* (1966) and *The Trip*, both starring Peter Fonda. Concentration on rape, orgies, gang-bangs, nudity and, in *The Trip*, hallucination brought on by LSD, caused the films to be condemned by NCOMP and barred abroad (e.g. in Great Britain), but they were spectacularly successful in the United States and represented a further loosening of the censors' stranglehold.

The spy genre began modestly, and without any particular expectation, with *Dr No* (1963), a tongue-in-cheek adaptation of Ian Fleming's espionage adventure, featuring public-school playboy James Bond, in which even the erotic details of the original were toned down, despite the presence of Ursula Andress. The fantasy formula and rough charm of Sean Connery caught on, and the Bond films (British-made and American-financed) turned into one of the cinema's most successful-ever series, topped by *Thunderball* (1967) and *Diamonds Are Forever* (1971), closely followed by *Goldfinger* (1964), *You Only Live Twice* (1967) and *From Russia With Love* (1964).

The secret of the Bond films' appeal was that

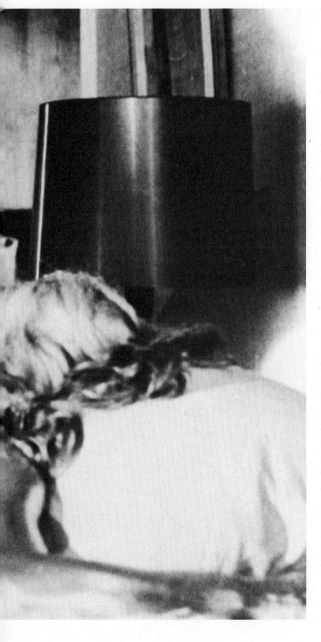

they offered vicarious sex and violence without guilt, and often spiced with sado-masochism. Their lack of realism and their high entertainment value, moreover, protected them from any serious confrontation with the censors. Spotting this, many producers jumped on the bandwagon. Columbia attempted a send-up version of Bond with *Casino Royale* (1967), a joke which misfired but was profitable none the less. Elsewhere, rival spy-heroes, strong on virility, appeared in force, including Matt Helm (played by Dean Martin) in *The Silencers* (1966), the cocky Flint (James Coburn) in *Our Man Flint* (1966), the bespectacled Harry Palmer (Michael Caine) in *The Ipcress File* (1965) and *Funeral in Berlin* (1967), 'The Men from UNCLE' (Robert Vaughn and David McCallum) in a tiresome series of TV spin-offs, and (a rare change of sex) *Modesty Blaise* (1965), incarnated on film by Monica Vitti.

Towards the end of the 'sixties a new kind of hero began to emerge, seemingly in deliberate contrast to the SuperBond image. This was the randy adolescent, setting out on his first sex safari and encountering wild beasts of unimaginable voraciousness. Peter Kastner played him in Francis Ford Coppola's *You're a Big Boy Now* (1967), and Barry Evans in the British equivalent, *Here We Go Round the Mulberry Bush* (1967). But his most successful manifestation was Dustin Hoffman in Mike Nichols's *The Graduate* (1967). Hoffman played a young, middle-class Jew who loses his innocence to the formidable Mrs Robinson (Anne Bancroft) and then complicates matters by falling in love with her daughter (Katharine Ross). Said David Shipman: 'Hoffman represented every youth trapped for the first time in the adults' world and the response of the world's youth catapulted him into superstar status.'[59]

More significant, though, was the entry of

Dean Martin and Beverly Adams in the Matt Helm spy-thriller *The Silencers* (Phil Karlson, 1966).

The Bed (1967), a Surrealistic, good-humoured celebration of uninhibited sexuality by avant-garde film-maker James Broughton.

Claudia Cardinale, earthy Italian star in the mould of Loren and Lollobrigida, in *The Legend of Frenchie King* (Christian-Jaque, 1971).

American film-making into the adults' world, as exemplified by mature, irreverent movies like *The Graduate*. In the face of intelligent, humorous film-making of this kind, Code Administrator Geoffrey Shurlock's hopeful pronouncement that, while no subject need be taboo, films should restrict themselves to 'the areas of integrity, good taste and a decent consideration for the sensibilities of the audience' no longer seemed particularly relevant.

Late in the 'sixties Valenti was forced to capitulate and abandon the Code altogether. It was replaced by a system of classification, despite the fact that only six years earlier the MPAA had pronounced that classification 'represents a dangerous infringement of the democratic American freedoms of communication and opinion and of the American tradition of parental responsibility'. The categories now in use were:

G – all ages admitted. General audiences.
GP – all ages admitted. Parental guidance suggested.
R – restricted. Under 17 requires accompanying parent or adult guardian.
X – no one under 17 admitted.

The administration remained tougher on sex than violence, true to the tradition of the Code. As early as January 1969, a commentator remarked that 'I rather suspect that the G category is really aimed against the portrayal of sex in films.' One member of the PCA resigned within six months claiming that there was too much concern with 'pubic hair and breasts'. Innocuous sex comedies devoid of full-frontal nudity were invariably rated X while violent films like *Straw Dogs* were accepted for the R category.

It was (surprisingly enough in view of its previous record) the British cinema which suddenly found itself in the van of permissiveness and social realism at the end of the 'fifties. For possibly the first time in their history, British feature films achieved international recognition and exerted a measurable influence on world cinema.

Several factors combined to produce this minor phenomenon, the most important being the massive cultural shakedown which, virtually at a stroke, lifted the drama of human relationships out of the comfortable middle-class drawing-room and dumped it rudely down in the working-class kitchen. At the same time, the new avant-garde directors like Tony Richardson, Lindsay Anderson and Karel Reisz (and even Establishment film personnel like Richard Attenborough) chose to make their films independently – just as their foreign counterparts, Bergman, Antonioni, and so on, had been doing – and their success encouraged American film-makers, traditionally shackled to the big studios, to do the same. American backers were suddenly anxious to pour huge helpings of dollars into British productions, or to set up lucrative co-productions (such as the James Bond films), while the film-makers for their part were only too happy to accept the freedom and scope for their artistic ambitions which these financial transfusions gave them.

More realism meant more explicit themes – particularly in the spheres of sex and violence – and the breaking of old cinematic taboos, and here, too, the climate proved suddenly favourable. The British censorship system (operated by the British Board of Film Censors [or BBFC]), although ineffably stuffy at times, had always been pragmatic and paternal and less influenced than America by a religiously-motivated, prurient sense of sin.

As early as 1908 'sex' films were being made in Britain. An advertisement in Kinematograph Weekly in that year referred to 'special for Gentleman Performances, Very Piquant Films and Lantern Slides', while the cinema's doubtful reputation had inclined the Electric Cinema in 1901 to proclaim its aim of showing only 'clean and moral pictures'. Calls for censorship were soon heard, but its eventual appearance came by a roundabout route.

The Cinematograph Act of 1909 was intended solely to establish safety precautions in cinemas which were vulnerable to fire hazards. Through loose drafting, however, the way was cleared for local authorities to impose conditions that were far removed from measures related to fire precaution. In 1911 the courts confirmed that the Act gave them the right to control film content. Already films were being subjected to widespread attacks in the press, while a number of chief constables declared 'with almost complete unanimity that the recent great increase in juvenile delinquency is, to a considerable extent, due to demoralizing cinematograph films'.

The rapid growth of local-authority activity encouraged the industry to seek a solution to the confusion and disruption of business that was ensuing. The trade organizations approached the Home Office, but failed to gain official support for the establishment of a national censor. In July, 1912, a meeting of exhibitors passed a motion that 'censorship is necessary and advisable' and the formation of the British Board of Film Censors was announced in November. It started work on 1 January, 1913, with the brief that it was to be 'a purely independent and impartial body, whose duty will be to induce confidence in the minds of the licensing authorities, and of those who have in their charge the moral welfare of the community generally'.

For some years the Board's situation remained precarious: the submission of films was voluntary and the autonomy of the local authorities threatened its existence. However, slowly at first, and more rapidly after the Home Office had given encouragement, the authorities began to adopt clauses in their licensing conditions that impelled cinemas to show only films certificated by the Board. By the end of 1924 the

Odile Versois and Diana Dors take to the streets in *Passport to Shame* (Alvin Rakoff, 1959).

James Fox is vamped by
Sarah Miles in *The Servant*
(Joseph Losey, 1963).

Dirk Bogarde as a man
whose homosexual past (in
the shape of Donald
Churchill) catches up with
him in *Victim* (Basil Dearden,
1961).

majority of authorities had acknowledged the Board in this way and the London County Council had introduced a set of conditions which were to form the basis of local-authority licensing for the future.

Originally the Board had only two invariable rules – no nudity and no representation of Christ – but a longer list of prohibitions was soon developed. There is no truth in the fiction that the Board has never had a written code; as early as 1917 the President, T.P. O'Connor, had evolved forty-three rules which he boasted 'cover pretty well all the grounds that you can think of'. They were indeed extremely re-strictive. On the subject of sex alone these rules prohibited the inclusion of unnecessary exhibi-tions of underclothing, of nude figures, offen-sive vulgarity, and impropriety in conduct and dress, indecorous dancing, excessively pas-sionate love scenes, bathing scenes passing the limits of propriety, subjects dealing with the premeditated seduction of girls, 'first night' scenes, scenes suggestive of immorality, situa-tions accentuating delicate marital relations, men and women in bed together, illicit sexual relationships, prostitution and procuration, scenes depicting the effect of venereal diseases, and incidents suggestive of incestuous relations.

This comprehensive list clearly ruled out any inclusion of sex in films to be shown in Britain. The Board saw its role in terms of 'eliminating certain subjects which are altogether unsuit-able for British audiences, and further of rais-ing the general standards of films exhibited in this country'. The policy was unashamedly paternalistic and the Board worked on the assumption that cinema audiences included 'a not inconsiderable proportion of people of immature judgment'.

The essential point was, as a later President pointed out, that for its first thirty-five years 'the policy of the Board was based on the principle adopted by the trade that the cinema should provide for a family audience'. To ensure that all material was suitable, certain aspects of life were therefore entirely eliminated from the screen. Any film that depicted 'mani-festations of the pursuit of lust', 'indelicate sexual situations' or 'women leading immoral lives' were banned. As Rachael Low has noted, 'drunkenness among women, brutality to women, fights between women, prostitution and procuration, "illegal operations", brothels, rape, confinements and puerperal pains were not just to be banned if "excessive" but were actually not to be mentioned at all. Girls were not made drunk or seduced, incest and the white slave trade did not exist.'

The sort of thinking that lay behind this extraordinarily extreme approach may be gathered from a statement made by a Home Secretary of the 'twenties, Sir William Joynson-Hicks: 'One side of this question, and one of terrible and far-reaching importance, is the effect of films produced either in America or in this country and exhibited in India and in the East, showing the white woman as an object of degradation . . . it is undoubtedly essential that all nations which rule in Eastern countries should see to it that the pride and character of their womanhood is maintained unimpaired.'

Very soon the Board was able to boast that its influence was 'having the desired effect of eliminating certain subjects which are alto-gether unsuitable for British audiences'. Ad-vances being made by film-makers abroad were entirely hidden from the British public and film-makers. Rachael Low has concluded that 'To some extent the very poverty of imagination in British film production, and the early con-tempt in which it was held, may have been due to the fact that people simply did not know what could be done, and in fact was being done abroad, with the film medium.'

The coming of Sound in the late 'twenties added to the concern felt about the strong im-pressions that films might make on their audiences. The problems of cutting Talkies led to the practice of studying scripts at the pre-production stage, and this gave the Board an even closer control on content.

Meanwhile sex was continuing to disturb the censors. In 1925 the Board announced that it wished 'to deprecate what seems to be a growing habit with actors of both sexes to divest themselves of their clothing on slight or no provocation', lamenting the tendency even for 'leading film actresses' to pull their dresses 'well off their shoulders'.

Six years later the Board was still inveighing on the same subject, criticizing those producers 'who delight to show the female form divine in a state of attractive undress', and who, for this purpose, 'drag in scenes of undressing, bathroom scenes and the exhibition of feminine underclothing' without any real need. The Board went so far as to conclude that 'the cumulative effect of a repetition of such scenes as can be described as "suggestive" is very harmful', although, as usual, no basis for this belief was stated.

By the following year it appears that such problems were over, for the Board was able to report that 'there is a beginning of a wholesome reaction in public opinion against the emphasizing of this sex-phase of life'. This prophecy was hardly fulfilled, but the Board continued to do its best to discourage films dealing with 'the sex elements in life' up to and after the war.

Shortly after the war the Board found itself with both a new president and a new secretary on the deaths of their predecessors. While there had already been four presidents, Brooks Wilkinson had been Secretary since 1912. His influence had been one reason for the Board's resistance to change: he continued to see his job in the terms in which he had created it. His departure meant the possibility of a new approach, and Wilkinson's successor, Arthur Watkins, was prepared to concede that the 'fifties offered a different set of conditions to those existing before the First World War. However, it was not essentially the personalities involved who, over the next fifteen years, were dramatically to alter the policy of the Board, but society and events which forced evolution upon them.

In Britain, as in America, the effects of affluence and, in particular, television had brought an end to the cinema as the main form of mass entertainment. By 1950 admissions had ceased to rise and were starting the rapid slide that continues today. In an attempt to appeal to audiences other than the family, which had hitherto been considered the only economic unit, the cinema was forced to venture into new areas.

In 1951 the X certificate was introduced, limiting audiences to people over the age of sixteen. The Board announced this as a move towards 'the reduction of censorship for adults to the minimum', but continued to affirm its intention to remove 'offensive and distasteful material which cannot be regarded as entertainment and which if not excluded would in the long run do harm to the cinema's claim to that universal patronage on which its economy rests.'

The industry felt the same way, for at first the new certificate was avoided as far as possible on the outdated theory that the cinema had to appeal to all the family. The Rank circuit released the only fourteen X films throughout the 'fifties, while ABC's total of fifty was heavily concentrated in the last two or three years. As a result, the certificate was limited to largely unprepossessing material and acquired a low reputation.

In 1957 John Trevelyan became Secretary and soon began to utter statements that contrasted powerfully with those of his predecessors: 'Censorship of the Arts may still be necessary, but it should exist only to stop what is dangerous and what could degrade and harm human personality.' Under pressure from the radically changing atmosphere in the arts, the

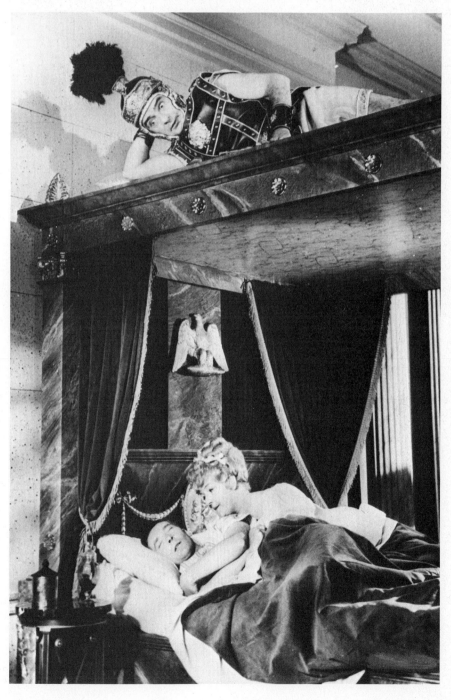

Kenneth Connor, Kenneth Williams and Joan Sims in *Carry On Cleo* (Gerald Thomas, 1964).

147

That special feeling

Recurring images of
erotic cinema: 3

Don Alvardo and Dolores
del Rio (*right*) in *The Loves
of Carmen* (**Raoul Walsh,
1927**). Erich von Stroheim
and Francilla Billington
(*centre, right*) in *Blind
Husbands* (**Stroheim,
1918**). *Onibaba* (*far right*,
Kaneto Shindo, 1964).
John Gilbert and Aileen
Pringle (*bottom*) in Elinor
Glyn's *His Hour* (**King
Vidor, 1924**).

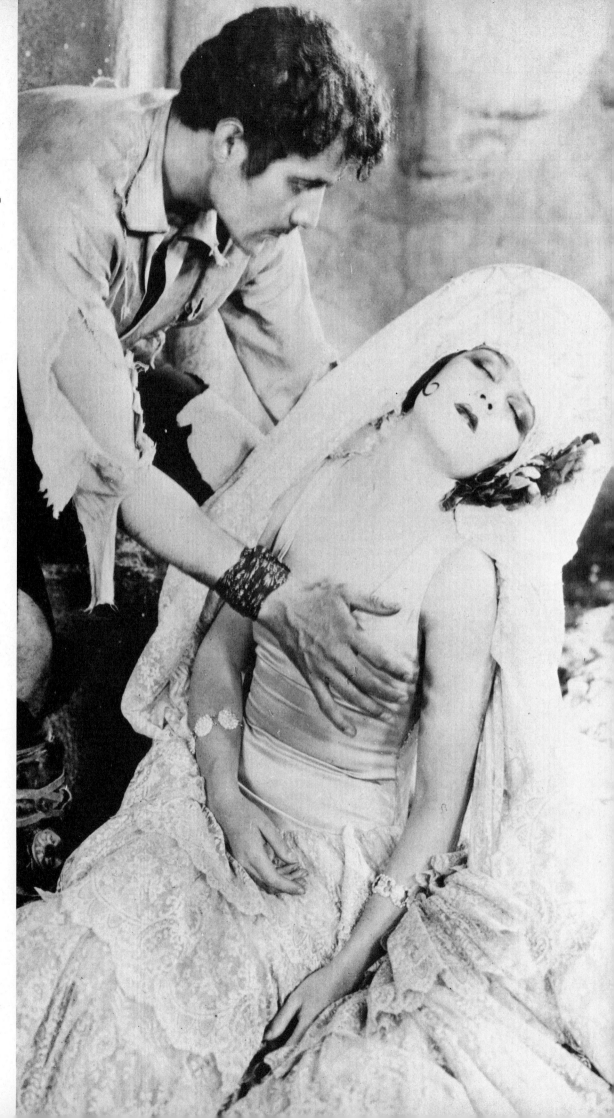

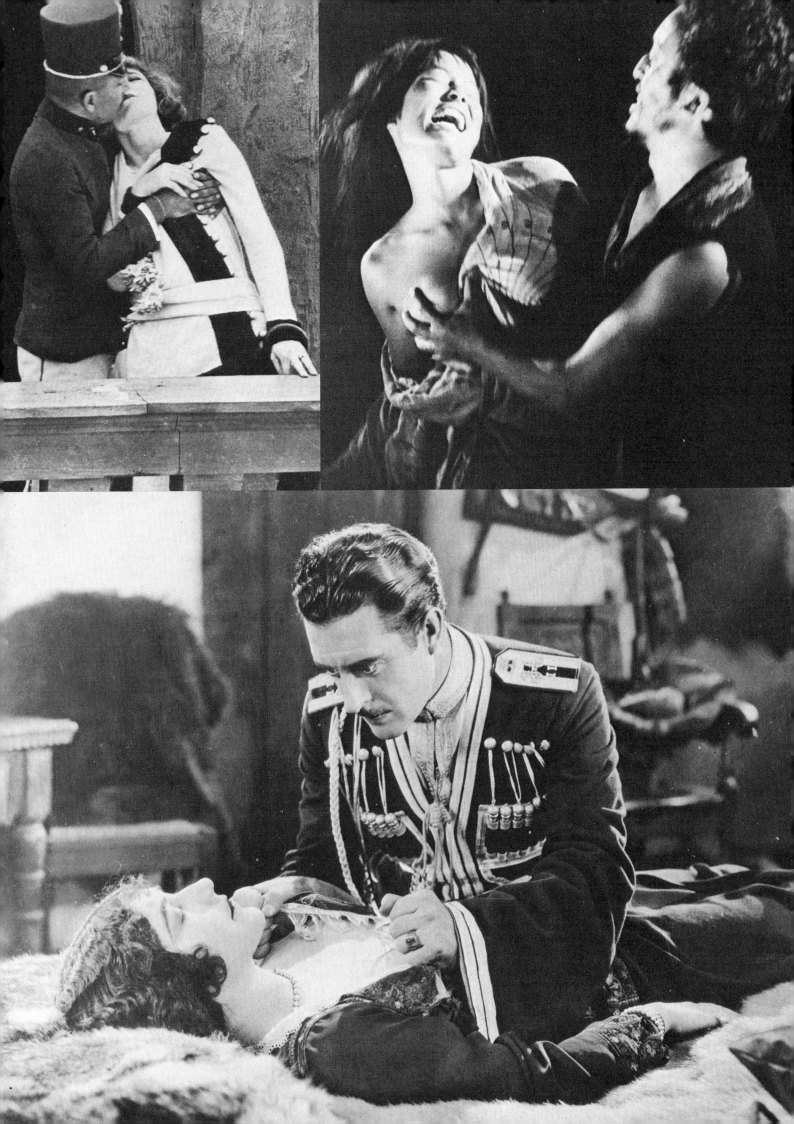

Yutte Stensgaard and Pippa
Steel in *Lust for a Vampire*
(Jimmy Sangster, 1970).

British censorship system was now ready to recognize an intelligent, responsible approach to sex, especially as it had a classification system (including the X category, for adults only) which would readily accommodate it without putting the morals of the whole nation at risk.

It was this attitude (plus, of course, the stimulating content of the films) which, in turn, encouraged American distributors to defy their own Code by showing the offending movies without a seal. They did this by forming quasi-independent subsidiary distribution companies not answerable to the Code's authority. There even came a point where over-exposure which had been cut from British films by the Board (such as the nude swimming scene in *Here We Go Round the Mulberry Bush*) was

retained for American distribution.

The first glimmerings of a harder, more serious approach to sex and other adult themes in the British cinema had appeared in the latter half of the 'fifties, although the films themselves weren't always much to write home about. There was a particular vogue for drab, doom-laden dramas about the evils of prostitution, among which *The Flesh is Weak* (1957) acquired an inflated reputation after running into censorship trouble. More typical was *Passport to Shame* (1959), which starred England's very own home-grown sex symbol, Diana Dors. Said the Monthly Film Bulletin (of the British Film Institute): 'This wildly incredible story introduced as a social document by Fabian of the Yard [a famous ex-Scotland Yard detective] must be the most wholeheartedly absurd prostitute drama yet.' This film and others like it were usually poor imitations of no less dismal Continental imports, such as *Girl of Shame* (1958, made by Veit Harlan, a one-time director of pernicious Nazi propaganda films) which tackled both prostitution and drug addiction, and *Dolls of Vice* (1958), a white-slave melodrama which came in for a good deal of scissorwork and drew some rare tongue-in-cheekiness from the Bulletin ('Several climaxes appear to have been cut by the censor').

Curiously, the critics' attitude to censorship at this time was often a good deal less bold than the films which suffered from it. When *Expresso Bongo* (1959), a mild send-up of the pop-music scene with a pimp (Laurence Harvey) as its main character, was given an A certificate, allowing children to see it in the company of adults, one commentator said: 'The censor seems to have viewed the film with an indulgent eye (and ear). Parents who take children should be warned to expect embarrassment.'[60]

A number of previously untouchable topics had begun to creep into movie plots, sometimes incidentally, sometimes as a principal theme. *Town on Trial* (1957) was a thoughtful crime drama in which detective John Mills explores the murder of a pregnant girl. *The Story of Esther Costello* (1957) depicted – though not too explicitly – the rape of a blind, dumb and deaf girl (played by Heather Sears). *A Question of Adultery* (1958) was about a sterile man who takes out a divorce action when his wife receives artificial insemination. *Sapphire* (1959) delved into race prejudice and miscegenation. *Too Young to Love* (1960) traced a fifteen-year-old's sufferings, from seduction through abortion to syphilis. *Never Take Sweets from a Stranger* (1960), *The Mark* (1961) and *Term of*

Trial (1962, with Laurence Olivier and newcomer Sarah Miles) were all centred on the seduction or assault of under-age girls. *Peeping Tom* (1960) was a more than usually explicit exercise in perversion and morbid sadism. And *No Love for Johnnie* (1961) dragged extramarital sex into the sacred world of politics.

The most significant breakthrough, perhaps – or at least the most controversial – was the recognition of homosexuality as a valid dramatic theme. It first cropped up as a crucial part of the plot in *Serious Charge* (1959), in which Anthony Quayle, as a vicar who runs a youth club, is falsely accused of assaulting a teenage boy. It was self-evident in *Oscar Wilde* and *The Trials of Oscar Wilde* (both 1960). And it was the underlying corrupting force in Joseph Losey's celebrated study of decadence, *The Servant* (1963).

The bravest film to tackle this tricky subject was *Victim* (1961), with Dirk Bogarde, which dared not only to have as its leading character a man with a homosexual past, but also to plead strongly and humanely for a repeal of the obnoxious laws which exposed homosexuals to the constant, terrifying threat of blackmail. Said Bogarde in an interview with Barry Norman in The Times: 'It was the first film to treat homosexuality seriously. It was the first film in which a man said "I love you" to another man. I wrote that scene in. I said "There's no point in half measures. We either make a film about queers or we don't." I believe that picture made a lot of difference to a lot of people's lives.'

Not least, as it happened, to his own, and not so much for the obvious reason that the theme had tarnished his heart-throb image. Suddenly, the hordes of adoring teeny-boppers who had made him the biggest British movie

Yvonne Mitchell (*centre*) as the sluttish wife in *Woman in a Dressing Gown* (J. Lee-Thompson, 1957), with Sylvia Syms and Anthony Quayle.

151

Above: Laurence Harvey and Simone Signoret in Jack Clayton's *Room at the Top* (1959).

Right: Richard Burton and Mary Ure in John Osborne's *Look Back in Anger* (Tony Richardson, 1959).

Opposite, top: Rachel Roberts and Albert Finney in *Saturday Night and Sunday Morning* (Karel Reisz, 1960).

Far right: Alan Bates tries to titillate June Ritchie with a nudie magazine in *A Kind of Loving* (John Schlesinger, 1962).

star ever to remain faithful to the native film scene, simply vanished into thin air. 'Overnight,' he said, 'I didn't have a single fan left – not because I had portrayed a homosexual (because in England the word "queer" used to mean that you weren't feeling very well, so they didn't get it anyway) as much as I had played the part of a man of forty-five, which was my real age. "You're old," wrote the shattered fans who could still bring themselves to put pen to paper. "You're older than my dad!"'

There were lighter aspects to the British cinema's more permissive mood at the end of the 'fifties. In 1959, for example, Britain had taken a belated cue from Swedish and other foreign imports and launched her first nudist-camp film, *Nudist Paradise*, an innocuous piece of supposed propagandizing on behalf of naturism, full of coy poses backed by an excruciatingly nudging commentary. So harmless was it considered to be, in fact, that it earned nothing more censorious than an A certificate, which meant that children (accompanied by an adult) could, if they so wished, get their first legitimate glimpse of the full female bosom in the cinema. There followed numerous similar celebrations of the goose-pimple, including one (*Some Like It Cool*, 1961) directed by Michael Winner.

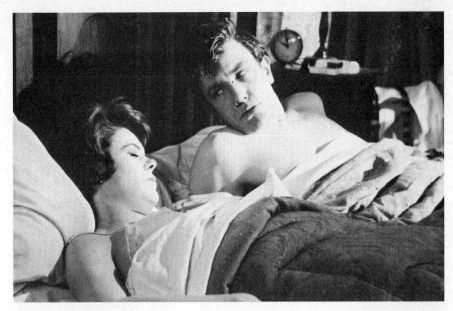

This watershed period in British film-making also saw the birth of two peculiarly indigenous genres – the *Carry On* . . . film and the Hammer horror movie. The seemingly never-ending series of farces produced by Peter Rogers, written by Talbot Rothwell and directed by Gerald Thomas began innocently enough with *Carry On Sergeant* (1958) and then got rapidly into its vulgar stride with *Carry On Nurse* (1959), *Carry On Teacher* (1959) and *Carry On Constable* (1960), since when it has blithely

Richard Harris attempts to break down Rachel Roberts's frigidity in *This Sporting Life* (Lindsay Anderson, 1963).

milked the same lavatorial jokes through more than a score of successive movies, without losing any popularity.

The appeal of the *Carry On* ... films lies in their uniquely English flavour, deriving partly from the traditions of bawdy British music-hall. What they most resemble, though, are Donald McGill's celebrated saucy seaside postcards, with their shameless emphasis on breasts, buttocks and *double entendres*. Barbara Windsor, opulently endowed doyenne of the *Carry On* ... films, could almost have stepped out of one of McGill's pink-cheeked drawings.

The Gothic horror film, previously the preserve of Hollywood, was first successfully moulded to the British market by Hammer in 1958 with Terence Fisher's *Dracula*, which apart from setting another interminable trend, ensured regular, lucrative employment thereafter for its two stars, Peter Cushing and Christopher Lee. Although blood and mayhem have always been the prime contents of the Hammer productions and their countless imitators, sexual sadism was never far from the surface and became an increasingly overt part of the proceedings as producers tried to wring yet more variations out of the Dracula and

Frankenstein themes – even to the point of transferring the traditional focus for the fanged bite from the jugular vein to the female nipple in *The Vampire Lovers* (1970)!

Dominating all these peripheral trends and developments, however, was the cultural revolution which temporarily transformed the British cinema from a medium of tired entertainment into an authentic branch of the social arts. The whirlwind of change had first blown up in the theatre, where John Osborne's epoch-making play, 'Look Back in Anger', had scythed through all the Establishment's concepts of what constituted Good Drama. The terms 'kitchen sink', 'angry young man' and 'anti-hero' were coined and became common currency, and a new, refreshing wave of social realism swept through British drama, literature and film-making.

Ted (later Lord) Willis was responsible for the first tentative steps towards the kitchen sink in the cinema, with adaptations of his plays *Woman in a Dressing Gown* (1957) and *No Trees in the Street* (1959). The first of these – about a sluttish, middle-aged woman unable to cope with her husband's infidelity with his secretary – retained a certain reputation as a

154

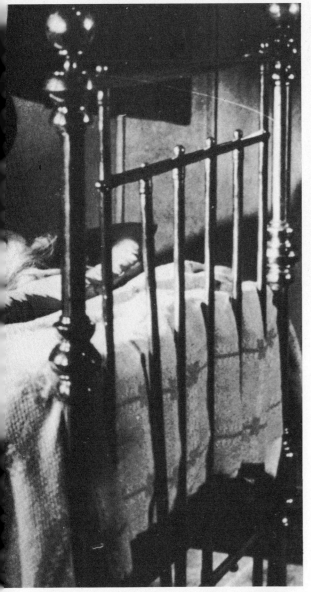

bold study of adultery and menopause among the working classes, thanks largely to a pivotal performance by Yvonne Mitchell, but neither film stood the test of time. *Woman in a Dressing Gown* was really little more than a poor man's *Brief Encounter*, while *No Trees in the Street*, a social problem picture about London slum life, never rose above being drab, hysterical and depleted. More importantly, though, both movies dared to depict, with some attempt at explicitness and authenticity, the life and problems – including the sexual hang-ups – of ordinary men and women.

The time was ripe for a much more audacious response to the new cultural climate, and in 1958 Jack Clayton duly obliged with his screen version of John Braine's *Room at the Top*. This told the cynical tale of Joe Lampton (Laurence Harvey), an ambitious clerk in

The aphrodisiacal eating scene from *Tom Jones* (Tony Richardson, 1963), with Albert Finney and Joyce Redman.

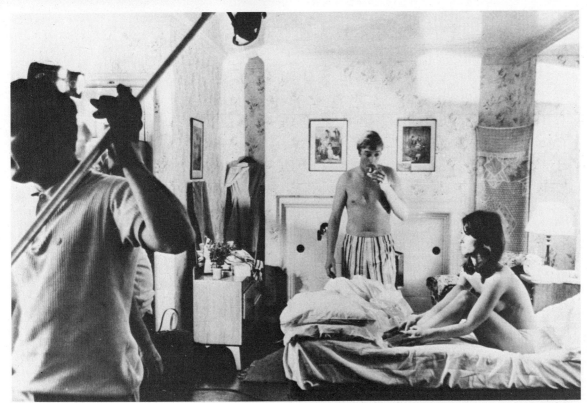

Michael Caine takes a break between seductions during the shooting of *Alfie* (Lewis Gilbert, 1966).

155

industrial Yorkshire who makes his boss's daughter (Heather Sears) pregnant in order to marry into the family wealth, despite his passion for his married mistress (Simone Signoret). Peter John Dyer spoke with mild disparagement of the film's 'slightly self-conscious determination to bring sex to the British screen',[61] but its significance went deeper than that. It was virtually the first reputable, critically acclaimed main feature to earn an X certificate and profit by it, and its success encouraged other respectable directors to tackle more adventurous themes in a proletarian setting.

With the flood-gates opened, British cinema suddenly came alive and kicking into the new decade. The progenitor of the whole revival, *Look Back in Anger*, was brought faithfully to the screen in 1959 by Tony Richardson, with Richard Burton as Jimmy Porter, the frustrated, embittered working-class intellectual who vents his scorn for the bourgeois Establishment on his pregnant, middle-class wife (Mary Ure), and has an affair with her best friend (Claire Bloom). This was followed in 1960 by another Richardson/Osborne collaboration, *The Entertainer*, with Laurence Olivier repeating his triumphant stage role as Archie Rice, faded pier-end comic and seducer of beauty queens. Shirley Anne Field played one such conquest, and Albert Finney had a small part as the younger son who dies in the abortive Suez campaign.

These two went on to star in the smash hit of 1960, Alan Sillitoe's *Saturday Night and Sunday Morning*, directed by Karel Reisz, the most uncompromising slice of working-class life up to that time. This saga of an irresponsible Nottingham factory worker (Albert Finney) who conducts a carefree affair with the wife (Rachel Roberts) of a colleague (Bryan Pringle) on the night shift and seduces a hard-bitten teaser (Shirley Anne Field) only to be trapped into marriage, contained some startlingly frank sequences, including an implied, tragi-comic abortion scene in which Rachel Roberts fails to dislodge her unwelcome foetus with a hot bath and a bottle of gin. Despite critical approval and the censor's indulgence, the film was too strong for some local authorities, who banned it.

The critical success of 1961 was another Tony Richardson film, *A Taste of Honey*, adapted from Shelagh Delaney's play about a teenage girl (Rita Tushingham) who is seduced by an itinerant Negro sailor (Paul Danquah) and cared for throughout pregnancy by an overt homosexual (Murray Melvin). This oddly romantic tale broke further new ground with its unabashed handling of miscegenation and Murray Melvin's camp, but quite serious, sympathetic and well-observed characterization as the homosexual. It was, strangely, Miss Delaney who later commented sadly that 'the cinema has become more and more like the theatre; it's all mauling and muttering'.

Similar in mood and frankness of theme was John Schlesinger's *A Kind of Loving* (1962), adapted from Stan Barstow's novel about a draughtsman (Alan Bates) who can't come to terms with his shotgun marriage to a girl (June Ritchie) he lusts after but doesn't love. This is claimed to be the first film in which a man is depicted buying contraceptives. Bates enters a chemist's shop with the intention of purchasing condoms but is overcome by shyness and emerges to present his eager friend (James Bolam) with a bottle of health tonic! This sequence was thought greatly daring at the time. More extra-marital pregnancy, with Leslie Caron the long-sufferer, occurred in Bryan Forbes's *The L-Shaped Room* (1962), which also tested another taboo with its clear references to lesbianism. *The Leather Boys* (1963) treated homosexuality more ambiguously with its story of a teenage ton-up boy who marries a

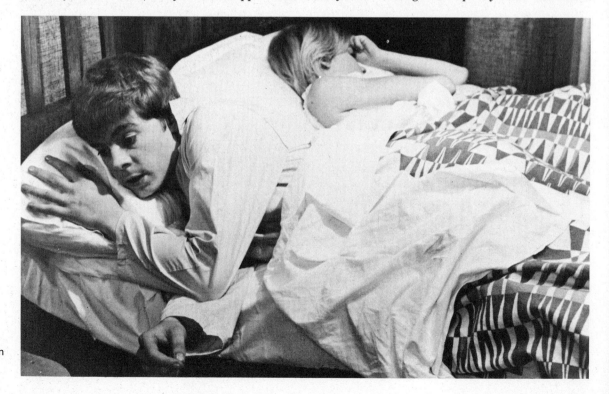

Frustration for young newlyweds Hywel Bennett and Hayley Mills, unable to consummate their marriage in *The Family Way* (Roy Boulting, 1966).

156

schoolgirl but abandons her for the companionship of a fellow motorcycle enthusiast.

The high point of this brief, vintage period of British social realism was reached in 1963 with Lindsay Anderson's film of the David Storey novel, *This Sporting Life*, about a Yorkshire miner who becomes a professional rugby player and nurses an intense but unfulfilled passion for his sexually turned-off, widowed landlady. The strength of Anderson's film, as with the others of its genre, lay in its candid, serious and totally adult approach to the sexual problems of its characters and the way they are affected by their social background. Extensive location shooting, ranging from dockside to dance-hall (and to which, despite their theatrical and/or literary origins, these pieces proved readily adaptable), added the extra dimension of reality.

As film-makers became more confident in their handling of erotic themes, and the censor, impressed with the artistic integrity of the new directors, became increasingly indulgent, so sex took on a more prominent and unashamed role in all types of films. Comedies and satires, in particular, began to have a field day. Sidney Gilliat's *Only Two Can Play* (1962, from the Kingsley Amis novel, 'That Uncertain Feeling') gave audiences a glimpse of Mai Zetterling's bare bottom in its story of a randy Welsh librarian (Peter Sellers) and his failure (in true British tradition) to consummate an affair with the willing wife of a local dignitary; and in *Live Now – Pay Later* (1962), Ian Hendry's door-to-door salesman gave his housewifely customers more satisfaction than they were likely to get from their hire-purchase agreements.

The comic blockbuster of the early 'sixties was Tony Richardson's ambitious, bawdy, trend-setting, multi-Academy Award-winning adaptation of Henry Fielding's satirical eighteenth-century novel, *Tom Jones* (1963). This free-wheeling affair, full of over-imitated cinematic tricks such as speeded-up action and characters talking to camera, made few concessions to conventional movie morality with its story of a bastard son (Albert Finney) who loves the daughter (Susannah York) of his adoptive father (Hugh Griffith) but can't resist sowing a few wild oats round the county.

The film became famous for its abandoned sexual encounters, for its superbly erotic, aphrodisiacal eating scene between Finney and Joyce Redman, and for the latter's deliciously wry glance at the camera (i.e. audience) on learning (erroneously, as it turns out) that the same Tom Jones with whom she has romped the night away is her very own son. In 1965, Terence Young tried to exploit the success of *Tom Jones* by adapting a trio of Daniel Defoe novels and calling the result *The Amorous Adventures of Moll Flanders*, but in spite of the obvious erotic charms of Kim Novak and the presence of a prestige cast, it was heavy going and proved only that Richardson's film had milked the formula dry.

Directors thereafter favoured sex comedies

Intruders Tony Beckley and Norman Rodway rape Suzy Kendall in *The Penthouse* (Peter Collinson, 1967).

with more modern settings. One of the most enjoyable was another by-product of the theatrical new wave, Ann Jellicoe's *The Knack* ('... and how to get it', 1965), directed by Richard Lester, a gentle satire on innocence and amorality about a shy young teacher (Michael Crawford) who learns his friend's (Ray Brooks) knack with girls and wins Rita Tushingham. Another character who had the 'knack' was *Alfie* (1966), Bill Naughton's Cockney philanderer, whose string of carefree seductions and line in candid sex-chat established Michael Caine's screen image and promoted him to international stardom.

Alfie inspired a brief mini-genre of jocular British comedies with serious socio-sexual undertones, including another Bill Naughton adaptation, *The Family Way* (1966), in which domestic circumstances make it hard for Hywel Bennett to consummate his brand-new marriage to Hayley Mills (who finally lost her celluloid innocence in a modest nude scene), and the over-modish *Georgy Girl* (1966), in which Alan Bates, having impregnated his girlfriend

Julie Christie in her Oscar-winning performance as John Schlesinger's *Darling . . .* (1965).

Charlotte Rampling), seduces her ugly-duckling room-mate (Lynn Redgrave) while she's away having the baby; James Mason, to complete the four-sided triangle, played a slavering sugar-daddy who lusts after Lynn. Eventually, and inevitably, the old-fashioned smutty British farce met the new permissiveness half-way to produce bland, polarized pictures like *Prudence and the Pill* (1968), a thin joke about a mother's contraceptive pills being swapped for aspirins.

As the 'sixties ran their course, British film-makers tried, with only limited success, to recapture the heady flavour of social realism with which the decade had so splendidly begun. Edna O'Brien's Irish romance, 'The Lonely Girl', filmed as *Girl with Green Eyes* (1964), about an innocent farmer's daughter (Rita Tushingham) who lives with a worldly, middle-aged writer (Peter Finch), was pleasant but novelettish. Another literary adaptation, Somerset Maugham's *Of Human Bondage* (1964), failed to retain the subtle eroticism of the original novel and became merely sordid, largely through the miscasting of Kim Novak as Mildred, the waitress turned prostitute. *Life at the Top* (1965), likewise, though it retained Laurence Harvey as Joe Lampton, was a pale and clumsy sequel to *Room at the Top*. An early Michael Winner effort, *The System* (1964), about casual seaside sex, was merely synthetic.

Anthony Simmons's *Four in the Morning* (1965), a double-tale about the sexual crises of two couples during one night, had pretensions which nearly came off, thanks to fine acting by Judi Dench, Norman Rodway, Joe Melia and Ann Lynn, and evocative Thames-side locations. Two adaptations of Nell Dunn's lively, observant books about life in the raw in South London, Peter Collinson's *Up the Junction* and Ken Loach's *Poor Cow* (both 1967), did good

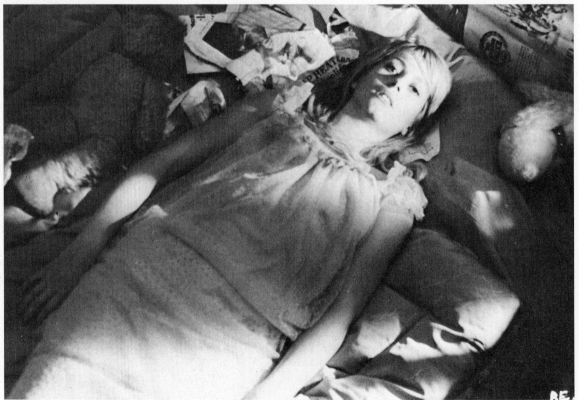

Roman Polanski's *Repulsion* (1965), with Catherine Deneuve as the schizophrenic whose rape fantasies drive her to murder.

158

business – the former exceptionally so – but lost much of the original's rampant eroticism. Another Peter Collinson drama, *The Penthouse* (1967), about a married man and his mistress tormented by psychopaths in an apartment, was simply an unpleasant and exploitative piece of sex-sadism, matched in pointlessness only by Jack Cardiff's *Girl on a Motorcycle* (1968), in which Marianne Faithfull emoted erotically in a riot of black leather and zips. Much better was David Greene's wry study of a novice policeman, *The Strange Affair* (1968), climaxed by a remarkably steamy bath scene involving Michael York and the nubile Susan George.

The British film with the biggest international reputation at this time was John Schlesinger's *Darling . . .* (1965), which cornered three Academy Awards, including one for its female star, Julie Christie. This succeeded by seeming to capture the trendy amorality of the times in its story of the rise and fall of a hard, ambitious young model (Julie Christie) who jilts her lover (Dirk Bogarde) and has an abortion, only to sink into depravity and a lonely marriage to a rich Italian nobleman.

Oddly enough, the most original talent to emerge on the British film scene in the latter half of the 'sixties was not a Briton at all, but an expatriate Pole called Roman Polanski. This former actor had made his reputation in Poland with a surrealistic short, *Two Men and a Wardrobe* (1958), and a disturbing feature, *Knife in the Water* (1962), which revealed his interest in the neurotic behaviour of people at sexual odds with each other. Yet his themes were regarded as bizarre and anti-social – 'the product,' according to the Polish Communist Party, 'of an over-stimulated and sick imagination' – and he deemed it prudent to leave his native country. Settling mainly in Britain, he has demonstrated in his English-language films an amused, sometimes cruel interest in people's sexual obsessions, emphasizing the sadistic and the perverse.

Repulsion (1965), with Catherine Deneuve, was a brilliant and horrifying study of schizophrenia in a girl pathologically revolted by sex, who has grotesque rape fantasies and ends up slaughtering her boyfriend and landlord in hideous fashion. *Repulsion* can also claim a dubious first for reproducing the sounds of orgasm most realistically, albeit off-screen! *Cul-de-Sac* (1966) had Donald Pleasence, as a pathetic transvestite, and Françoise Dorléac, as his French wife (permitted a muted nude scene by the censor), forced to harbour wounded criminals. And *Rosemary's Baby* (1968), made in the USA and Polanski's first commercial success, delved into the more erotic areas of black magic (the censor objecting to one brief scene in which Rosemary, played by Mia Farrow, is tied to a bed prior to impregnation by the Devil; the rape was acceptable but not the bondage). Latterly, Polanski's standing suffered somewhat following a badly botched satirical horror movie, *Dance of the Vampires* (1967), and a tedious *Candy*-style sex fantasy, *What?* (1974), although his highly subjective version

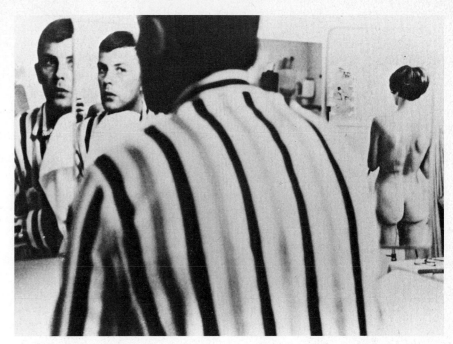

of *Macbeth* (1971) contained some interesting ideas, including a youthful, naked Lady Macbeth (Francesca Annis).

Permissiveness in British movies took one more major step forward in the final years of the 'sixties when the first transient shots of full-frontal female nudity were passed by the censor. The total ban on nudity had survived until 1950. After that date it began to be gradually eroded, first in foreign films like the Swedish *One Summer of Happiness*. In the mid-'fifties there was a spate of American, and later British, nudist films. At first the Board had refused to pass these, but when local authorities accepted them in large numbers, it was forced to change its policy. Over the following ten years even greater expanses of flesh were allowed, but strict limits were still operative in 1964 when the President noted that 'clearly the exhibition of human genital organs would in general be objectionable, but not (unless offensively pictured) breasts, chests, or buttocks. Nor should

Sven-Bertil Taube and Agneta Ekmanner in Jonas Cornell's *Hugs and Kisses* (1966), the first film in which the British Board of Film Censors gave its official blessing to pubic hair.

David Hemmings's sexual romp with a pair of photographic models in *Blow-Up* (Michelangelo Antonioni, 1967) gave British audiences their second glimpse of pubic hair.

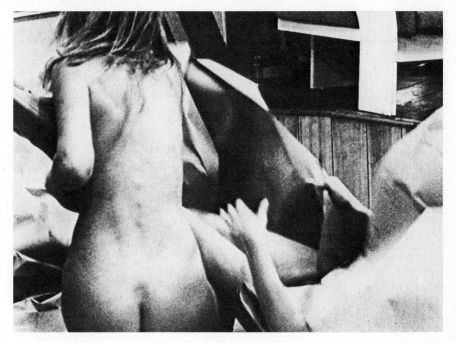

the sexual act be implied, nor physical caresses.' By this time nudes were even admitted in 'dramatic or other' films, provided that 'the sight of the nude is not prolonged', though 'there might be objection to full breasts in such circumstances'.

This double standard seems comical but it is not entirely illogical. Part of the Board's function is to protect films from prosecution, and while nudist and other sex films appeal to a small and pre-selected audience in specialized cinemas, other films may be seen by a wider section of the population, more likely to be offended or shocked if not actually corrupted.

Somehow the Board must gauge public opinion, although, in effect, it is more concerned with judging what local authorities will allow, for they hold the statutory power and are theoretically supposed to represent the wishes of the electorate. In fact throughout the 'fifties and 'sixties the authorities were more liberal than the censors. Many films banned by the Board were passed for local exhibition up and down the country, while reversals in the other direction were extremely rare. Yet few local authorities aroused controversy or opposition as a result of their actions.

The female full-frontal breakthrough came not in any dubious products of the sexploitation market, but in three highly regarded films by reputable film-makers, Jonas Cornell's *Hugs and Kisses* (1966), Antonioni's *Blow-Up* (1967) and Lindsay Anderson's *If . . .* (1968).

Hugs and Kisses, said John Trevelyan later, was the turning-point as far as the pudendum was concerned. The vital scene was one in which a woman is shown standing and admiring herself before a mirror, her pubic hair plainly revealed. At first, the BBFC cut the shot, but later reinstated it, thus making pubic hair acceptable thereafter on both stage and screen.

Blow-Up, however, in which female pubic hair is briefly revealed during a mini-orgy scene involving photographer David Hemmings and two models, was of particular interest because of its timing. The Board of Film Censors were in the middle of a public row caused by their decision to cut a similar glimpse of pubic hair from a Yugoslavian film which, being by an unknown director and having no critical pedigree, they had dismissed as of no account. This was Dusan Makavejev's *The Switchboard Operator* (1967), which was quickly recognized by the *cognoscenti* as a film of some merit and not one to be lightly snipped at by the censor. Embarrassingly for the Board, in the midst of the controversy *Blow-Up*, which had met with their approval on artistic grounds, pubic hair and all, entered distribution and made their decision on *The Switchboard Operator* look patently ridiculous.

Such errors of judgment had been almost inevitable since the middle of the decade when the Board made a major break with tradition and began to take quality into consideration. Trevelyan was loath to interfere with films of real merit, but the new approach also involved more pragmatic motives, for it was clearly felt that more intellectual audiences could be allowed a stronger helping of sex on the grounds that they were less likely to be shocked or offended. In addition the paternalistic belief that the less educated were more corruptible still remained. Trevelyan later said, 'We used

The fuss over Eva Ras's pubic hair in *The Switchboard Operator* (1967) brought fortuitous fame to talented Yugoslav film-maker Dusan Makavejev and led to a more tolerant attitude to censorship in Britain.

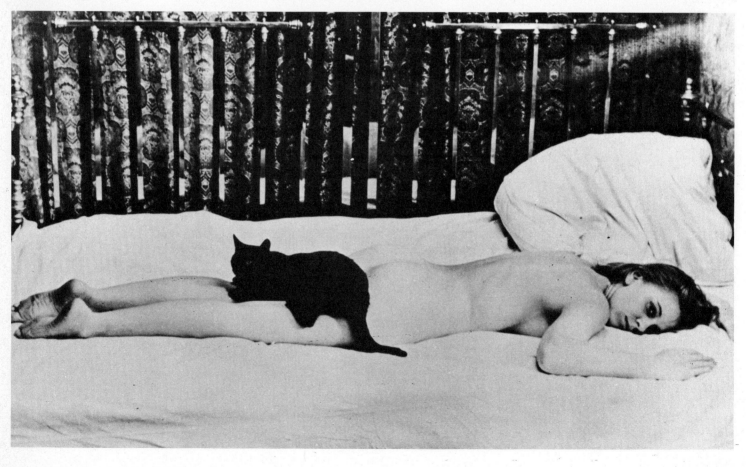

at this time to be more generous to sex scenes in films with foreign dialogue than to films with English dialogue, since the former usually had a more limited distribution, normally only to art theatres, and were less likely to produce criticism.'

This policy naturally led to difficulties in deciding which films merited this special treatment. The Board, with no particular qualifications as film critics, tended to rely to some extent on the reputation of the director and this can lead to an underestimation of films by relatively unknown makers. *The Switchboard Operator* (or *Love Dossier* as it was first called) was submitted to the Board by a small company with the accompanying message: 'I am sending you a film which has a few tits in it. I don't think much of it but I can sell it to the sex theatres.' Trevelyan and his colleagues were similarly unimpressed and made considerable cuts.

Nevertheless the Board's new approach led to a much greater freedom in its decision-making, and while it may be impossible to defend logically, its results have been beneficial. The affair of *The Switchboard Operator* had a happy

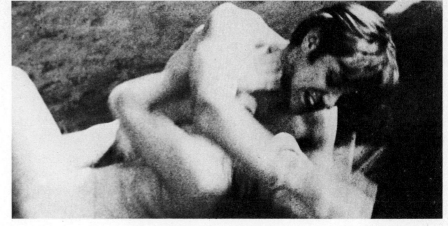

outcome too. The effect on British censorship was that much more beneficial, for the Board immediately relaxed its attitude to female nudity, gave its blessing to Christine Noonan's full exposure in *If . . .* , and adjusted itself to taking a far more lenient line on the sexual content of the films in the fast-approaching 'seventies.

Malcolm McDowell made explicit love to a briefly full-frontal Christine Noonan in this fantasy sex scene from Lindsay Anderson's *If . . .* (1968).

From Europe with Love

The liberated film-makers of Continental Europe continued to set world cinema trends in the 'sixties from both an artistic and an erotic point of view. The trick – still only half understood in Britain and America – was to make art and eroticism go hand in hand, thus allowing sex to ride profitably on the back of respectability.

Not that the best directors necessarily took this equation into account – they merely harnessed their artistic instincts to the exploration of themes which interested them most, and sex in human relationships naturally came high on their list. There was, it is true, a ceaseless outpouring from the Continent of worthless, drab, unrevealing dramas, purporting to be social documents, about prostitution, unmarried mothers, homosexuality, smalltown immorality, and so on, but these were simply an inevitable, exploitative by-product of the success formula stumbled upon by doyens like Bergman, Fellini, Antonioni and their peers.

The importance of these master film-makers to the English-speaking cinema was threefold: they expanded the artistic and erotic possibilities of movie-making and inspired emulation; they demonstrated that art, as well as sex (but usually the two combined), could equal profits; and they helped to eradicate the more senseless repressions of British and American censorship (although the censors of both countries still rallied occasionally to fight a rearguard action against what they regarded as liberty-taking).

The 'sixties began in a flurry of controversy and inconsistency as the first wave of critically acclaimed but sexually ultra-liberated foreign films reached the British and American markets,

some of them several years old. Bergman's delightful study of young love leading to disillusionment, *Summer with Monika*, made in 1952, was given an A certificate (children accompanied by adults) in Britain, despite a decorous but revealing shot of Harriet Andersson stepping into a lake with nothing on. Claude Chabrol's *Les Cousins* (1958) was permitted to preach the message that sensuality and unfettered eroticism are good for you. *The Case of Dr Laurent* (1957) was climaxed by a real-life, unblinkingly photographed childbirth – a deliberate act of medical propaganda. And *Huis Clos* (made in 1954), though inexplicit in visual terms, explored without undue interference Sartre's hellish triangle of impotence, lesbianism and nymphomania. Louis Malle's *The Lovers* (1958), on the other hand, hit a censorial nerve with its adulterous love-making scenes between Jeanne Moreau and Jean-Marc Bory; these were, in fact, poetic, romantic and quite modest, but had, nevertheless, to be re-edited for English eyes.

French film-making, as the above selection indicates, was particularly bold and influential at this time. Alain Resnais, one of the major talents of the *nouvelle vague*, depicted candid love-making between a Japanese man and a Frenchwoman in his multi-layered allegory of peace, love and war, *Hiroshima Mon Amour* (1958), and followed it with his celebrated, enigmatic, implicitly erotic *L'Année Dernière à Marienbad* (1961). Jean-Luc Godard, after his dazzling début with *Breathless*, explored the status of sex in and out of marriage, particularly as it relates to women, in such polemics as *Une Femme Mariée* (1964), *Masculin-Féminin* (1966) and *Deux ou Trois Choses que Je Sais d'Elle*

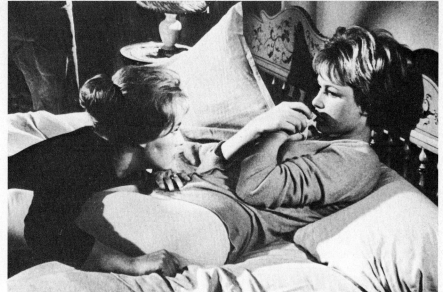

(1966). François Truffaut consolidated a more popular and lasting reputation with his dazzling study of an offbeat *ménage à trois*, *Jules et Jim* (1961), which anticipated his later, good-humoured explorations of the fragility of sexual relationships in *La Peau Douce* (1964), *Baisers Volés* (1968) and *Domicile Conjugal* (1970). Chabrol caused a small stir with his melodrama about lesbianism and bisexualism, *Les Biches* (1968). Marcel Camus enjoyed some temporary fame with his *Black Orpheus* (1958), a sensuous, occasionally bare-bosomed modern version of the Greek myth, set in Rio de Janeiro at carnival time and played entirely by black actors. Claude Autant-Lara scored a box-office success with *The Green Mare's Nest* (1959), best known and most typical of a rather silly French sub-genre devoted to bucolic rape and farmyard sex.

And Roger Vadim with his 'taste for carefully calculated eroticism'[62] soldiered blithely and stylistically on, secure in the knowledge that (as one critic said of *La Ronde*) he 'certainly knows how to photograph his ladies'. His ladies in the 'sixties – Bardot having moved on – included Annette Stroyberg, whom he directed in *Les Liaisons Dangereuses* (1960), and Jane Fonda, who undressed for him in *La Ronde* (1964), *The Game is Over* (1966) and his lively comic-strip fantasy, *Barbarella* (1968), before rebelling against the exploitation of women as sex objects. *Barbarella*, it is revealing to note, shocked audiences with its frank, freewheeling sex scenes, launched with a weightless space-strip and climaxed by a sequence in which Miss Fonda survives a machine designed to execute people by giving them prolonged orgasms. Yet only six years later it was shown on British television and provoked barely a single word of protest. Vadim's work eventually sank into absurdity with *Pretty Maids All in a Row* (1970 – Rock Hudson as a homicidal seducer of college nymphs) and *Don Juan* . . . , his 1974 reunion with Bardot. Margaret Hinxman has summed him up best – as a director 'whose films are on occasion less distinguished than his gift for remoulding interesting actresses

In Roger Vadim's *Les Liaisons Dangereuses* (1960) Jeanne Moreau solved the problem of her husband's infidelity by seducing the woman (Annette Vadim, formerly Stroyberg) she suspected he was falling in love with.

Jeanne Moreau and Jean-Marc Bory in Louis Malle's *The Lovers* (1958). Their bathtime love-in was lyrical as well as hygienic, but it had to be toned down for British release. In the States, a Supreme Court decision cleared it uncut and paved the way for greater freedom on American screens.

163

Spread a little happiness

Recurring images of
erotic cinema: 4

Glynis Johns (*right*) in *The Chapman Report* (George Cukor, 1962). Jeanne Moreau (*far right*) in *Mademoiselle* (Tony Richardson, 1965). Elliott Gould (*bottom*) in *Getting Straight* (Richard Rush, 1969).

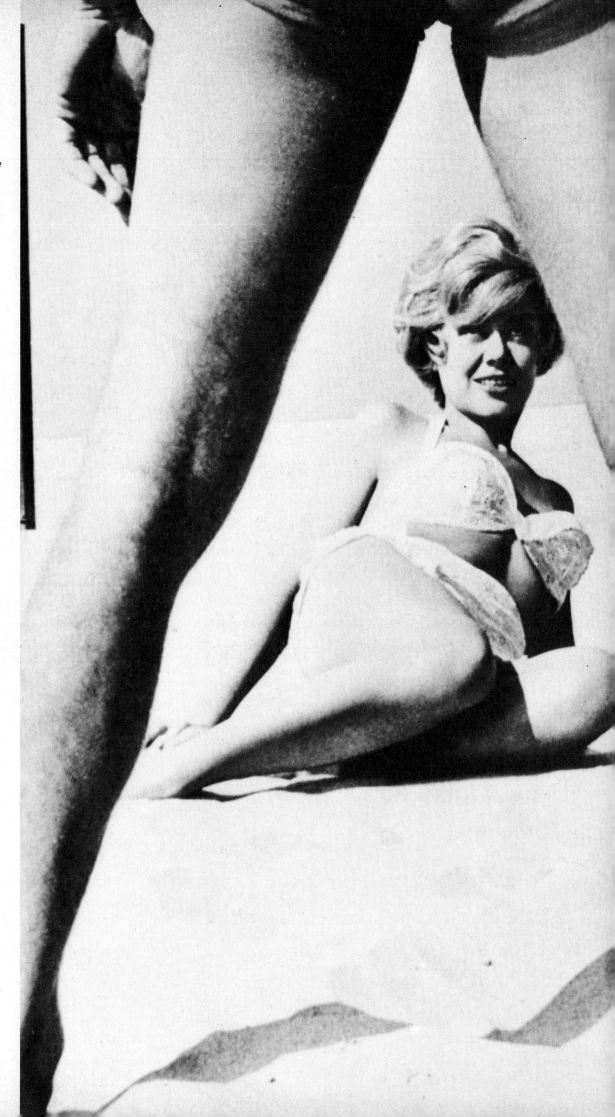

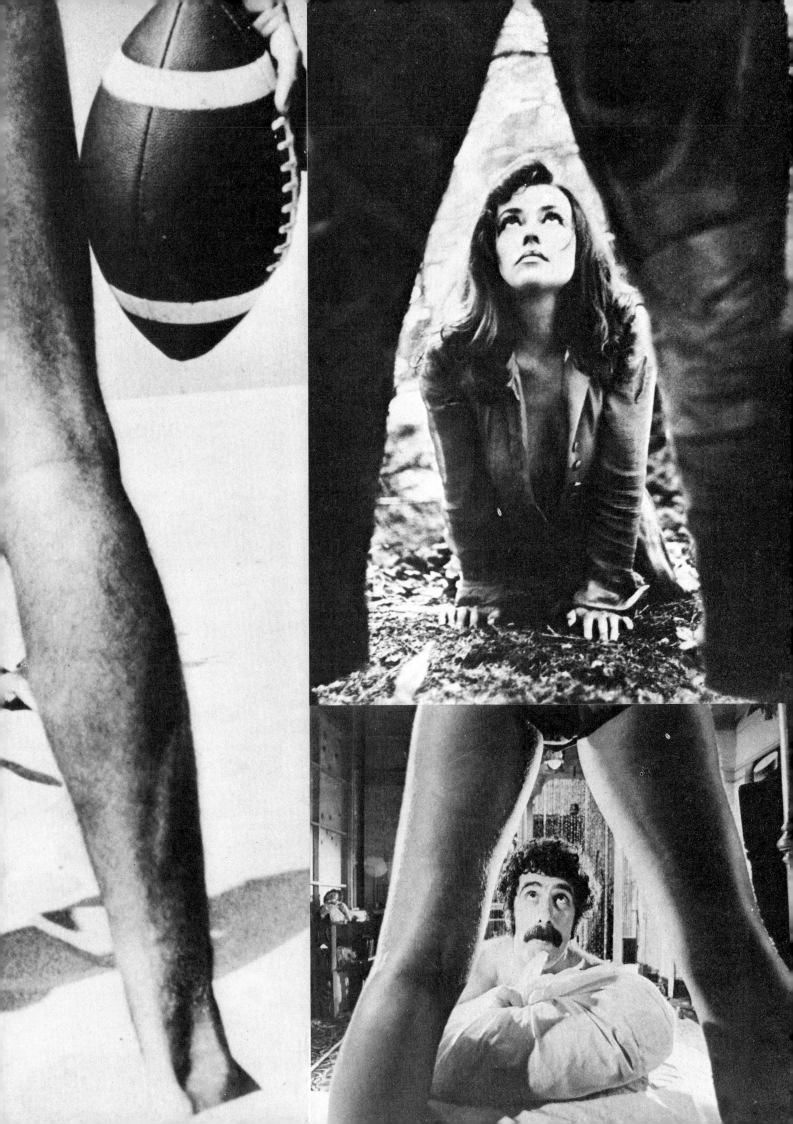

into sex symbols . . . and then marrying them.'[63]

Luis Buñuel, semi-exiled Spanish director, made many of his films in France, including his great popular success, *Belle de Jour* (1967), in which Catherine Deneuve played a woman who, finding her husband's attentions inadequate, becomes a high-class whore during the afternoons.

French censorship being principally concerned with political matters, sex and nudity generally had an easy ride in French films, but under De Gaulle's régime, a puritanical backlash began to create new problems for moviemakers. An extreme case was Jacques Rivette's *La Religieuse* (1966), which offended the Catholic Church by mixing sex and religion in its story of a nun (Anna Karina) driven to suicide by lesbianism and other worldly corruptions. The theme was handled responsibly and unsensationally by Rivette, and the film was twice approved by the official French censor, but Catholic pressure caused it to be banned. Only after a threat by sixty French directors to boycott the Cannes Film Festival was Minister of Culture André Malraux prompted to find a face-saving solution, but the film remained

Part-time prostitute Catherine Deneuve prepares to satisfy Francis Blanche's desires in *Belle de Jour* (Luis Buñuel, 1967).

Anna Karina as the nun beset by worldly corruption in *La Religieuse* (Jacques Rivette, 1966).

166

Tor Isedal about to rape
Birgitta Pettersson in *The
Virgin Spring* (Ingmar
Bergman, 1960).

Gunnel Lindblom as Ingrid
Thulin's nymphomaniac sister
and Birger Malmsten as the
barman she picks up for a
one-night stand in *The
Silence* (Bergman, 1963).

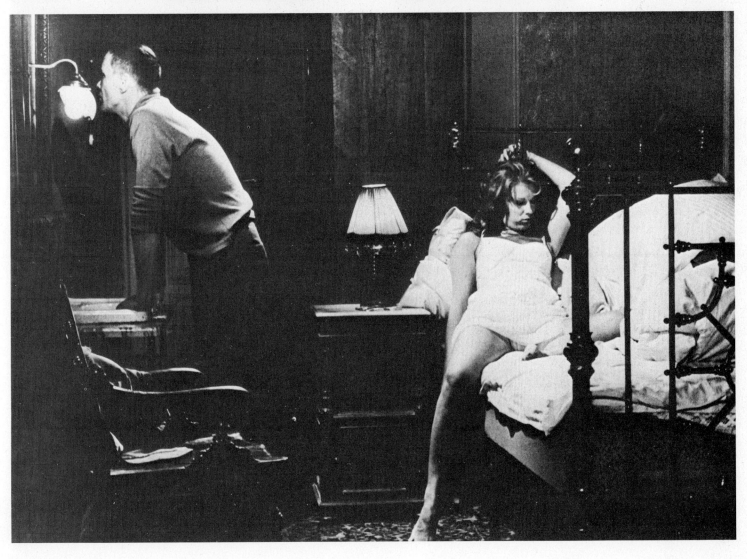

unseen outside France for two years.

The acknowledged leaders of the erotic revolution in the 'sixties were the Scandinavians – in particular Sweden. One of the most controversial films of 1960 was Swedish, Ingmar Bergman's *The Virgin Spring*. This austere, fourteenth-century folk-myth about the murder by herdsmen of the innocent daughter of a landowner contained a brutal rape sequence which, though photographed with skill and no trace of salaciousness, lost several shots in the American-released version and practically disappeared from that shown in Britain. Bergman went on to make his sombre trilogy about human relationships crippled by repression, sexual incompatibility and spiritual barrenness: *Through a Glass Darkly* (1961), *Winter Light* (1963) and *The Silence* (1963).

The third of these ran a gamut of explicit erotic sequences which even the Swedish censors mulled over for a long period before consenting to its release. The film is about two sisters, Ester (Ingrid Thulin) and Anna (Gunnel Lindblom), who have had an incestuous lesbian relationship but have become totally alienated. Anna has nymphomaniacal tendencies and, stimulated by the sight of a couple copulating in a cinema, picks up a barman and makes love to him in front of her sister and young son. Ester, suffering from a breakdown, resorts to drink and masturbation, the latter graphically (though dispassionately) conveyed by Bergman's camera. Sweden and Germany eventually accepted the film's sexual content uncut, but elsewhere it suffered varying amounts of cropping. In Britain, censor John Trevelyan simply warned Bergman to tone down the film before sending it over, and the resulting hybrid lacked many of the original's erotic details.

Per Oscarsson – though incestuously in love with Bibi Andersson in *My Sister, My Love* (Vilgot Sjöman, 1966) – still finds time for the local whores.

Bergman has never again depicted sex as explicitly as in *The Silence*, although *Persona* (1966) had moments of intense erotic activity, and *Cries and Whispers* (1973) contained one notorious scene in which a woman mutilates her vagina with a piece of broken glass. The strong, underlying eroticism in many of his films, however, helped to create a climate in which serious exploration of overtly sexual themes could take place relatively unhampered.

A far less subtle director than Bergman, Vilgot Sjöman, aroused a good deal more controversy with his blatant depictions of multifarious sex. His record of censorial rows began with *491* (1966), a study of delinquency which included homosexual seduction, perversion with a prostitute, and clear hints of bestiality. The Swedish censor board, extraordinarily, banned it completely. Sjöman appealed eventually to the Swedish parliament, and his film

was finally cleared with a few cuts and some tampering with the soundtrack. Sjöman complained: 'The censorship board is working to some very strange rules, judging films by an Ingmar Bergman from one moral standpoint and films by other directors on different ones. What Bergman shows is "great art", but if another director shows the same thing, it seems to be pornography.'[64] *491* predictably had an even harder time getting shown in the States.

My Sister, My Love (1966), an aesthetically superior and occasionally lyrical study of incest between an eighteenth-century nobleman (Per Oscarsson) and his sister (Bibi Andersson) proved more acceptable, but Sjöman's next film, *I Am Curious – Yellow* (1967), caused as much controversy as any film during the decade, principally for its extensive scenes of fully fledged intercourse and total male and female nudity. The Swedish censors, perversely, balked mainly at the film's strongly left-wing political stance, but passed the film uncut, whereupon it drew enormous audiences. Elsewhere, the film was either banned or the unprecedented sex scenes were radically cut before distribution, the British censor docking a full eleven minutes (including a scene of rear-entry copulation and the full-frontal nudity).

A Danish film, Johan Jacobsen's *A Stranger Knocks* (1960), had also portrayed the complete sex act, including orgasm (albeit entirely simulated, the actors wearing clothes throughout), thereby unwittingly advancing the cause of anti-censorship in America. When New York refused to show the film, the US Supreme Court ruled, correctly, that the orgasm was the film's dramatic as well as sexual climax and essential to the plot, and passed the film uncut – declaring at the same time that the New York censor board had no legal standing.

Led and inspired by the bleak eroticism of Bergman on the one hand and the provocative permissiveness of Sjöman on the other, the

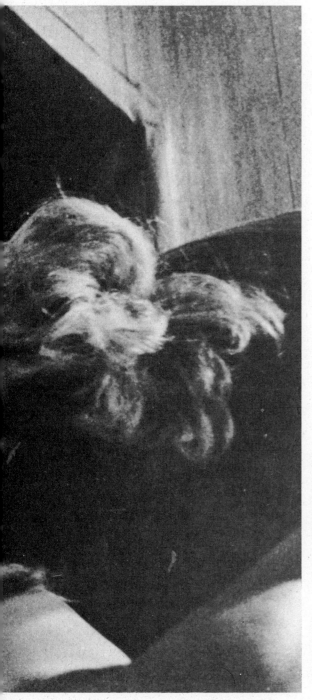

Lena Nyman and Borje Ahlstedt in the most sexually explicit film of the 'sixties, *I Am Curious – Yellow* (Sjöman, 1967).

169

Scandinavians continually proved themselves throughout the 'sixties the most uninhibited of the world's film-makers when it came to showing sex on the screen. Lars Magnus Lindgren's *Dear John* (1964), a concentrated study of a brief but unhesitant love affair between a middle-aged man (Jarl Kulle) and a waitress, was notable for its candid dialogue, and for the obvious enjoyment its leading characters got from their sex play. Feminist Mai Zetterling's *Night Games* (1966), which included among its themes an ambiguous Oedipal relationship, boyhood masturbation and homosexuality, shocked Americans to such an extent that it was barred from the San Francisco Film Festival. And Lars Görling's *Guilt* (1965) provided one of the earliest glimpses of a man's penis. Finnish director Jörn Donner, meanwhile, built up an international reputation (or perhaps notoriety) and established a

large following of admiring young film-makers with his unrestrained sex adventures, *To Love* (1964), *Black on White* (1968) and *Portraits of Women* (1970).

Denmark made an impression in the 'sixties far out of proportion to the small size of its film industry with such films as Palle Kjaerulff-Schmidt's nudity-packed *Weekend* (1963) and Knud Thomasen's *Venom*. The latter contained footage from an actual hard-core blue movie which, being essential to the plot, was simply scratched out rather than cut in some countries.

One of the most successful Danish sex films from this period was the relatively stylish comedy, *Seventeen* (1965), the adventures of a randy but inexperienced adolescent (Ole Søltoft) who is initiated into the pleasures of sex by a variety of willing ladies. Many of the scenes, including fairly explicit nude love-making in a number of positions and facial

Christina Schollin and Jarl Kulle as the happy lovers in *Dear John* (Lars Magnus Lindgren, 1964).

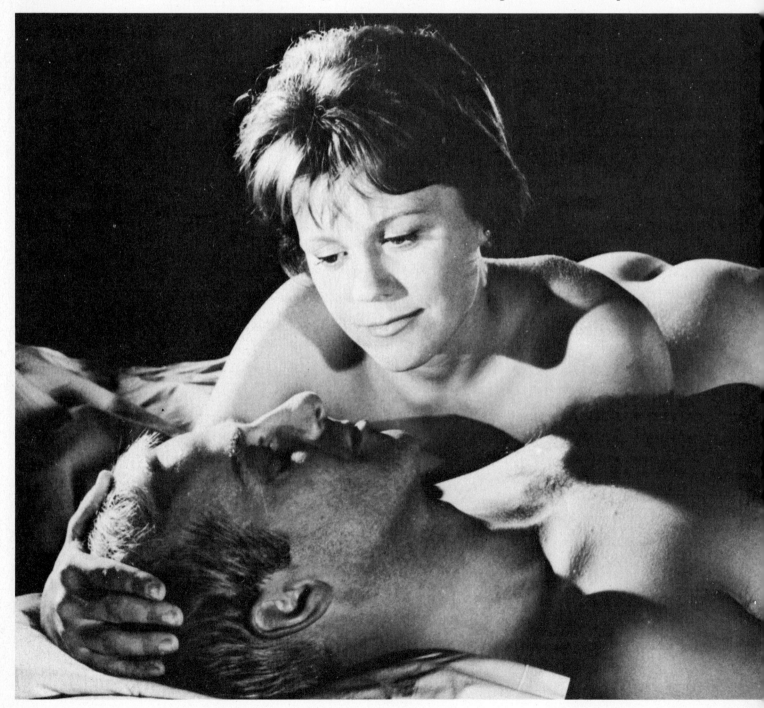

orgasm reactions, as well as an implied (if not actually observed) erection, were too revealing for the British Board of Film Censors, who refused to pass the film without cuts. The distributors managed to exploit the situation by getting the film approved for showing in its complete form by the Greater London Council, and then, having milked the highly profitable publicity dry, making compromise cuts agreed with the BBFC for general release outside London.

Italy, like Sweden, began the 'sixties in controversial fashion with films depicting rape. One of these was Vittorio De Sica's internationally acclaimed *Two Women* (1960), which won Sophia Loren an Oscar, but also had a number of censorship boards reaching for their scissors. The offending scene was a gang-rape in which a refugee mother and daughter (Loren and Eleanora Brown) are violated in a church

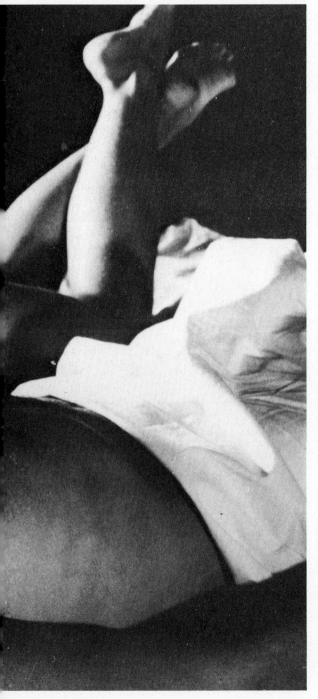

by a squad of Moroccan soldiers in the closing stages of the Second World War. Although the camera concentrated mainly on facial shots and the rape's aftermath, the British censor, for one, found plenty to cut. Another rape scene, in Luchino Visconti's *Rocco and His Brothers* (1960), was rendered harmless in the States by being darkened to a degree which made it virtually impossible to discern what was going on.

The true liberators of sexual attitudes on the Italian screen in the 'sixties, however, were Federico Fellini and Michelangelo Antonioni. Fellini's films emphasize very powerfully the corruptibility of love and the ugliness of both lust and repression, and they are fundamentally pessimistic, showing 'a world without love, people who exploit others, a world in which there is always an ordinary person who wants to give love and lives for love'. Since the grand decadence and depravity of *La Dolce Vita* and the satirical voluptuousness of the Anita Ekberg episode of *Boccacio '70*, Fellini's films have become more obsessively autobiographical and steeped in sexual fantasy (notably *8½*, 1963, and *Juliet of the Spirits*, 1965). At the same time, his characters and images have become more and more grotesque, as demonstrated by the monstrous beings who inhabit the erotic nightmare of *Satyricon* (1969) and the ogrish prostitutes who parade before the young hero of *Roma* (1972), Fellini's scathing satire on life in the Italian capital.

Antonioni shot to fame with his 'erotic adventure story', *L'Avventura* (1960), in which he established his themes – the impermanence and barrenness of sexual relationships, and the frustration of women trapped in a bourgeois society – and perfected his ascetic technique of detachment and cold observation: almost the opposite, in fact, of Fellini. With *La Notte*

The mutual deflowering of Ole Søltoft and Ghita Nörby in Annelise Meineche's *Seventeen* (1965).

(1960) and *L'Eclisse* (1962), he completed a trilogy begun by *L'Avventura*, and these films remain his collective masterpiece. In his later films, particularly *Blow-Up* and *Zabriskie Point* (1969), the underlying eroticism of Antonioni's themes is less subtle and his sex scenes are more explicit, although there is still a strong feeling of dehumanization in the scene in *Blow-Up* in which David Hemmings 'makes love' to a model with his camera, bringing her near to a sexual climax with a series of swiftly taken, lens-thrusting snapshots on his studio floor.

There was also, happily, some light relief to be had from Italian attitudes to sex. One of the funniest and most successful comedies to emerge during the decade was Pietro Germi's *Divorce – Italian Style* (1961), in which Marcello Mastroianni, as a slightly seedy baron, plots to rid himself of his fat, moustachioed wife – with the law's connivance – so he can marry his pretty young cousin.

The influence of the major European film directors of the 'sixties – particularly those of France, Italy and Scandinavia – was radical and wide-ranging, and by the end of the decade there was barely a single film industry in the world which could not, with impunity, depict some degree of sexual activity on the screen

with reasonable explicitness and authenticity. Even the Eastern bloc proved capable of producing an occasional example of delightful and disarming erotica, particularly, thanks to a period of political relaxation, Czechoslovakia.

Among the best to reach Western cinemas was Milos Forman's *A Blonde in Love* (1965), a bitter-sweet story about a young factory girl's brief affair with a pianist, which includes a nude love-making sequence that is both sensual and discreet. Even better was Jiri Menzel's *Closely Observed Trains* (1966) which, remarkably, won an Academy Award. This wartime tragi-comedy of a young partisan whose impotence is cured (in a remarkably candid love scene) by a willing railway conductress, is chiefly and justly famous for a sequence in which a lecherous stationmaster rubber-stamps the bare bottom

of one of his conquests to denote mission accomplished.

Japan, too, ever ready to imitate Occidental trends and attitudes, swept away old taboos and began to introduce overt eroticism into both its commercial and serious films, often with violence an added ingredient, as in Kaneto Shindo's *Onibaba* (*The Hole*, 1964), about the sexual rivalry of a woman and her daughter-in-law who murder wounded Samurai and sell their armour, and Hiroshi Teshigahara's *Woman of the Dunes* (1964), an allegory about love, passion and survival.

And yet, even by the end of the 'sixties the erotic progress made by the commercial cinema was as nothing compared to the sexual stampede which was to take place during the next few years.

The bizarre fantasy sequence from Antonioni's *Zabriskie Point* (1969), in which the youthful love-making of Mark Frechette and Daria Halprin causes the Arizona Desert to blossom forth with copulating couples.

173

It did not take the cinema's commercial substrata long to recognize the pocket-lining possibilities of the greater freedom of expression enjoyed by movies from the 'fifties onwards, and the legitimate cinema was increasingly infiltrated by films which set out cynically to exploit the public's appetite for eroticism on the screen.

Efforts in this direction in the 'fifties were mainly devoted to finding an acceptable format in which to show nudity. (American hypocrisy and ambivalence towards nudity was neatly and self-deprecatingly satirized by Shelley Winters, who said: 'I think it is disgusting, shameful and damaging to all things American. But if I were twenty-two with a great body, it would be artistic, tasteful, patriotic, and a progressive, religious experience.')

Continental films – especially those of France, Italy and Scandinavia – already exposed the bare flesh of their female stars with considerable alacrity, but in Britain and America the wheels of tolerance turned more slowly. The only American films which had so far succeeded in showing publicly, and without censure, a degree of nudity were a number of pseudo-ethnological documentaries about non-white cultures (black breasts in their natural, native environment being considered less corrupting

Garden of Eden (1954), pronounced decent by the New York Court of Appeals, launched the tidal wave of nudist-camp films in Britain and America.

to gaze upon than white ones) and a handful of cheaply re-created, shoddily photographed burlesque shows containing striptease acts. Even in the latter, exposure often stopped discreetly short of total toplessness.

The taboo against nudity was eventually challenged by giving it a setting which was essentially unerotic – the nudist camp. There had been some tentative precedents for this, including a whole sub-genre of foreign films (the French had even attempted a comic version of a nudist-camp film, *L'Ile aux Femmes Nues*, in 1952) and, more interestingly, an American production of 1933 called *Elysia*, generally considered to be the first of its kind. But the crunch came with a skilfully made semi-documentary, shot in a Florida nudist colony, entitled *Garden of Eden* (1954).

This was considered indecent by the New York censors and banned throughout the state, the judgment being that 'the motion picture depicts in color the life in a nudist camp with views of nude men, women and children, singly and in pairs, walking, talking, swimming and playing together. . . . In addition the picture contains specific protracted scenes of women in unwholesome, sexually alluring postures which are completely unnecessary to – and, in fact, a radical departure from – the activities of the nudist camp depicted. For example, there is a dream sequence where the principal actress, a comely young lady, completely disrobes in full view of the audience. . . .' The producer, Walter Bibo, fought the decision, claiming that his film had educational value, and in 1957 he was exonerated by a New York Court of Appeals ruling which said that 'Nudity in itself, and without lewdness or dirtiness, is not obscenity in law or in common sense.'

This declaration was adopted as a fundamental freedom by American film-makers, who quickly abandoned their careful, documentary approach to nudism and began to fill outdoor sets with uniformly attractive, well-endowed models and strippers and call the result things like *Daughters of the Sun* (1962). Eventually, in a 1966 production, *The Raw Ones*, total, full-frontal male and female nudity was depicted for the first time in a nudist-camp film, although it was hardly ever programmed owing to cinema managers' fear of prosecution.

Garden of Eden was the first nudist film to be shown in Britain with a British Board of Film Censors' certificate, leading the way for a spate of European imports, such as the two Swiss features, *Isle of Levant* (1957) and *Around the World with Nothing On* (1958), and the first home-grown example, *Nudist Paradise* (1958). And so, rather curiously, while films of quality were being treated leniently, Trevelyan, Secretary of the BBFC, was also tending to be generous to films at quite the other end of the market. Speaking of the proliferation of sex

*Three Nuts in Search of a
Bolt* (Noonan, 1964) with
Mamie Van Doren.

pictures in Scandinavia, Germany, America
and elsewhere which was a major feature of the
'sixties, he said, 'We were as reasonable as
possible with these films, taking into account
that there was a demand for them, and that
since their publicity usually indicated what
kind of films they were, the people who would
object to them would probably not go to see
them.' However, even in the permissive early
'seventies the Board continued to cut those
films clearly aimed at the limited 'dirty-
mackintosh' market. Sex films from Germany,
Sweden and France were usually cut first by
distributors and then by the censors. Indeed, as
these productions became more and more
explicit, importers were increasingly having
trouble finding material that would survive
British censorship and still be exhibitable.

Still, after *Nudist Paradise* in 1958 Britain
proceeded, somewhat improbably, more or less
to take over the sunshine movie genre, turning
out a long string of flesh-operas disguised as
naturist propaganda in the early 'sixties.
Occasionally these were glossy and reasonably
well made, like *Sunswept* (1961) and Michael
Winner's *Some Like It Cool* (1960), or employed
a genuine documentary approach, like *Search
for the Sun* (1962), which examined the past
and present philosophy of nudism in Britain
and showed some historic clips of the Speil-
platz colony. But they were, for the most part,
cheap, unforgivably dull tit-and-bum parades,

175

coyly photographed and rarely redeemed by by the pulchritude of their players. Answering to such titles as *The Nudist Story* (1960), *Nudes of the World* (1961), *Naked as Nature Intended* (1961), *My Bare Lady* (1962), *Take Off Your Clothes and Live* (1962), *Eves on Skis* (1963), *The Reluctant Nudist* (1963) and *It's a Bare, Bare World* (1964), these films generally shared a common theme: shy secretary (or clerk) reluctantly fetches up in nudist camp, finds personality blossoms when clothes are abandoned, and falls for boss/colleague who has, unbeknownst, been going there for years.

The nudist-camp genre rapidly fizzled out as equivalent amounts of flesh began to be exposed far more aesthetically in mainstream features. There were attempts to find another formula for the gratuitous presentation of nudity, including

hooking otherwise forgettable movies on to the impressive physiques of big-name sex stars like Jayne Mansfield ('I have fine, healthy, normal girlish impulses and I always make sure to obey them') and Mamie Van Doren – as producer Tommy Noonan did in, respectively, *Promises, Promises!* (1963) and *Three Nuts in Search of a Bolt* (1964). But although these films were successful at the box-office, not even Jayne or Mamie could thereafter claim special mammary attention in an increasingly topless world. By the end of the 'sixties, simple nudity no longer had the power to shock, and exploitation of it as often as not reached the frivolous level of Allen Funt's Candid Camera exercise, *What Do You Say to a Naked Lady?* (1969), which tested (for laughs) the reactions of people encountering a naked girl in the street.

One of the least pleasant but most persistent by-products of the more tolerant movie atmosphere was a repellent cycle of voyeuristic, pseudo-anthropological 'documentaries' which sensationalized various bizarre happenings throughout the world, usually with a grotesquely violent or sado-sexual emphasis. The first, most notorious and technically the best of these was *Mondo Cane* (1961), an Italian-made hotch-potch of supposedly true incidents cruelly designed to catch mankind with its trousers down. The catalogue of depravity and degradation, loosely soldered with a commentary claiming spurious sociological connections between the various incidents, included the gorging of geese in Strasbourg to produce prime *pâté de foie gras*, a New Guinea native woman suckling a pig at her breast, hysterical female fans tearing the clothes off actor Rossano Brazzi, naked, rapacious tribal women pursuing an eligible male, and so on *ad nauseam*.

Critic John Gillett called *Mondo Cane* 'a hymn to death and mutilation', but it played a highly profitable tune at the box-office and imitation was instant and rife. The directors of the film, Gualtiero Jacopetti and Franco Prosperi, made a whole career out of the genre, following up their first production with *Women of the World*, a chauvinistic nude show which made little pretence at being other than gratuitous voyeurism.

Spin-offs inspired by the success of the Jacopctti movies included further Italian efforts with interchangeable titles like *Women by Night* (1962) and *This Shocking World* (1963); a string of equally unsubtle American hybrids, such as *Sexy Proibitissimo*, *Mondo Freudo* and *Mondo Bizarro*; and some feeble but curious 'investigations' of undercover vice in London by British imitators, including *West End Jungle* (which failed to secure a certificate from either the BBFC or the London County Council) and *London in the Raw* (1964). Even Claude Lelouch essayed a dubiously motivated study in feminine behaviour with *La Femme Spectacle* (*Paris in the Raw*, 1964). As late as 1969 the genre was still a viable proposition, as the returns from Marcello Avallone's excessively tedious *The Queer . . . the Erotic* demonstrated. This was a hypocritically high-minded study of sexual attitudes in Europe's more permissive societies (sex education for children in Germany, an orgiastic wake in Sweden, a homosexual marriage in Rotterdam, and so on) contrasted with erotic rites in African countries, including a public celebration of the sex act.

Jacopetti and Prosperi kept their own pot boiling with *Mondo Cane 2* (1965), *Africa Addio* (1965, more tribal sensationalism from the Dark Continent), and *Uncle Tom* (1971). The last of these was a particularly repulsive piece of exploitation disguised as a factual reconstruction of the abuses of slavery in America's Deep South. Concentrating on the more bestial and erotic aspects of its theme (selective breeding, feeding from troughs, etc.), the film in fact looked more like a logistical exercise in how much naked flesh could be crammed into a wide-angle lens (hundreds of naked, superbly built Haitians were employed to portray the slaves) – a massively cynical reminder of the old Hollywood ethic that you can show as many tits as you like so long as they're primitive and black.

The cutting of the film from 130 minutes to 90 for British distribution sheds an interesting sidelight on modern censorship attitudes. The Board of Film Censors recognized that *Uncle Tom* was a blatant and particularly offensive example of the exploitation of an emotive theme, yet did not want to run the risk of appearing to take up either a pro- or anti-racist stance (a rule of the Board is to remain politically uninvolved) by banning it outright. It therefore hacked sufficient footage out of the film to render it, in effect, commercially unviable.

Another kind of documentary emerged at the end of the 'sixties as a result of Denmark's virtual abandonment of film censorship – the investigation of pornography for 'sociological' purposes. One example, *Sexual Freedom in Denmark* (1970), was in fact a report on the

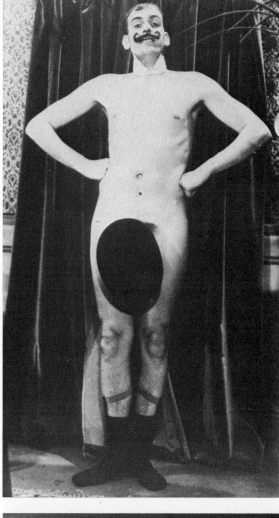

Left and below: Pornography and censorship satirized by Gabriel Axel in *Danish Blue* (1968). This documentary about the relaxation of censorship in Denmark cut little ice with censors elsewhere, most of whom banned it.

Lesbian cabaret act from
Sexus.

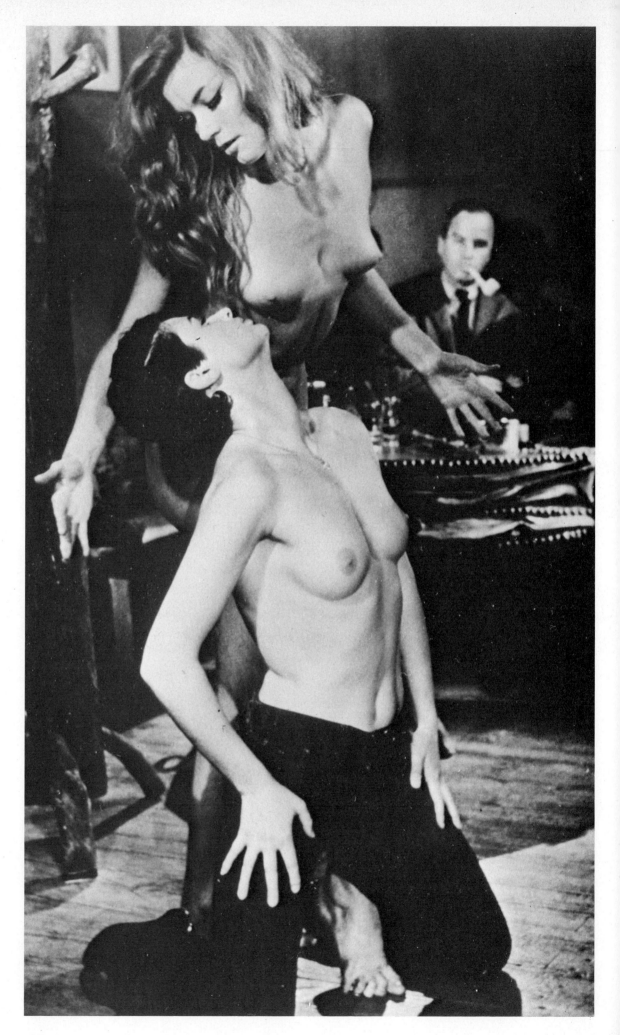

lifting of censorship in that country, although the principal excuse for making this and others of its type – such as *Pornography in Denmark* (1970) or *Pornography: Copenhagen 1970* (1970) – was to include blue-movie footage or sex-show activity on the pretext that they were essential 'informational' elements of the documentary. These thinly veneered sexploitation vehicles cut little ice with the British censor, but found a legitimate market in the States on the grounds that they had 'redeeming social values' and avoided appealing to 'prurient interest' – two precepts which had been the subject of court rulings.

Earlier, Gabriel Axel had made a comedy documentary about the relaxation of censorship, *Danish Blue* (1968), which again received no certificate in Britain, but was much admired by critics when shown at Derek Hill's New Cinema Club, a membership-only organization (now defunct) dedicated to the breakdown of film censorship. The humour, aimed at the clumsy antics of a nation dutifully practising pornography almost as a state religion, was a little heavy at times, but nevertheless apt and a welcome change from the pretentiousness of the pseudo-sociological products it was parodying.

A related, and equally ambivalent genre, which also came strongly into vogue in the late 'sixties, was that embracing sex-education films. These were considerably more explicit than anything previously intended for public exhibition and caused some hard thinking by the British censor, but, as sex education was by now common in schools, it would have seemed odd to ban this material even for adults. Numerous books had been published without serious complaint, and, while the Board had never admitted that what is available in book form should be acceptable on the screen, there was strong reason to believe that those in need of sex education were unlikely to get it from books.

Nevertheless the Board was unable to make up its mind over these films. Some it banned, others were passed after great deliberation and some misgivings. Others were not passed but local authorities were advised that the Board was not strongly opposed to them and were almost invited to pass them. On a number of occasions films were submitted to the local censors, some of whom accepted them, thus encouraging the Board to follow suit. Many local councils grew increasingly irritated at this apparent inconsistency on the part of the Board, while others became aware, for the first time, of their real power in relation to film censorship. The episode probably played some part in the growth of local-authority interference that was to follow. As far as sex-education films were concerned, the end result was that most were ultimately passed, and by the time the genre lost favour, some considerable fortunes had been made, and new aspects of sexual behaviour had been seen on British screens. In America, they qualified under the 'redeeming social values' ruling.

The first, phenomenally successful examples came from Germany, beginning with *Helga* (1967), which tried, by dramatizing the sexual adventures and hang-ups of a (presumably) typical young German woman, to emphasize the importance of courtship, marriage, preparation for motherhood, childbirth, etc. A sequel, *Michael and Helga* (1968), continued the process with Helga 'happily' married, but its speciousness drew a bitter outburst from an anonymous reviewer in the Monthly Film Bulletin: 'As in *Helga* and the rest, statistics are twisted to fit a particular thesis, the tone is irritatingly patronising throughout, and the mixture of ponderous dialogue and overt titillation is offensive. It's surely about time someone called a halt to these gross distortions of sexual fact and fantasy. As for Helga, if she is representative (as she is undoubtedly supposed to be) of German womanhood, German men have a good reason to wish that Dr Kinsey and his disciples had kept their theories to themselves.'

These criticisms of the *Helga* series could apply equally to the similar *Oswalt Kolle* cycle (which included *The Wonder of Love*, 1967, and *Sexual Partnership*, 1968), though the *Kolle* films added another convention to the format – the panel of doctors and 'experts' commenting cosily on the various erotic problems presented. These pundits featured more prominently in the better, slightly less nudging movies which concentrated clinically on techniques of love-making and its psychologically remedial effects, notably the German *Freedom to Love* (written and directed by respected sexologists Doctors Phyllis and Eberhard Kronhausen) and *Anatomy of Love*, and the Swedish *Language of Love*. All of these explored graphically, and with much practical advice from the experts, the various aspects of a satisfactory or problematical sex life – coital positions, masturbation, contraception, impotence, frigidity, use of vibrators, oral sex, and so on.

Anatomy of Love was chiefly remarkable also for a 'balletic' set-piece in which a couple copulate in time to Ravel's 'Bolero', the lovers and the music reaching their climaxes simultaneously. *Language of Love* was by far the most overt of the sex-education films, portraying (among other things) erection, actual intercourse (as opposed to simulation) performed on a revolving platform like a cake stand, cunnilingus (as a remedy for premature ejaculation), and the fitting of female contraceptives. It was also, at times, guilty of sublime absurdity, particularly in the American-dubbed version: in one of several dramatized vignettes designed to demonstrate sexual hang-ups in marriage, a husband rejects his wife's advances with the excuse, 'I've had the boss on my back all day'!

Outside Germany and Sweden, production of sex-education films was desultory and, in some instances, inevitably and transparently exploitative. *The Molesters* (1966), for example, was a thoroughly bogus affair claiming to be a clinical study of voyeurism, fetishism, flagellation, child molestation, and other aberrations.

Mixed bathing

Recurring images of
erotic cinema: 5

Gina Lollobrigida (*right*) in
Solomon and Sheba (**King
Vidor, 1959**). Mick Jagger,
Anita Pallenberg and
Michèle Breton (*far right*)
in *Performance* (**Donald
Cammell and Nicolas
Roeg, 1970**). Martine
Carol (*bottom, right*) in
Lucrèce Borgia (**Christian-
Jaque, 1952**). Claudette
Colbert's famous bath of
asses' milk (*bottom, far
right*) in *The Sign of the
Cross* (**Cecil B. De Mille,
1932**). Legend has it that
the milk curdled under
the blazing arc lights and
formed a crust on the
surface. A visitor,
mistaking the result for
a marble floor, attempted
to walk across it, and
found himself up to his
neck in rancid cheese.

Erica Gavin in *Vixen* (1969), most lurid of Russ Meyer's highly charged sex melodramas.

teach them the real facts of life in their own schools.

In America, the 'educational' tag on a movie could also operate, it was discovered, in favour of fiction films. A key case concerned the Danish-made *Without a Stitch* (1960), which recounted the sexual experiments undertaken by an attractive girl suffering from frigidity. The Los Angeles Customs authorities objected to the film and tried to have it banned. It was successfully defended, however, on two counts: it did not, as the Los Angeles Customs Office claimed, exceed 'contemporary community standards' (another legal yardstick used in judgments on films) since equally uninhibited films like *I Am Curious – Yellow* had been showing for months in Los Angeles unremarked; on the other hand it did (and a female social scientist was able to persuade the court to this effect) offer the same advice to its heroine as a responsible clinic would have given under the circumstances described in the film. It had, therefore, 'redeeming social values', which meant that it could be passed for exhibition.

Meanwhile, in Britain, more extreme examples of sexploitation found another outlet in the private-member clubs which had appeared in the early 'sixties. Clubs such as the Gala and Compton chains avoided the licensing regulations by restricting admission to members. They were therefore able to show films not passed by either the Board or the local censors, although the threat of common-law proceedings meant that most such films were cut anyway, and went only a little further than the 'official' product. Far from considering this a loophole, Trevelyan actively encouraged the development, feeling that the existence of the club would remove some responsibility from the Board by providing an alternative form of exhibition for unacceptable films. He was thus tacitly agreeing that the Board's role was now restricted to that of 'protecting the mass undiscriminating cinema audience from unwelcome shock'.

For the most part, however, sexploitation was handled far more warily in the fiction films of the 'sixties than in their 'documentary' counterparts, simply because (with the exception of isolated examples like *Without a Stitch*) it was more difficult to find a valid sociological excuse for depicting nudity and eroticism therein. The more blatant 'nudie' films and movies of obviously lurid intent, like West Germany's *Dolls of Vice* (1958) or France's *Paris Vice Patrol* (1958), were therefore largely restricted to the club cinemas and dirty-mac circuit. Nevertheless, the gap between what was becoming permissible in the legitimate, mainstream cinema and what could be got away with in sexploitation movies was narrowing rapidly, as evidence of which the occasional stray sex film acquired a more public reputation than might have been expected.

An extreme example of a club movie wandering into the public arena was *Moonlighting Wives* (1968), a dismal American sex drama about bored housewives taking up whoring in

Britain managed some conventional examples of the genre, including Terry Gould's *Love Variations* (1969), a well-meaning but ineffectual (and motionless) demonstration of about forty coital positions. Less obviously 'educational' was *The Perfumed Garden* (1969), a tasteful visual representation of the celebrated Persian love manual, with a commentary culled from the original text as translated by Sir Richard Burton.

A stir was caused in Britain in the early 'seventies by a controversial short film made privately and strictly for limited educational use by a Birmingham school-teacher, Dr Martin Cole. This innocuous, indifferently made little movie demonstrated in simple terms the physiology of boys and girls at puberty, showed a boy's and man's penises flaccid and erect, and contained a sequence showing a female teacher masturbating – but because it was aimed at schoolchildren, the film provoked an outcry among parents and educational authorities, and Dr Cole was suspended from his job. After taking his case to court, Dr Cole was exonerated and reinstated, but not before the whole affair had provided a perfect example of the prurience and double standard of a society prepared to allow its children to be exposed daily to cynical sexploitation through the media, yet take violent objection to any serious attempt to

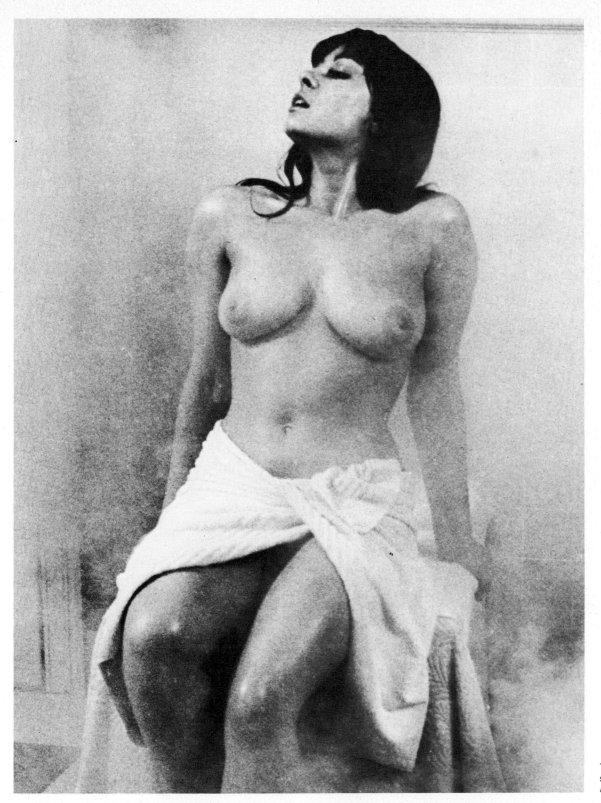

the afternoons, which was so heavily cut in
Britain as to be rendered both sexless and
meaningless. More acceptable and more
successful was *The Notorious Daughter of
Fanny Hill* (1965), the first American costume
sex film, so it was claimed, whose scenes of
simulated love-making were considered particularly daring at the time it originally appeared.

The most popular sexploitation features
came, not surprisingly, from the Continent
with Denmark and Germany prominent as
usual. The Danish *I, A Woman* (1965) was one
of the first successes in this field. It used a
superficial study of nymphomania as an excuse
to expose as much of Essy Persson's impressive
physique as it possibly could, and became a big
hit on both sides of the Atlantic, although in
Britain it had to settle for a certificate from the
Greater London Council after the Board had
refused it one.

The unattractive hero of *Seventeen*, Ole
Søltoft, found himself, after the phenomenal
success of that venture, being typecast as a
sexual beginner seeking initiation, in a series
of nudging, largely unerotic comedies which
included *Song of the Red Ruby* (1970), *Bedroom
Mazurka* (1970) and *Danish Dentist on the Job*
(1971). The better, more lightweight erotic

Edy Williams taunts a noticeably unenthusiastic David Gurian in Russ Meyer's spoof sexploiter for Twentieth Century-Fox, *Beyond the Valley of the Dolls* (1970).

comedies, such as *Elbow Play* (1969) and the comparatively amusing and high-spirited *Do You Want to Remain a Virgin Forever?* (1968), came from Germany; while it took a co-production team from Austria, Hungary and Italy to come up with the most popular sexual romp of them all, *The Sweet Sins of Sexy Susan* (1967), which generated a whole cycle of virtually indistinguishable sequels.

Britain's film-makers, as usual, climbed on the bandwagon in their own good time and in their own familiar half-hearted way, achieving in such inept imitations of the genre as *Sweet and Sexy* (1970) what sexploitation expert Kenneth Thompson described as 'a peculiar and significant fatuity'. There was little improvement in *Monique* (1970), about a French au pair girl who has sexual relations with both her employers, husband and wife, but at least Malcolm Leigh's *Games That Lovers Play* (1970), for all its arch awfulness, looked like an

original, home-grown product rather than a cheap copy of a foreign import. (Leigh's film also had the odd distinction of casting Richard Wattis, archetypally prudish civil servant in countless British comedies, as an insatiable sexual athlete who can only get satisfaction with two women at once.)

An earlier British sex movie of more than passing interest was *The Yellow Teddybears* (1963), which had few merits as a film, but which had, enterprisingly, capitalized on highly controversial press reports about a group of schoolgirls who signified their loss of virginity by wearing small golliwogs on their lapels. The film substituted teddybears for golliwogs and threw in pregnancy and attempted abortion for good measure.

The one film-maker who demonstrated to perfection how blurred were the lines between sexploitation and the commercial cinema at the beginning of the 'seventies was Russ Meyer.

184

This ex-Second-World-War cameraman made his reputation in Hollywood first as a skilful photographer of glamour girls, then as the originator of a formula for making nude films which were acceptable to the censors. His method, first demonstrated in *The Immoral Mr Teas* (1959), was simply to fill the screen with the most delectable bodies he could find, concentrating on breasts and bottoms, and keep it all strictly at arm's length – a voyeuristic exercise, in other words, with no sexual activity.

Mr Teas, for example, was about a man who, as a result of an anaesthetic administered for a tooth extraction, undresses with his eyes every girl he sees. The film was prosecuted from time to time, but always won, on the premise already established that nudity *per se* is not obscene. The reputation of *Mr Teas* grew along with its box-office returns and inspired an avalanche of imitations over the next half-dozen years, as well as encouraging mainstream film-makers to begin inserting nude shots into their more 'legitimate' products. Meyer's own follow-ups included *Eve and the Handyman* (1961) and the satirical *Wild Gals of the Naked West* (1962).

Meyer himself realized that the sexless nude film had a limited life, that audiences would soon demand something more stimulating than untouchable flesh, and in 1963 he set a new trend with *Lorna*. This was a violent, sensational melodrama about a much-desired backwoods girl in America's Deep South, still strong on nudity, but with the added ingredients of lust, rape, explicit sex and murder. 'I realized the nudies had had it,' said Meyer. 'Women had been presented in every conceivable way. There was nothing left to the imagination. Now there was required, in addition to the exposure of flesh, some sort of simple story. So from *Lorna* on, I have concentrated on action melodramas, violence and sex, presenting lovemaking in the most realistic manner, and, when the situation required, photographing our actresses pretty much in the nude.'[65]

Again, imitation (and prosecution) was widespread, Meyer showing the way with such sagas of bloody excess as *Motor Psycho* (1965); *Faster, Pussycat! Kill! Kill!* (1966), about a gang of psychopathic girls who kill men for kicks; *Cherry, Harry and Raquel* (1969), which includes (unusually for Meyer) a glimpse of male frontal nudity; *Rope of Flesh* (1969); and – most controversial of all – *Vixen* (1969), which, in the space of a year, was prosecuted twenty-three times across the States on charges of obscenity, pornography and committing a public nuisance. A measure of the explicitness of *Vixen*'s nymphomaniac theme and the frequency of its couplings can be gauged by the fact that the British censor cut it down from seventy-one minutes to forty-seven.

Appropriately, it was Meyer who was chosen,

Laura Antonelli in *Venus in Furs* (Massimo Dallamano, 1968), a piece of German sexploitation which pressed a rather thin claim to being based on the Sacher-Masoch novel of the same name.

in 1970, to effect the final fusion between sexploitation and mainstream film-making. This he did by agreeing to make *Beyond the Valley of the Dolls* for Twentieth Century-Fox, a desperate measure by Richard Zanuck to revive his company's ailing finances. The result was an outrageously camp, gratifyingly funny pastiche of pornography, about a busty, all-female rock group getting endlessly laid in Hollywood, packed with nymphomaniacs and homosexuals, and brought to a hilariously gruesome climax by a homicidal transvestite. Meyer even found an opportunity to mock his sponsors by playing the Twentieth Century-Fox fanfare during a decapitation sequence.

Fox used Meyer again in 1971 for the Irving Wallace adaptation, *The Seven Minutes* (i.e. the average time it supposedly takes a woman to achieve orgasm), about the unsuccessful prosecution of an allegedly pornographic novel. But instead of sensationalizing an exploitable subject and indulging his taste for excess, Meyer used the assignment as an opportunity for yet another transition. He concentrated relatively seriously on the anti-censorship argument he was trying to put across, and kept nudity and explicit sex to a minimum.

William Rotsler, in his book 'Contemporary Erotic Cinema', puts the case more strongly: 'Russ Meyer . . . has *never* made a pornographic movie and his latest films don't even have nudity. The brief "pornographic" scene used as such in *The Seven Minutes* was not pornographic at all, but so powerful is the Meyer touch that you *think* it is, or might be!' The creator of *The Immoral Mr Teas* had, it seems, become the Moral Mr Tease – but not before he had helped to set Hollywood on the path towards a degree of permissiveness which even in 1971 no one could have thought possible.

New Stars for Old

The star-system was pronounced dead by almost everyone, but as of the moment of writing everyone is talking about Liza Minnelli in *Cabaret* and she made the covers of Time and Newsweek simultaneously. Contrast the unfortunate Julie Ege, a British starlet. The Sunday Times reported in February 1971 that in less than two years 1,657 column inches had been devoted to her of which only $3\frac{1}{2}$ inches consisted of "critical appraisal of her film roles". The movie world may have endured a series of convulsions which now and then seemed fatal: but some things don't change.'

Thus spake David Shipman in the introduction to the second volume of his massive work, 'The Great Movie Stars', in 1972. The old Hollywood star-system, it is commonly held, finally died in the 'sixties, along with studio contracts (and studios), gossip columns and the mass audience. Or did it? Shipman suggests that, despite the revolution in film production methods, little has changed in the 'seventies with respect to the way film personalities are handled; superstars continue to be fêted; starlets still strive for maximum exposure (in every sense).

As usual, the truth lies somewhere in the middle. The system is certainly dead – no longer are stars 'made' (or broken), nor do they have their 'images' maintained by a vast studio publicity machine. Stars there certainly are, however – less thick on the ground, perhaps, and diminished somewhat in stature, but there, nevertheless, to add lustre to a film and sometimes a dash of sex appeal.

Curiously, Shipman's examples are not the most typical of enduring modern stardom, though they serve to illustrate how the star set-up has changed: Liza Minnelli's reputation and popularity rested on one well-received film and cooled rapidly with the lack of a successful follow-up; Julie Ege, on the other hand, is a rare contemporary throwback (like Raquel Welch) to the days of the sex symbol, able to function as a 'star' almost without making movies as long as the custodians of her image keep the media well fed with publicity material and revealing photographs.

The star shakedown began in the 'fifties when the major stars, led by James Stewart, broke away from the studios which held them in thrall and started to control their own financial destinies, signing contracts which were as much to their own advantage as to those who employed them. At the same time, they began to bother less about their off-screen image, some insisting that their private lives be regarded as private, others openly flouting false moral conventions by declaring a candid interest in free love or simply living together – and all with little protest from the press. The sex symbol thus became largely redundant, since all stars were sex stars in the sense that they happily and naturally engaged in the act of love both off the screen and on. Only the Burtons, mainly because of a continuously stormy domestic life coupled with a show of old-fashioned financial extravagance, retained any measure of gossip-value.

On the debit side, stars lost the security of the studio system. Whereas in the so-called Golden Age, a studio would be obliged to underpin a fading or off-form star with clever publicity and regular employment in decently made A-features (just as, conversely, a couple of charismatic stars – say James Cagney and Joan Blondell in *Blonde Crazy*, 1931 – could lift a film out of mediocrity by their presence), from the 'sixties actors were generally only as good or as popular as their last film.

It was perfectly possible, therefore, for Ryan O'Neal to soar to stardom in the phenomenal, freakishly successful *Love Story*, only to flop dismally in his next movie, *The Wild Rovers*. With a few exceptions (Steve McQueen, Clint Eastwood, Robert Redford and Charles Bronson maintained pulling power at the box-office, but few others do – not, for example, Elizabeth Taylor, surprisingly enough), the films became more important than the stars, and in many cases the directors, too, came to exceed their actors in importance and attraction. Thus, where one used to speak in terms of a Clark Gable movie or a Greta Garbo film, one would talk today of a sex movie or a Peckinpah film.

The stars of the 'seventies, therefore, were no longer larger than life or 'glamorous' in the well-groomed, soft-focus sense; they were no longer exotic gods and goddesses living out fantasy existences; they no longer wished to be idolized or even recognized (except, maybe, as good actors). The accent was now on a serious, intelligent approach to the professional job of acting a part. Even in a popular open forum, many modern stars would deliberately eschew the glib, studio-prompted response to questions about their lives and careers. Paul Newman once half-embarrassed, half-impressed a National Film Theatre audience in London by weighing up carefully and in long, multi-second pauses even the simplest, most trivial questions put to him before answering.

It is ironic that the term 'superstar' should have been coined in an era when claimants to the epithet were so distinctly rare (Brando, perhaps? Streisand?). Even the survivors from

John Richardson and Raquel Welch in *One Million Years BC* (Don Chaffey, 1966).

187

an earlier age – Wayne, Stewart, Grant, Crawford, Davis, Lancaster, Peck, Fonda – seemed to
have diminished a fraction or two in star stature,
with the compensation that they seemed con-
sciously to turn in better *performances* than
they used to and appear more accessible and
human. One cannot imagine thirty or so years
ago a star saying to a public audience, as Burt
Lancaster did, 'I like to get up early and go
running. Some people choose masturbation to
get their blood circulating in the morning – me,
I run in the park!'

At the same time, there are many good actors
on the modern screen who are simply that –
good actors – whereas, in the age of the major
studios and the long-term contract they would
have been carefully cosseted and cultivated
and groomed into steady, dependable stars.
James Garner springs most readily to mind,
along with George Segal and Rod Taylor.

The way in which attitudes to stardom have
changed over the years is admirably summed up
by two statements by two superstars, one old,
one new. 'Actresses,' said Mary Pickford,
'should realize that when they deliberately
choose a public career, they have no right to
disappoint the public – and no right to privacy.
As a toy of the public, that's part of the price.'
Said Robert Redford: 'I owe an audience a
performance, nothing more.' To which one
should perhaps add a characteristic piece of
sarcasm from the arch-enemy of privacy-
invaders, Marlon Brando: 'Once you are a star
actor, people start asking you questions about
politics, astronomy, archaeology and birth
control.'

The one major star who successfully bridged
the generation gap between the old and new
Hollywoods, retained a glossy, glamorous
image, and skilfully preserved a dual claim as
sex star and serious actress was Elizabeth
Taylor. Said Shipman: 'More than any other
star in the history of the cinema, her private
life has been public property; during the 'sixties
it was almost impossible to pick up a newspaper
without some item about her. This was
intriguing. Her life was, and probably still is,
exciting. Her beauty is unquestioned. Her
talent is something else.'[66] Her association
since 1958 with steamy, erotic roles (*Cat on a
Hot Tin Roof*, *Suddenly Last Summer*, *Butterfield 8*, and so on) and her knockabout public
affair with Richard Burton, subsequently
leading to an equally turbulent marriage and
divorce, helped to keep her younger com-
petitors in the shade. Latterly, though, her
film roles have grown progressively dismal,
culminating, in *Ash Wednesday* (1973), in an
ill-advised part as a raddled, menopausal
socialite who undergoes radical cosmetic sur-
gery and rediscovers sex.

In early '74, the only modern actresses who
could remotely pretend to superstardom on a
similar level to Elizabeth Taylor were Barbra
Streisand and Jane Fonda. Gossip-columnist
Sheilah Graham described Streisand as 'crude,
unpolished little Barbra, the poverty-shriven
ugly duckling who made it by sheer guts all the

way from a Brooklyn tenement to the cathedral-
like shrine that Garbo built in that far-flung
outpost of culture, Beverly Hills'. That was
soon after she had taken the movie city by
storm in her first film, *Funny Girl*, which won
her a predictable Oscar and set her on the road
to winning just about every popular entertainment award going – all, as she put it, 'without
having my nose fixed, my teeth capped, or my
name changed'. The ugly duckling was, of
course, a stunningly attractive swan, and one
of the few actresses of the 'seventies who can
convey deep sexual feeling without stripping to
the buff, which she has steadfastly refused to do
in her movies. One of the best moments in *The
Way We Were* was her 'seduction' of an un-
witting, semi-conscious Robert Redford who
has passed out in her bed.

Jane Fonda started her career in pleasant,
harmless light comedy roles, but became famous
by going to France and displaying her splendidly
lissom form in films (directed by her then
husband Roger Vadim) like *La Ronde* (1964), *La
Curée* (1966) and *Barbarella* (1968). Said Time:
'Such Vadim-witted flicks were 25 per cent
titillation, 75 per cent marzipan; but because
they were 100 per cent Jane, they were worthwhile'. Eventually she reacted against the roles
she had been playing, regarding them as anti-
feminist, and took up an aggressively anti-
exploitation stance. She even expressed regret
at having played the prostitute in *Klute* (1971),

although she made the character intensely real and sympathetic and won an Oscar for her troubles.

Jane Fonda's personal rebellion had deep roots; Hollywood had tried to mould her into a sex symbol from the start. Her figure – best shown, perhaps, in *Klute* – though superb in the eyes of most men, met with disapproval from studio chiefs who thought her breasts too small. She was peremptorily ordered into falsies which she wore in her films for several years; moguls stated baldly that they weren't investing their money in a flat-chested actress! She later recalled: 'I was not the material for movie stardom. My cheeks were too fat, my hair was the wrong colour; they plucked my eyebrows, put lipstick on, changed my hair – then I got the message about the falsies.' One director even objected to her chin and wanted it broken and reset! Little wonder she deserted America for the more appreciative attentions of Vadim.

Most of Jane Fonda's generation of actresses ultimately rebelled against being regarded purely as sex symbols, though they accepted the explicit portrayal of sex as an integral part of many of the roles they played. Even Stella Stevens, who, because of her blonde hair, substantial figure and pretty/sexy face, seemed destined to pop up occasionally simply as a reminder of Monroe, found herself in worthwhile roles, such as Jason Robards's ex-whore girlfriend in Peckinpah's *The Ballad of Cable*

Hogue. Similarly, Ann-Margret, for a long period typecast in salacious teenager roles, suddenly emerged as an actress to be reckoned with in the part of Jack Nicholson's rapacious lover in *Carnal Knowledge* (1971); and Tuesday Weld, Hollywood's 'baby beatnik', made a similarly good impression in *The Cincinnati Kid* (alongside Ann-Margret) and *Pretty Poison*.

Another emergent star of *Carnal Knowledge* was Candice Bergen, whose perfectly chiselled features and elegant build marked her down for cool but volcanic roles, in which, she noted with some cynicism later, she always seemed to

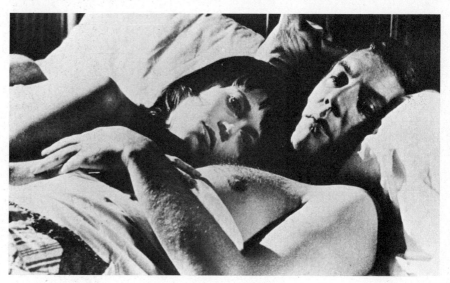

Right: Julie Christie: 'warm and protective . . . sunny and desirable' (David Shipman).

Far right: Jacqueline Bisset in *The Grasshopper* (Jerry Paris, 1969).

Ali MacGraw and Ryan O'Neal in *Love Story* (Arthur Hiller, 1970).

be simulating sexual climax: 'I may not be a great actress, but I've become the greatest at screen orgasms . . . ten seconds of heavy breathing, roll your head from side to side, simulate a slight asthma attack and die a little!'

Prominent among other actresses who were beginning to overshadow the established, 'old-fashioned' sex stars such as Elke Sommer, Ursula Andress and, of course, Raquel Welch – as much for their own strong sex appeal as their obvious histrionic talent – were Faye Dunaway, Katharine Ross, Ali MacGraw and Jacqueline Bisset. Of these, Jacqueline Bisset, surprisingly, emerged as the most sensual and versatile. 'Under the star system twenty-odd years ago,' said John Huston, 'she would have been a monarch.' Her gamine modesty and spontaneity and ability to convey deep affection, combined with the best kind of soft English physique and good looks, made her among the most desirable of modern actresses – at her best in *Secrets* (1971), in which she shared a startlingly abandoned lovemaking scene with Per Oscarsson, and François Truffaut's superb *Day for Night* (1973).

The 'sixties and early 'seventies saw a resurgence of British actresses fully equipped in all respects to compete with their American counterparts, often in the steamiest roles, yet often conveying at the same time a certain intellectual quality. Glenda Jackson led a field which included Vanessa Redgrave and Susannah York (but not Susan George, whose

James Coburn coping manfully in *Pat Garrett and Billy the Kid* (Sam Peckinpah, 1973).

talents are more emphatically physical, though supremely so) if only for being the least inhibited about stripping off, which she did successively in *Women in Love* (1969), *Sunday, Bloody Sunday* (1971) and *The Music Lovers* (1971). A British actress with more conventional star qualities, but a smaller international standing is Julie Christie, who found few outstanding film roles after her Oscar-winning achievement in *Darling*, but has stayed in the public consciousness thanks to a well-publicized liaison with Warren Beatty and, latterly, a controversial and very beautiful nude lovemaking sequence with Donald Sutherland in *Don't Look Now*.

While old hands like Frank Sinatra, Dean Martin, Kirk Douglas, and even John Wayne continued (to the increasing embarrassment of their audiences) to win the girl, a new breed of male hero arrived on the scene, better adapted to the violence and casual sex called for in the films of the late 'sixties and 'seventies. Less romantic, more laconic than his predecessors; tough, virile, sometimes brutal like Lee Marvin, or cheerfully amoral like James Coburn – whether cop, criminal or Westerner; and frequently saddled with all kinds of hardware in the shape of guns and fast cars. The most

Lee Marvin in *The Professionals* (Richard Brooks, 1966) – 'more male than anyone I have ever acted with,' said Jeanne Moreau.

191

Paul Newman attempts to seduce a far-from-willing Patricia Neal in *Hud* (Martin Ritt, 1962).

popular archetypes for this model of hero became Clint Eastwood, Charles Bronson and Steve McQueen.

Bronson's strong appeal and vast international following are astonishing in view of his credentials. He was well into middle-age with a long career as a screen heavy behind him, specializing in mean gangsters, Apaches and occasional tough-but-tender, good-bad guys, before he suddenly rocketed to world popularity, topping box-office polls in France, Japan and South America. Despite his rugged, rough-hewn, self-confessedly ugly appearance, Bronson's attraction is self-evident – he simply exudes sex appeal on the one hand, while at the same time cultivating an invariably cool, controlled, strong, silent image with which male audiences can easily identify. Nevertheless he rejected permissive trends such as nudity: 'Stripping naked is not entertainment,' he is reported as saying. 'It's for the voyeurs, and I'm damned sure I'm not going to let them get kicks from seeing me totally nude.'

McQueen is equally unconventional and difficult to analyse. His wizened, simian face is

Charles Bronson, the cinema's most bankable star, in *Chato's Land* (Michael Winner, 1971).

pleasant enough in a Sinatra-ish way, but it's no oil-painting, while his small, tough, wiry physique is hardly one's conception of how a sex star should be constructed. Yet he clearly has what all the great screen stars have had, irrespective of their acting talents: old-fashioned charisma – and never more strongly in evidence than in *The Great Escape*, a vast, multi-star war epic which the neat, athletic McQueen completely dominated. Shipman has got nearest to the magic of the man: 'Steve McQueen can act with the back of his head. He can act without doing anything.... He has only to appear on the screen to fill it. He may be doing nothing important – waiting under a clock, coasting along in a car, catching a ball in a baseball mitt – but there's never any doubt he is a copper-bottomed, gold-plated star.'

In *Magnum Force* (1973), this pretty little Japanese chick gazes up at Clint Eastwood's six-foot, five-inch frame and says: 'How does a girl get to go to bed with you?' He replies, 'Try knocking on the door.' They've only known each other for about half a minute, making it one of the swiftest screen seductions on record, and it illustrates the fact that Eastwood's sex

Clint Eastwood as The Stranger in *For a Few Dollars More* (Sergio Leone, 1965).

Steve McQueen – 'a copper-bottomed, gold-plated star'.

appeal is instant and uncomplicated. He is the conventional tough-guy *par excellence* – handsome, laconic, cynical, determined and independent; clearly a man capable of wiping out half the male population of Mexico (as he did as the cigarillo-smoking Man with No Name in the first successful 'spaghetti' Westerns, *A Fistful of Dollars*, 1964, and *For a Few Dollars More*, 1965); clearly a man to be idolized by other men and worshipped by women.

A less rugged, more refined, almost intellectual image is presented by the two other dominant male stars of the modern screen – Paul Newman and Robert Redford. They discovered when acting together – as in *Butch Cassidy and the Sundance Kid* (1969) and *The Sting* (1973) – that a special empathy exists between them, yet they represent different generations of stars and each is uniquely attractive. Newman is – or was when he concentrated on acting and less on directing – closer to the Brando generation of method actors; Redford, on the other hand, has qualities which could make him the first true star of the 'seventies, 'one of those rare stars,' said an American critic, 'who could sum up, all by himself, the spirit of his time.'

His star quality and sex appeal radiate from his devastating good looks and enormous acting talent, yet he is a complete loner, the antithesis of the old-fashioned star. 'I am not,' he has declared firmly, 'a Hollywood man', and proved it by turning down hatfuls of plum parts (including Dustin Hoffman's in *The Graduate*, John Cassavetes's in *Rosemary's Baby* and George Segal's in *Who's Afraid of Virginia Woolf?*) and getting himself sued by Paramount

for breaking a contract. He is a rebel, a recluse and a romantic ('I don't like sexless love or loveless sex, but I believe in love first') – the right qualifications, perhaps, for the star of the future.

Like Redford, Dustin Hoffman is a new-look star, sufficiently versatile to play a sexual innocent (as in *The Graduate*), a centenarian (*Little Big Man*, 1971) or a crippled con-man (*Midnight Cowboy*, 1969). Gene Hackman is in the same mould, yet represents a further variation – the character actor as star, with a paradoxical ability to render himself almost totally anonymous while acting everyone else off the screen (as in *The French Connection*, 1971, and *The Conversation*, 1974).

Donald Sutherland and Elliott Gould, stars of *M*A*S*H* (1970) and *S*P*Y*S* (1974), similarly cannot be defined in old, conventional star terms: they are not quite romantic leads, nor are they outright character actors; they aren't handsome or ugly; and they're never typecast. (Perhaps for them and their like a new term should be coined – like anti-star.) Al Pacino – a pocket edition of Dustin Hoffman – and Jon Voight are two more young stars who have been lucky enough to land strong, varied roles: Pacino in *The Godfather* (1972), *Scarecrow* (1973, with Gene Hackman) and *Serpico* (1973); Voight in *Midnight Cowboy* (as the hopeful Texan stud looking for a lay in New York), *Deliverance* (1972) and *Conrack* (1974).

One comforting chunk of beefcake surfaced among all these brash new faces: husky Burt

194

Reynolds, grandson of a full-blooded Cherokee Indian and the likeliest-looking chest-barer since Clark Gable. Reynolds crashed the fame-barrier in 1972 by agreeing to pose starkers, full-frontally, in *Cosmopolitan* magazine's centre-fold. In fact, he kept one coy hand strategically placed in front of his genitals, but the pic caused enough stir (and admiration) to launch him on his film career, which included impressive performances in *Fuzz* (1972) and *Deliverance*.

Perhaps the most interesting of America's 'seventies male stars will turn out to be Jack Nicholson, a seasoned actor who laboured long and hard in ludicrous horror movies (*The Raven*, 1963, was one of the less shaming examples) before earning overnight fame in *Easy Rider* (1969). *Carnal Knowledge* and *Five Easy Pieces* (1970) confirmed his considerable talent and spotlighted him as a star with a very special sex appeal, deriving from his cynicism, world-weariness, and tough, almost Bogartian attitude to women.

One of the most dazzling, most revered personalities of the early 'seventies was the extraordinary Bruce Lee, an American-born karate expert whose athletic good looks and extraordinary virtuosity in the art of *kung-fu* made him the superstar of the myriad martial-

Above: Sidney Poitier, Katharine Houghton and Spencer Tracy in Stanley Kramer's sugary tub-thumper about miscegenation, *Guess Who's Coming to Dinner* (1967). For years, Poitier was Hollywood's solitary black hero, until the Harlem action men took over in the 'seventies.

Left: Jack Nicholson, director, working on *Drive, He Said* (1970).

Opposite, top: Burt Reynolds in *Fuzz* (Richard A. Colla, 1972).

Opposite, bottom: Jon Voight with Brenda Vaccaro in *Midnight Cowboy* (John Schlesinger, 1969).

Richard Roundtree as *Shaft* (Gordon Parks, 1971).

arts films which flooded the world's screens, most famously in *Fist of Fury* (1973) and *Enter the Dragon* (1973). It was shortly after the latter that Lee suddenly died, allegedly from an internal haemorrhage brought on by over-exertion in the film's fight scenes, to be mystically mourned by thousands of distraught fans, just as Rudolph Valentino and James Dean had been before him.

A more permanent, more significant trend in American films was the rise of the Negro star. For many years, only one black actor, Sidney Poitier, could claim to have made the big-time in movies, although singer Harry Belafonte supplied some occasional competition. Poitier's first serious rival was ex-footballer Jim Brown, who specialized in bare-chested action roles in fast-moving adventures like *100 Rifles* (1968,

opposite Raquel Welch, a notable breakthrough in black-white couplings). Then came the first *Shaft* films (1971 onwards), with Richard Round-tree as the lusty Harlem troubleshooter, the model for countless urban thrillers intended for black audiences, in which the whites were understandably the villains. White director Martin Ritt partially restored the balance with his lyrical, liberal portrayals of the Negro lot in *Sounder* (1972) and *Conrack*, with the sympathetic Paul Winfield emerging as an attractive new star.

Outside America, the established stars continued to hold sway, although in England a handful of pleasant young actors like Michael York, Edward Fox, Malcolm McDowell and Hollywood refugee Richard Chamberlain were beginning to forge solid reputations. The biggest names in Britain were Sean Connery, Michael Caine and the handsomely scarred Oliver Reed. Connery had shaken off the sexy Bond image, along with his toupee, and was picking more serious parts – most notably in *Zardoz* (1974), opposite Charlotte Rampling. Reed, on the other hand, saw himself as the saviour of British films, England's only true superstar. 'There is no such thing,' he said, 'as a humble actor. Do you know what I am? I'm English and successful and good – that's what. Destroy me and you destroy the British film industry. Keep me going and I'm the biggest star you've got.'

Caine was, by contrast, a paragon of modesty. 'I wasn't successful until I was thirty,' he told one interviewer, 'so I had thirty years to figure out what I was going to do with it. I was very set in my character. I looked at actors who failed. One of the reasons they failed was that they

Alain Delon in *Borsalino* (Jacques Deray, 1970).

196

changed with success until they were no longer what they had been. Success in my case is based on being very natural and recognizable. A man of my age can look at me and think, "Jesus Christ, he's just like me." It's identification, you see.'[67]

Continental stars with traditional sex appeal were suddenly few and far between in the 'seventies. France had its triumvirate of Jean-Paul Belmondo, Alain Delon and Jean-Louis Trintignant, while the amiably lugubrious Marcello Mastroianni continued to undermine the myth of Italian virility with his amused portrayals of seedy lechers, culminating in the poxy nobleman of Polanski's *What?* (1973) who can only get turned on when he's dressed in a tiger skin or *carabinieri* uniform and whipped by a pretty girl.

The most enduring and respected European star turned out to be the one-time idol of the English teeny-boppers (who 'never left a cinema without crawling out under some police horse's withers') Dirk Bogarde, whose recollection of his brief brush with Hollywood wittily sums up the absurdity of the declining days of the star

system: 'Twentieth Century-Fox were buying up everyone. They were going to call me Ricardo . . . something or other Spanish, and I was going to have to do a crash course in Spanish so that I could be discovered in Mexico for some extraordinary reason – I think they'd got enough Englishmen at the time. And the contract stipulated that after a certain period of time I would have to marry one of the girls on the list who were also under contract to them!' No wonder he said some years later, as he lay on the floor in an Italian studio on the set of *Night Porter* (1974) with his fly buttons undone and Charlotte Rampling sitting on top of him: 'Film-making is no job for a grown man.'

Above, left: Marcello Mastroianni in *Blow-Out* (Marco Ferreri, 1973).

Above: Jean-Paul Belmondo. After seeing him in *Breathless* (1959), Pauline Kael called him 'probably the most exciting new presence on the screen since the appearance of Brando'.

Whatever Next?

It was in the early 'seventies that the dividing line between what was traditionally acceptable in legitimate commercial film-making and what had previously been regarded as fit only for the private sexploitation market began to blur. In the spheres of sex and violence, despite the beginnings of a moral backlash, the cinema reached an unprecedented peak of permissiveness. In Britain, at least half of the films passed by the BBFC carried an X certificate (the rest being evenly divided between AA, A and U). The family audience barely existed: certainly the major circuits could not survive on this fare. Increasingly they were forced to resort to appeals to the various minority audiences and sex films were able to emerge from their previous relative obscurity. And in America, hard-core pornography finally and legally entered the realm of public exhibition (although generally speaking, in direct contrast to the British cinema, the Americans tended to indulge violence but clamp down on sex).

There were two reasons for this strictness over sex and nudity in America. Firstly, there was, as we have seen, Catholic pressure. Although companies found devious ways to make profitable G-rated films, the power of the Church remains as long as it has the ear of the forty million plus Catholics in the USA. Secondly, the Production Code cannot ban films: the X certificate covers all pictures that cannot be passed in other categories and companies can X-rate films themselves without ever submitting them to the PCA. There are, therefore, many hundreds of small cinemas which show X films, normally of a sexual nature, that could not be shown in Britain at all. The celebrated 'pornographic' films like *Deep Throat* and *The Devil in Miss Jones* were only the tip of a very large iceberg which appeared after the courts severely reduced the powers of local censors in 1965. The enormous success of *I Am Curious – Yellow*, which in 1968 had been seized by the Customs, declared obscene by a

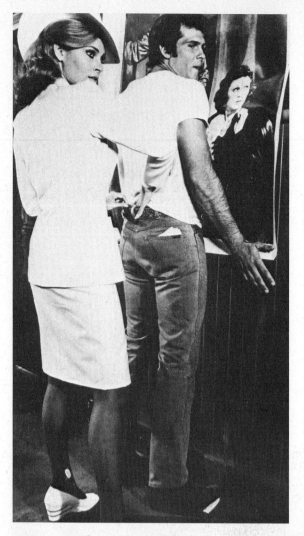

Raquel Welch as *Myra Breckinridge* (Mike Sarne, 1970) and Roger Herron as the stud she is about to rape with a dildo.

New York jury, but cleared on appeal, led to the importation of a large number of foreign films of a more dubious nature but defended none the less as having 'redeeming social values'.

Following the first glimpses of pubic hair in *Blow-Up* and *If . . .*, the final months of the 'sixties saw a further sweeping away of old taboos, albeit with a touch of the censors' brakes being applied here and there. Lesbianism – hinted at lightly in *The Prime of Miss Jean Brodie* (1968) – became a clearly stated theme in *The Killing of Sister George* (1968), even though the climactic scene – the seduction of Susannah York by Coral Browne – was scythed out by the British censor (some local authorities fearlessly reinstated portions of it). Male homosexuality also began to be treated more and more overtly, first of all in *Staircase* (1969), which (rather misguidedly) cast Richard Burton and Rex Harrison as bickering queer barbers, and then much more uncompromisingly in William Friedkin's adaptation of *The Boys in the Band* (1970), which introduced some of the plainer four-letter words in the English language to the screen for the first time. 'Who,' asks Cliff Gorman, in his brilliant portrayal of the most effeminate of the homosexual group as they gather for a soul-searching party, 'Who do you have to fuck to get a drink around here?'

Other homosexual manifestations to occur in movies around this time included an elliptical but unmistakable male fellatio scene in John Schlesinger's *Midnight Cowboy* (1969) when Jon Voight, as a broke and disillusioned Texas stud, importunes in a New York cinema;

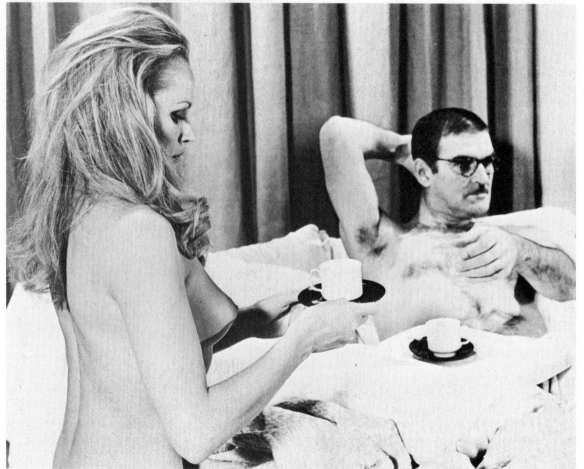

Ursula Andress and Stanley Baker in *Perfect Friday* (Peter Hall, 1970).

Racquel Welch's anal rape, with the aid of a dildo, of an athletic but stupid young stud in *Myra Breckinridge* (1970); the buggery by backwoodsmen of Ned Beatty in *Deliverance* (1972) and, of course, the celebrated full-frontal nude wrestling match by discreet, flickering firelight between Alan Bates and Oliver Reed in Ken Russell's *Women in Love*. These were the first substantial shots of the penis in a feature film and reflected the abandon with which filmmakers were now prepared to fill the screen with nudity whenever the opportunity arose.

Glenda Jackson stripped for the first (but not the last) time in *Women in Love*, and so did Jenny Linden; Ursula Andress pranced full-frontally across the screen in *Perfect Friday* (1970); and two of Britain's more delectable chests – Judy Geeson's and Helen Mirren's – were bared in, respectively, Peter Hall's *Three into Two Won't Go* (1968) and Michael Powell's *Age of Consent* (1969); Geeson also undressed for a nude swim with Barry Evans in *Here We Go Round the Mulberry Bush*, while Mirren made a magnificent full-frontal staircase descent in Russell's *Savage Messiah* (1972).

It is worth mentioning that, despite all the daring nudity in *Women in Love*, the film's most effectively erotic moment is that in which Alan Bates splits and caresses a fresh fig during a picnic and discusses its symbolic properties with his female companions.

Sexual themes positively abounded, some of them innovatory, some simply consolidating more daringly earlier breakthroughs. *Easy Rider* essayed a sexo-psychedelic LSD trip in a churchyard; *Bob and Carol and Ted and Alice* (1969) staked a claim to being the first candid comedy – and a very funny one – about hippy ideals of free love and partner-swapping; Frank Perry's *Last Summer* (1969), about adolescent sex, contained toplessness and a rape; *The Liberation of L.B. Jones* (1969) worked an implicit castration into its theme of miscegenation and murder, while miscegenation was played for laughs in *The Landlord* (1970); and Mike Nichols's *Catch 22* (1970) proffered a splendid full-frontal shot of Paula Prentiss standing on a raft. Nichols's film also depicted fellatio, between a GI and a prostitute in a darkened doorway.

The first stirrings of youthful sex was a theme sensitively and amusingly handled by Robert Mulligan in *Summer of '42* (1971), which contained a variation of the familiar condom-buying scene in which the two boys (Garry Grimes and Jerry Houser) who are the heroes of the film are too embarrassed to make their vital purchase. In another scene, one of the boys gets carried away by his first experience of sex on a beach, and exhausts himself with several repeat performances. And in yet another, wittily observed, Garry Grimes contentedly and excitedly caresses his girlfriend's upper arm throughout an entire cinema performance thinking it is her breast. The only false note in the film is struck by the climactic scene, in which Garry Grimes, still a virgin, makes love to a distressed war widow (Jennifer

Coral Browne, Beryl Reid and Susannah York as the lesbian triangle in *The Killing of Sister George* (Robert Aldrich, 1968).

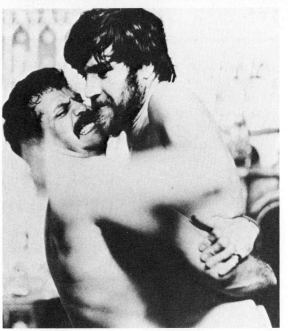

The full-frontal nude wrestling match between Oliver Reed and Alan Bates in D.H. Lawrence's *Women in Love* (Ken Russell, 1969).

Robert Culp (*second from right*), Natalie Wood (*second from left*), Elliott Gould (*left*), and Dyan Cannon as *Bob and Carol and Ted and Alice* (Paul Mazursky, 1969).

Judy Geeson as the provocative teenager who disrupts the peaceful, middle-aged marriage of Rod Steiger and Claire Bloom in *Three Into Two Won't Go* (Peter Hall, 1968).

O'Neill) for whom he has long nursed a secret infatuation.

The biggest controversy at the beginning of the decade was caused by a Danish adaptation of Henry Miller's novel *Quiet Days in Clichy* (his *Tropic of Cancer* had also been filmed, but less provocatively). The film was prosecuted in America on the grounds that it went 'beyond customary limits of candor'. It was certainly cheerfully amoral, like its source, as it followed its hero's efforts to feed both his hunger and his lust while living in poverty in Paris. There was a great deal of nudity, some of it male full-frontal (though not erect, when, in context, it should have been – a frequent and silly convention in serious sex films), and one close-up of actual penetration during lovemaking – but probably what gave most offence was the opening credits sequence in which a title says: 'It was a time when cunt was in the air', and the word 'cunt' appears, graffiti-wise, written several times over the sky in a shot of Paris. The court decision was eventually to pass the film since it did not 'appeal to the prurient'. A Californian judge declared that 'Bearing in mind the increasing frankness in society in matters pertaining to sex and nudity, and the possible artistic merit of the film, I find that the film appeals to the normal interest in sex and nudity which the average person has in such matters.' This judgment was not echoed in Britain by the Board of Censors, who rejected the film completely. Eventually, three years later, it was passed by the Greater London Council.

There was no controversy at all over two British films which came out more or less simultaneously and purported to be comedies located precisely in the groin. One was called *Percy*, and was about a penis transplant and the sexual adventures subsequently enjoyed by its new owner (Hywel Bennett); the other was called

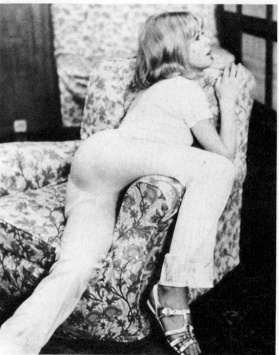

The Statue, starred David Niven, and focused on the question of whether or not a sculptress had used another, better-endowed model for the vital part of a nude statue of her husband. Both films were effectively emasculated (to use an appropriate word) by the fact that in neither case did one so much as glimpse an example of what they were about.

Mike Nichols's *Carnal Knowledge*, at least, had the courage to tackle some taboo themes in its story of two college friends (Jack Nicholson and Art Garfunkel) who love the same girl (Candice Bergen), and of how social ignorance and repression, and their own emotional inadequacies lead to sexual misery. In an early scene, the friends discuss explicitly how one of them has been masturbated by Candice Bergen;

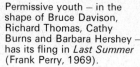
Permissive youth – in the shape of Bruce Davison, Richard Thomas, Cathy Burns and Barbara Hershey – has its fling in *Last Summer* (Frank Perry, 1969).

later on, Garfunkel produces a condom prior to making love to Miss Bergen – the first appearance of a sheath in a commercial feature film; and the final scene shows Nicholson, virtually impotent, going through a ritual with a prostitute which ends in fellatio, the only way he can enjoy sex.

Themes, or scenes, began to repeat themselves, with variations, in 1971. Glenda Jackson writhed nude on a railway carriage floor in an agony of sexual frustration in Ken Russell's *The Music Lovers*, an outrageous fantasy about Tchaikowsky's homosexuality and inability to consummate his marriage. She was indirectly involved with another homosexual in John Schlesinger's finely controlled *Sunday, Bloody Sunday*, about a charming, bisexual young man (Murray Head) who commutes between his mistress (Miss Jackson) and his male lover (Peter Finch) and their frustration at having to share him.

The Boys in the Band was displaced by an immeasurably more powerful portrayal of homosexual groups, *Fortune and Men's Eyes* (1971). Set in a Quebec prison, this disturbing, factually based drama vividly recounted the corruption of a heterosexual convict trapped in a tough, potentially vicious homosexual society. In one horrifying scene a weak, put-upon prisoner is gang-banged by his fellow inmates; in another, the 'hero' is blackmailed by his cellmate into accepting him as his lover for the duration

of the remainder of his prison sentence.

Just as sensational in theme – though delightfully sensitive in its handling – was Louis Malle's *Dearest Love* (1971), in which a young teenager has his first sexual experience with his own mother: a beautifully controlled, convincing and totally unsalacious film.

Susannah York was seduced back into lesbianism by Elizabeth Taylor in *Zee and Co.* (1971), a desperate ploy by the latter to win her husband (Michael Caine) back from Susannah's illicit arms.

A minor breakthrough was scored by Nicolas Roeg's superbly photographed *Walkabout* (1970), the story of a young brother and sister's survival in the Australian desert, which earned nothing more restrictive than an A certificate from the censor despite a full-frontal shot – admittedly utterly charming – of Jenny Agutter bathing nude in a shallow pool. Milos Forman's comedy, *Taking Off* (1971), also achieved a small advance, this time on the language front, by being permitted to retain uncut in Britain a hilarious, beautifully sung folk-song called 'Ode to a Screw' in which every line of lyric contains the word 'fuck'.

A much more significant piece of progress was notched up by Dusan Makavejev's brilliant satirical fantasy extolling the theories (the main one being that social and political oppression stem from unfulfilled sexuality) of Wilhelm Reich, *W.R. – Mysteries of the Organism* (1971).

This contained not only extensive nudity and exuberant lovemaking, but also the commercial cinema's first erection, in a scene in which a girl takes a plaster cast of a man's erect penis.

One of the most delightfully bawdy sex films of the 'seventies was Pier Paolo Pasolini's *The Decameron* (1970), which captured superbly, in a series of graphically ribald sketches, performed mostly by non-professional actors, the spirit of Boccaccio. Among the best was one about a man who achieves rear entry into another man's wife by pretending to change her into a horse; and another about a gardener who seduces (or is seduced by?) a whole convent of nuns. An attempt by Pasolini to repeat the formula with his version of *The Canterbury*

Tales (1972) was, alas, a total failure; where *The Decameron* was bawdy and funny, the *Tales* was merely tasteless and grotesque, in spite of explicit nudity and shots of (for example) simulated homosexual intercourse (again, with a limp penis).

The great controversy of 1971 occurred in Britain and concerned the judgment of new censor Stephen Murphy on three separate films, *The Devils*, *Straw Dogs* and *A Clockwork Orange*, all of which came out in relatively quick succession and caught the new man rather unfairly on the hop. Coincident with Trevelyan's retirement in 1971 there was a renewal of pressure to increase censorship. This movement was associated with a turn to the right in British politics and a reversal of the liberalism that had characterized the 'sixties. It was also a reaction to the very different material that was now emanating from America, still the major source of films for this country.

The Devils proved to be Ken Russell's most tasteless, hysterical and unpleasant film, an account, supposedly, of the sexual possession of the nuns of Loudon during the reign of Louis XIII. A catalogue of grotesque tortures and sexual excesses, with Vanessa Redgrave (as mad Sister Jeanne) frenziedly masturbating in her cell, *The Devils* met with scant approval from the new censor who came down hard on it – though not hard enough for some people.

The trouble started when Murphy subsequently allowed Sam Peckinpah's immensely gory *Straw Dogs* and Stanley Kubrick's intrinsically violent *A Clockwork Orange* a fairly easy passage to the cinema. Critics and public alike made spurious comparisons between the films and the apparently arbitrary decisions made by the censor. Many people, horrified by the mayhem in *Straw Dogs*, felt it should have been cut much further; the same with *Clockwork Orange*, especially the phallic murder sequence and the mugging scenes.

Straw Dogs had, in fact, lost a good deal of its violence (all of which remained in the American version), but only a few seconds had been snipped from the rape scene (most of which was cut from the American version), leading to confusion in some minds about the form the attack upon Susan George had taken, i.e. whether she had been buggered or simply entered from the rear, as was in fact the case. Many enemies of the Board of Censors took the opportunity to attack it at this very vulnerable time in an attempt to unseat Murphy, but he

Art Garfunkel and Candice Bergen as repressed sweethearts in *Carnal Knowledge* (Mike Nichols, 1971). She relieves his frustration with masturbation.

Hywel Bennett having his new equipment tested in *Percy* (Ralph Thomas, 1971), an arch British comedy about a penis transplant.

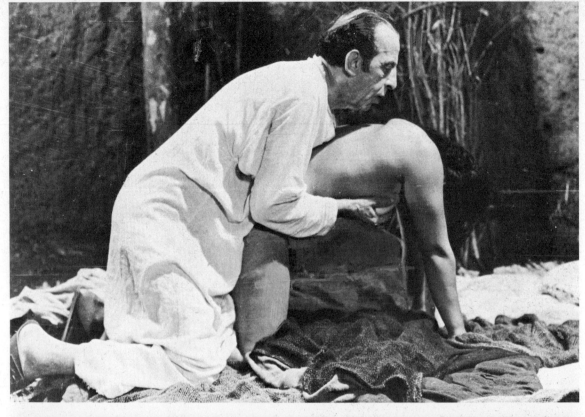

Right: The 'Don Gianni' episode from Pier Paolo Pasolini's *The Decameron* (1970), in which a priest convinces a peasant that he can turn his wife into a horse. When she is naked and on all fours he 'adds the horse's tail'.

Opposite: Michael Green as 'Queenie', who does a full-frontal drag striptease in *Fortune and Men's Eyes* (Harvey Hart, 1971), a harsh study of homosexuality in a Quebec prison.

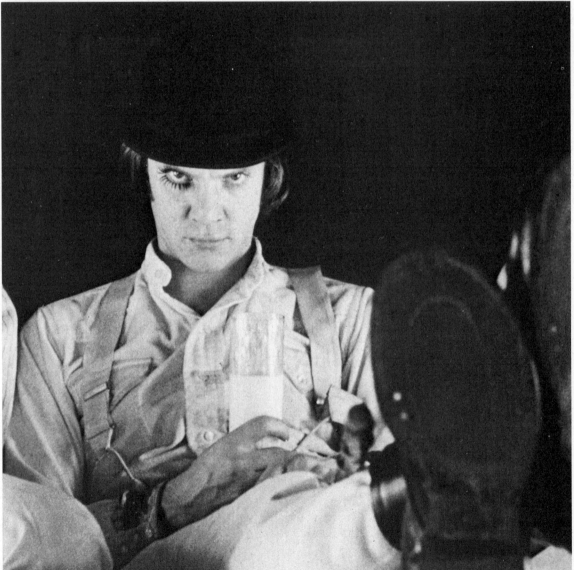

Right: Malcolm McDowell in *A Clockwork Orange* (Stanley Kubrick, 1971).

Opposite: Jagoda Kaloper in *WR — Mysteries of the Organism* (Dusan Makavejev, 1971).

204

survived, and in retrospect his decisions appeared to be based on sound aesthetic judgment of the films concerned.

However, 1971 remains a potent instance of the constraining factor of public opinion. It is well known that the public is more concerned about sex and bad language than it is about violence, while British groups like the Festival of Light and the National Viewers and Listeners Association are almost solely concerned with sex and can exert disproportionate pressure by playing off one medium against another. After the traumas of 1971–2, there was little immediate likelihood of the Board relaxing its standards to any marked degree. The GLC or Greater London Council's liberalism (always vulnerable to political circumstances) and the existence of members-only clubs (so strongly threatened by the Conservative administration of 1970–4) remained as important alternatives in the face of severity on the part of the Board.

An almost incessant storm raged throughout

Ken Hutchison attempts to rape Susan George in *Straw Dogs* (Sam Peckinpah, 1971).

the early 'seventies round the films of Andy Warhol – or to be more accurate, of his colleague and active cameraman, Paul Morrissey. Most of Warhol's product is regarded as 'underground' material, although some of his films (which 'usually run for several hours and are totally boring except to the initiated', says Leslie Halliwell) have a strong following, including *Sleep* (1963), *Blow Job* (1964), *My Hustler* (1965), *The Chelsea Girls* (1966) and *Blue Movie* (1969).

Morrissey's first film for Warhol as director was *Flesh* (1968), a coherent, absorbing, accessible study of a young man (Joe Dallesandro, constant star of Warhol/Morrissey movies) who hustles for homosexuals in New York for a day in order to pay for his wife's girlfriend's abortion. It is candid and explicit, peopled with transvestites and homosexuals, contains a brief, casual shot of an erection, and has a fellatio sequence. The Board of Censors, then under John Trevelyan, could not justify giving

the film a certificate, but encouraged the distributors to approach the reputable Open Space Theatre to give it club-controlled screenings. However, a member of the public complained that *Flesh* was obscene and over thirty policemen descended on the theatre in February, 1970, in order to seize the film and charge its exhibitors under the Obscene Publications Act. A tremendous row followed, as much over the peremptory police action as anything else. The outcome was that the obscenity charge was dropped on the grounds that films were not subject to the Obscene Publications Act, but the theatre was heavily fined for admitting non-members to see the film. *Flesh* subsequently ran to predictably packed houses at a London cinema and ensured good audiences for any future Morrissey films.

The next was *Trash* (1970), a powerful anti-drugs tract in which Dallesandro played a man who has been rendered sexually impotent by hard drugs. The Board again refused a

206

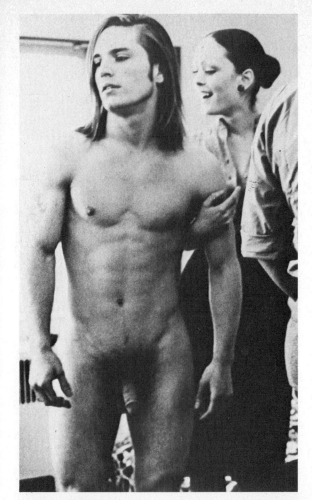

certificate (Stephen Murphy's first decision of note), claiming that the message was not obvious, that there was an implication of approval for soft drugs, and that some scenes could give offence, namely 'the opening fellatio, close shots of the needle in the drug-addict's arm, and the famous masturbation-with-a-beer-bottle sequence'. After a long period of haggling (and refusal to show the film by most local authorities approached), the distributors agreed to cut the film, and it was fortuitously launched at a time of public outcry over plans to televize a documentary about Warhol (although the latter, when it was finally transmitted, proved to be so pretentious and tedious that most of the good publicity was nullified).

A third Morrissey film, *Heat* (1971), a smoothly made, almost 'commercial' feature vaguely sending up *Sunset Boulevard*, with Dallesandro as an ex-juvenile star ambitious to get back into pictures, was passed after elimination of a scene showing a dim-witted young man constantly masturbating and enjoying fellatio (later passed intact by the GLC).

Compared with the candour of a Warhol/Morrissey film, even the cruder erotic features from the 'seventies look bland, and this would certainly apply to *Portnoy's Complaint* (1972), a clumsy adaptation of Philip Roth's celebrated book about a young Jew who sublimates his insecurities in masturbation. Also heavy-handed was Michael Winner's peculiarly moribund exercise of 'prologuing' Henry James's

Joe Dallesandro and Jane Forth between takes of *Trash* (Paul Morrissey, 1970).

Dallesandro and Sylvia Miles in *Heat* (Morrissey, 1971).

Claude Faraldo's *Themroc* (1972), about a man (Michel Piccoli) who rebels against his drab, working-class existence, makes love to his sister (Béatrice Romand), incarcerates his mother (Mme Herviale), and turns his apartment into a cave.

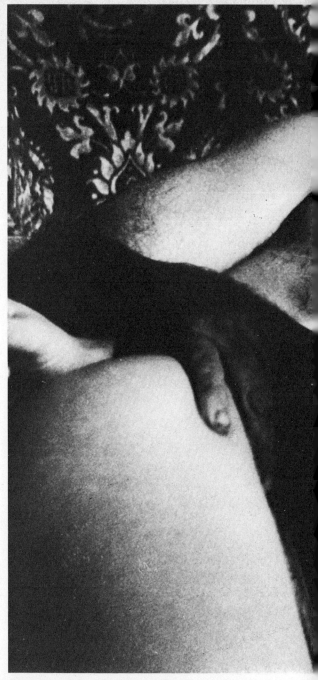

story, 'The Turn of the Screw', which came out as *The Nightcomers* (1971). It did, however, have one remarkably tempestuous sex scene between Marlon Brando and Stephanie Beacham, strongly laced with sado-masochism.

A welcome comedy appeared in 1972, from the original hands of Woody Allen, with the excessively long title, *Everything You Always Wanted to Know About Sex* *But Were Afraid to Ask*. This took the form of a hit-or-miss series of sketches illustrating points from a sex manual, the funniest of which were a spoof horror movie, complete with crippled retainer transformed into a monster by an experimental four-hour orgasm; and a fantasy which imagines the inside of the body as a scientific operations room staffed by little men in white coats, all co-operating in a joint bid to complete a satisfactory seduction which the 'body' is undertaking in a car.

Animation at last discovered sex, most notably in the full-length feature cartoons, *Fritz the Cat* (1971) and *Heavy Traffic* (1973), a pair of bawdy, often crude satires on Harlem tenement life of which a convention seems to be that you can get away with a lot more erotic excess in a piece of animation than you can in an ordinary film.

The next controversy to follow the Warhol disputes surrounded a film by Bernardo Bertolucci – *Last Tango in Paris* (1972). This study of despair, loneliness and lust, pivoting on a casual affair between a recent widower (Marlon

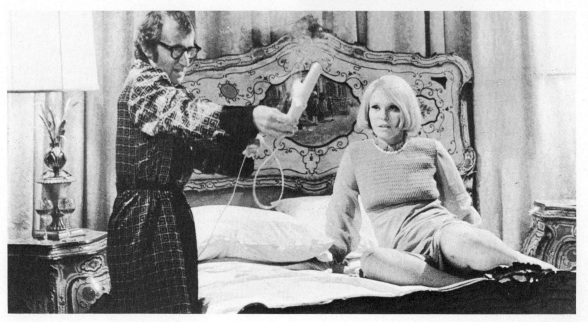

Woody Allen with combustible vibrator in his own comedy, *Everything You Always Wanted to Know About Sex* *But Were Afraid to Ask* (1972).

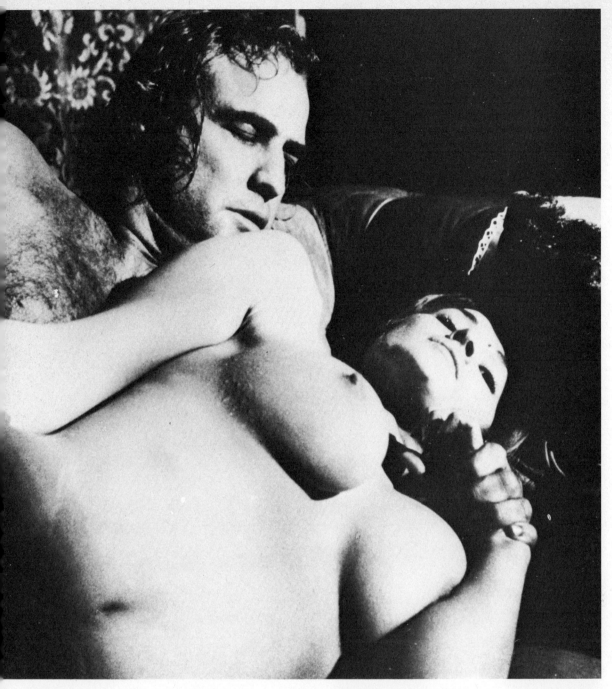

The violent, impassioned, sado-masochistic sex scene between Marlon Brando and Stephanie Beacham in *The Nightcomers* (Michael Winner, 1971).

Brando) and a girl (Maria Schneider), became notorious for its candid sex scenes, although they took up no more than about ten minutes of the film's two-hour length. One of them, however, involved anal entry, complete with butter (although Brando kept his trousers on throughout), and another called for a brief speech full of bestial images during an anal grope.

The Board trimmed the Butter Scene, as it became known, but otherwise left the film intact, angering the various reactionary organizations, such as the Festival of Light, devoted to stricter censorship of the media. A curious Central Criminal Court 'loophole' judgment by the Lord Chief Justice in 1974, stating that films *could*, after all, be prosecuted under the Obscene Publications Act, gave the hardliners some hope, however, that a private prosecution taken out against *Last Tango* by a retired Salvation Army worker might result in its being banned.

A further prosecution was taken out by Mrs Mary Whitehouse, a leading pro-censorship figure, against another controversial Continental film, *Blow-Out* (1973), a fantasy in which a group of people shut themselves in a house and eat themselves to death, with full wind accompaniment, pauses for defecation, and sex on the side. The prosecution, having been taken out under the Vagrancy Act and not the Obscene Publications Act, failed, but the judge made it clear that he thought parts of the film were obscene.

Meanwhile, in the United States, the breakdown of formal censorship paved the way in the 'seventies for much stronger meat than that which was causing reactionary hackles to rise in Britain. 'Nudie' films and soft-core pornography had for some while been filtering on to the nation's cinema screens, care being taken only to ensure that the strict laws against obscenity in advertising were not transgressed.

It was only a matter of time, therefore, before someone would take the plunge and set a dish of hard-core pornography before the public. This came in the surprisingly palatable form of *Deep Throat*, one of the most controversially successful films in cinema history. With total explicitness, and a shade or two more skill than is usually displayed in hard-core pornography, *Deep Throat* developed the amusing idea of a girl unsatisfied by sex until she discovers that her clitoris is in the back of her throat.

The actress who played this biological freak, Linda Lovelace, acquired sufficient fame from *Deep Throat* for her name to be recognized even by thousands of Britons who had yet to see her film, and even deemed it worthwhile to visit London and discuss censorship in Britain. Miss Lovelace became the object of a small but hilarious joke cult, among the best of which was the rumour that her follow-up movie was going to be a remake – *Guess Who's Coming – for Dinner*.

Gerard Damiano, who made *Deep Throat*, was also responsible for its most celebrated and lucrative successor, *The Devil in Miss Jones* (1973) – described by William Rotsler as a 'modern existentialist drama' and 'the most determinedly anti-erotic film I've ever seen . . . they do virtually everything in the book, including oral sex with a snake. . . . The anal sex that was prominent in . . . *Deep Throat* is shown

here almost as a way of life. . . . Afterwards, I felt like going to a Disney movie to wash my mind out.'

More respectfully admired by hard-core initiates was the Mitchell Brothers' (*Behind*) *The Green Door* (1972), about a woman's bisexual orgy fantasies. Its star, Marilyn Chambers, expressed the sex actors' ethos in an interview with Rotsler: 'So many couples come to see *The Green Door*, it's amazing! I've heard a lot of people say, "God, we went home and we hadn't screwed for so long and *jeez*, it was out of sight!" To me that means I'm doing a good job. If people get turned on by it, then it's groovy.' She also summarized the American censorship situation with admirable succinctness: 'The rating system kills me. If a guy cuts off a woman's breast it is rated R. If a guy *kisses* it, it's rated X! How absurd!'

However, the threat of backlash hung over this whole lucrative arena. The Nixon administration had, from the first, been determined to make a vigorous effort to reverse the trend of the previous decade. After the election of 1968, the complexion of the Supreme Court rapidly changed as men known to be out of sympathy with the liberalism of the Warren era were appointed. In rejecting the report of the Commission on Obscenity and Pornography in 1970 Nixon made his own attitude very clear: 'The warped and brutal portrayal of sex in books,

Marlon Brando and Maria Schneider in *Last Tango in Paris* (Bernardo Bertolucci, 1972).

plays, magazines and movies, if not halted and reversed, could poison the wellsprings of American and Western culture and civilisation. . . .'

In New York, Mayor Lindsay tried to clean up Times Square but was rebuffed by the courts who ruled that the revoking of licences was prior restraint and therefore unconstitutional. Early in 1973, Nixon presented an Anti-Obscenity Bill that seemed likely to affect wide sections of the film industry, for prison was threatened for anyone who handled material that 'represents any act of sexual intercourse, flagellation, torture or violence; shows any explicit close-up of a human genital organ; or makes any advertisement notice, announcement, or other method by which information is given as to the manner in which any of the obscene material may be procured'. Safeguards protecting material with an 'artistic, scientific, or literary purpose' seemed weak, given the broad framing of the Bill.

Shortly afterwards the Supreme Court reversed its earlier judgment that the constitution protects obscene matter, and argued that local community standards rather than national standards should be applied, thus opening the way for a resurgence of local censorship. Exhibitors were promptly prosecuted for showing films like *Carnal Knowledge*, *Paper Moon* and *Last Tango in Paris*.

The MPAA organized opposition to protect the industry from such local action, and

Heavy Traffic (1973), Ralph Bakshi's second animation feature (*above*), parodying the violence, vulgarities and excesses of tenement New York. Sex had first come to animation in the 'twenties with Max Fleischer's creation, Betty Boop (*left*). Betty was once banned by the New York Supreme Court as being 'permanent outrage'.

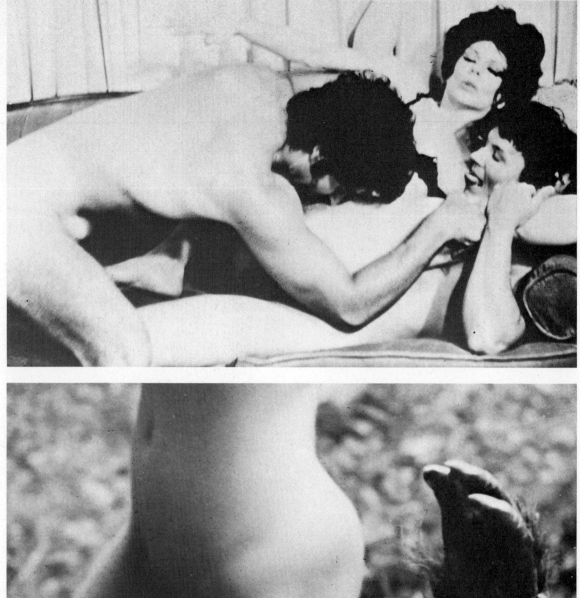

'The True Story of the Beast
of Gevaudan' — an episode
from Walerian Borowczyk's
Immoral Tales (1974). This
controversial sketch —
expected to fall foul of even
the most liberal censor — tells
of a shepherdess who is
chased through a forest by a
bear-like beast with an
enormous (and eminently
visible) phallus. She is
caught and raped by the
beast, but after a while she
begins to enjoy the
experience and becomes the
aggressor, eventually
wearing her attacker out.

212

received some encouragement when the New York Supreme Court threw out cases against four films on the grounds that there was no way of knowing whether the majority of the population of the city would regard them as obscene or not. Within a few months the Supreme Court was indicating that it might amplify or redefine its decision in an effort to combat the confusion that had arisen. Much, of course, hinged upon general political developments in America and whether the campaign against 'obscene' films would go down with the Nixon administration.

By mid-'74 Britain had not dared to emulate America by introducing hard-core pornography into its cinemas, and given the state of the law and the eagerness of watchdogs to invoke it, the day when that would happen looked a long way off. It seemed ironic, therefore, that some distribution in the States was still subject to censorship and that the exquisite nude love scene between Julie Christie and Donald Sutherland in *Don't Look Now* (1973), untouched by censor's hand in the British version, was scissored out for American release. Meanwhile, it was intriguing and encouraging to note that the explicit but very discreet lovemaking in *Siddartha* (1973) drew from the British censor nothing more severe than an A certificate.

Every revolution produces a reaction, and there have been signs in the United States, with business in some sex cinemas down by 60 per cent, that even hard-core pornography is a passing phase at the public level. If this is so, what will replace it? One frightening answer is suggested in Guardian correspondent Richard Roud's observations after watching Dusan Makavejev's *Sweet Movie* (1974) at the Cannes Film Festival: '*Sweet Movie* features, you could say, urination and defecation. Not to forget a great deal of vomiting. Curious that these bodily functions should turn out to have been the last taboo to go, that sexual intercourse seems to have less thrill value than the digestive and excretory functions. But I expect the psycho-analysts could explain that.'

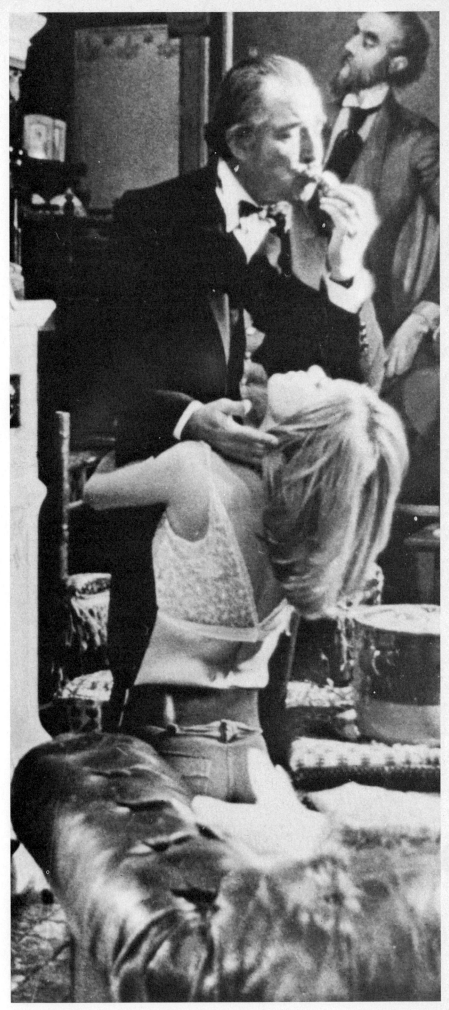

ACKNOWLEDGMENTS

List of Sources

[1] 'The Eye of the Movie' by Henry Alan Potamkin, quoted in 'Saint Cinema: Selected Writings 1929–70' by Herman G. Weinberg. DBS Publications, New York, 1970. Vision Press, London, 1972.

[2-5] 'Million and One Nights' by Terry Ramsaye. Simon and Schuster, New York, 1964 (3rd printing). Cass & Company, London, 1964.

[6] 'The Pin-up: A Modest History' by Mark Gabor. Universe Books, New York, 1972. Andre Deutsch, London, 1972, and Pan Books, London, 1973.

[7] 'The Haunted Screen: Expressionism in the German Cinema and the Influence of Max Reinhardt' by Lotte H. Eisner. Thames and Hudson, London, 1969 (published with new material). University of California Press, Berkeley, 1969. Originally published by Le Terrain Vague, Paris, 1952, under title 'Ecran Demoniaque'.

[8] 'Amour-Eroticisme et Cinéma' by Ado Kyrou. Le Terrain Vague, Paris, 1957.

[9-12] 'Million and One Nights'. See above.

[13] 'Sex, Psyche Etcetera in the Film' by Parker Tyler. Horizon Press, New York, 1969. Pelican Books, London, 1971. Copyright Parker Tyler.

[14] 'Sex in the Movies' by Alexander Walker. Pelican, London and New York, 1968. First published as 'The Celluloid Sacrifice' by Michael Joseph, 1966.

[15, 16] 'The Parade's Gone By' by Kevin Brownlow. Martin Secker and Warburg, London, 1968, and Abacus Books, London, 1973. Knopf, New York, 1968, and Ballantine, New York, 1969.

[17] 'The Autobiography of Cecil B. De Mille' by Cecil B. De Mille and D. Hayne. Prentice-Hall, New York, 1959. W. H. Allen, London, 1960.

[18] 'The Movie Moguls: An Informal History of the Hollywood Tycoons' by Philip French. Weidenfeld and Nicolson, London, 1968, and Pelican Books, London, 1971. Henry Regnery, Chicago, 1971.

[19] 'Saint Cinema'. See above.

[20] 'The Movie Moguls'. See above.

[21] 'Saint Cinema'. See above.

[22] 'Million and One Nights'. See above.

[23] 'Romantic Adventure: The Autobiography of Elinor Glyn'. Nicholson and Watson, London, 1936.

[24] Rudolph Leonhardt, quoted in 'The Haunted Screen'. See above.

[25] 'The Filmgoer's Companion' by Leslie Halliwell. Avon Books, New York, 1971. Paladin, London, 1972.

[26, 27] Quoted in 'The Wit and Wisdom of Hollywood: From the Squaw Man to the Hatchet Man' by Max Wilk. Atheneum, New York, 1971. Cassell, London, 1972.

[28-31] 'Clark Gable' by René Jordan. Pyramid, New York, 1973.

[32-34] 'Saint Cinema'. See above.

[35] 'The Filmgoer's Companion'. See above.

[36-38] 'Eros in the Cinema' by Raymond Durgnat. Calder and Boyers, London, 1966. Hillary, New York, 1966.

[39] 'The Haunted Screen'. See above.

[40] 'Amour-Eroticisme et Cinéma'. See above.

[41] 'Saint Cinema'. See above.

[42, 43] 'Ecstasy and Me: My Life as a Woman' by Hedy Lamarr. W. H. Allen, London, 1967. Taplinger, New York, 1966.

[44] 'My Wicked, Wicked Ways' by Errol Flynn. G. P. Putnam, New York, 1959. Heinemann, London, 1960, and Pan Books, London, 1972 (3rd printing).

[45] 'Howard: The Amazing Mr Hughes' by Noah Dietrich and Bob Thomas. Fawcett World Library, New York, 1972. Coronet, London, 1972.

[46] 'The Pin-up'. See above.

[47] 'Amour-Eroticisme et Cinéma. See above.

[48] 'The Wit and Wisdom of Hollywood'. See above.

[49] Quoted in 'The Citizen Kane Book' by Pauline Kael. Bantam Books, New York, 1971. Martin Secker and Warburg, London, 1971, and Paladin/Granada, London, 1974. Originally a New Yorker article called 'Raising Kane'.

[50] 'The Filmgoer's Companion'. See above.

[51] 'Hitchcock' by François Truffaut. Simon & Schuster, New York, 1967. Martin Secker and Warburg, London, 1968.

[52] Tennessee Williams.

[53] 'Great Movie Stars' (vol 2) by David Shipman. Angus & Robertson, London, 1972. St Martin's Press, New York, 1973.

[54] 'Stanley Kubrick Directs' by Alexander Walker. Harcourt Brace Javanovich, New York, 1971. Davis-Poynter, London, 1972, and Abacus, London, 1973.

[55, 56] 'Sex in the Movies'. See above.

[57] British Film Institute's Monthly Film Bulletin.

[58] 'The History of Sex in Cinema' by Arthur Knight and Hollis Alpert. Series of twenty articles in Playboy magazine, 1965–8.

[59] 'The Great Movie Stars'. See above.

[60] British Film Institute's Monthly Film Bulletin.

[61] British Film Institute's Monthly Film Bulletin.

[62] 'Dictionary of Film Makers' by Georges Sadoul. University of California Press, Berkeley, 1972.

[63] 'The International Encyclopedia of Film', edited by Dr Roger Manvell. Michael Joseph, London, 1972. Crown, New York, 1972.

[64] Quoted in 'The History of Sex in Cinema'. See above.

[65] Quoted in 'The History of Sex in Cinema'. See above.

[66] 'Great Movie Stars'. See above.

[67] Films Illustrated, November, 1973.

Thanks

The authors were helped by many people in many ways during the writing of this book, but they are especially grateful to the following: Jo Sandilands of Honey magazine, who enthused about the original idea; Fred Newman, Graham Donaldson, Graham Sellors, Michael Prideaux, Sarah Reynolds, Mundy Ellis and others at Phoebus Publishing who gave various forms of assistance, forbearance and encouragement; John Baxter, Kevin Brownlow and other contributors to Phoebus's 'The Story of the Movies'; Susan Pascall, who let her husband 'get on with it'; Rosemary Stark, who was true to type; Homer 'Pudding' Smith, for providing warmth and comfort in moments of stress; Sheila Whitaker; Guy Phelps; Mary Jackson; Jane Mercer; Kenneth Thompson; Mary Davies and John Fitzmaurice; John Raisbeck, Steve Jenkins, Elizabeth Heasman and the Stills Collection of the National Film Archive; the National Film Archive Catalogue; the Information Department and Book Library of the British Film Institute; Stephen Murphy and the British Board of Film Censors; the John Kobal Collection; the Radio Times Hulton Picture Library; Mrs Cecilia De Mille Harper and Mrs Florence Cole of the De Mille Foundation; Mary Corliss of the Museum of Modern Art Film Department; BBC Television, for showing the right old movies at the right time; and Sigmund Freud, without whom . . .

In addition to the numerous books, publications, journals and other sources mentioned in the text and notes, the following proved particularly useful:
'The British Film Catalogue 1895–1970' by Denis Gifford. David and Charles, Newton Abbot, 1973. McGraw-Hill, New York, 1973.
'Contemporary Erotic Cinema' by William Rotsler. Penthouse/Ballantine, New York, 1973.
'The Filmgoer's Companion' by Leslie Halliwell. MacGibbon and Kee, London, 1970 (revised edition). Avon Books, New York, 1971.
'Films of Cecil B. De Mille' by Gene Ringgold and DeWitt Bodeen. Citadel, New York and London, 1969.
'Gotta Sing Gotta Dance – A Pictorial History of Film Musicals' by John Kobal. Hamlyn, London and New York, 1970.
'The History of Sex in Cinema' by Arthur Knight and Hollis Alpert. Series of twenty articles in Playboy magazine, 1965–8.
'The Moguls' by Norman Zierold. Avon Books, New York, 1972.
'The Movies' by Richard Griffith and Arthur Mayer. Simon and Schuster, New York, 1970 (revised edition). Spring Books, London, 1971.
'See No Evil' by Jack Vizzard. Simon and Schuster, New York, 1970.
Sundry editions of Films Illustrated, Cinema and TV Today, Films and Filming, and the British Film Institute's Monthly Film Bulletin.
JP and CJ

The Hamlyn Publishing Group gratefully acknowledges MGM. Warner Brothers, 20th Century-Fox, Paramount, RKO, Universal, Republic, Columbia, United Artists, UFA, the Rank Organization, British Lion, Ealing Studios, Woodfall and Walt Disney.

INDEX

215

217